D1191395

cognition,
curriculum,
and
comprehension

cognition,
curriculum,
and
comprehension

John T. Guthrie, Editor
International Reading Association

ira international reading association
800 barksdale road   newark, delaware 19711

Copyright 1977 by the
International Reading Association, Inc.

Library of Congress Cataloging in Publication Data
Main entry under title:
Cognition, curriculum, and comprehension.

Based on a seminar organized and sponsored by the
International Reading Association held in Newark, Del.
in 1975.

Bibliography: p.

1. Reading—Congresses. 2. Reading comprehension—
Congresses. 3. Language arts—Congresses. I. Guthrie,
John T. II. International Reading Association.
LB1049.95.C63   428.4   77-24012
ISBN 0-87207-520-6

Contents

CONTRIBUTORS

Irene Athey Chairperson, Center for Development, Learning and Instruction, College of Education, University of Rochester, Rochester, New York

Isabel Beck Research Associate and Director of Reading Curriculum Development, Learning Research and Development Center, University of Pittsburgh, Pittsburgh, Pennsylvania

John B. Carroll Kenan Professor of Psychology and Director, L.L. Thurstone Psychometric Laboratory, University of North Carolina, Chapel Hill, North Carolina

Lawrence T. Frase Chief, Learning Division, Basic Skills Group, National Institute of Education, 1200 19th Street, N.W., Washington, D.C.

Cheryl Hansen Itinerant Master Teacher, Montgomery County Intermediate Unit, Special Education Center, 1605B W. Main Street, Norristown, Pennsylvania

Lois Hood Department of Psychology, Program on Development and Learning, Teachers College, Columbia University, New York, New York

Karlyn Kamm Developmental Specialist, Wisconsin Research and Development Center for Cognitive Learning, University of Wisconsin, Madison, Wisconsin

Thomas Lovitt Professor, Experimental Education Unit, Child Development and Mental Retardation Center, University of Washington, Seattle, Washington

Wayne Otto Professor and Chairperson, Department of Curriculum and Instruction, University of Wisconsin, Madison, Wisconsin

Charles A. Perfetti Associate Professor of Psychology, Learning Research and Development Center, University of Pittsburgh, Pittsburgh, Pennsylvania

Russell G. Stauffer Professor Emeritus in Education, University of Delaware, Newark, Delaware

Gita Wilder Senior Research Associate, Division of Educational Studies, Educational Testing Service, Princeton, New Jersey

Foreword

This volume represents a confluence of significant current trends in the scientific study of reading processes and practical aspects of curriculum design. These major trends include the interactive relationship between reading research and instructional practice; the emergence of an increasingly systematic field of curriculum design; an increased concern with instruction in the more complex competencies of reading; and the potential contribution of new theories of human cognition to understanding these complex outcomes of education.

In the past, books on the psychology of reading identified existing experiment and theory and attempted to draw implications from this information for reading instruction. There was the implicit acceptance that innovations in practice proceeded in a sequence from basic research to applied research, to development, to application and practice. In contrast, this book makes it apparent that this conception of a linear progression from science and practice is overly simplistic. By bringing together researchers in cognitive psychology and psycholinguistics and experts in curriculum design, the volume appears to recognize the fact that research and development are mutually dependent matters. Researchers need the direction and discipline that come from contact with real-world problems, and developers need to express their problems in researchable terms. This mutual engagement invigorates both enterprises and sharpens the focus of work in both research and development.

Systematic principles and procedures for instructional development have begun to appear with increasing frequency in textbooks and university courses. This growing interest in instructional development as a systematic field is evident in this book. The chapters by curriculum developers show an awareness of a potential knowledge base that can provide heurisitic guidance in their work. They are experienced and wise enough, however, to realize that psychological principles provide only a basis on which the artistry and intuition of the instructional developer must be imposed. The message delivered is that it is important to consider the information provided both by theory-based laboratory investigation and by study of the educational practices of outstanding teachers.

Highlighted in this book is the concern with the advanced competencies of reading and verbal literacy subsumed under the general name of comprehension. Comprehension abilities have not been as carefully analyzed as the supposedly simpler decoding skills. As a result, there is less general agreement about the objectives of advanced reading instruction. The increased attention to reading comprehension reflects both social and scientific changes. Socially, it reflects more intense demands for higher standards of literacy in the population. The new challenge for education is to teach competencies that enable individuals to use advanced comprehension skills—to read unfamiliar text in order to gain new information, to draw inferential judgments from text rather than accept directly stated information, and to interpret complex text so that it can be related to knowledge already acquired. The scientific basis for increased attention to comprehension results from the emergence of an increasingly strong psychology of human cognition. The relatively recent changes in predominant theoretical conceptions in psychology—a change from empty organism stimulus-response theories to conceptions of human nature concerned with active internal cognitive processes and structures—have generated an increased interest and capability to investigate and understand the complex processes of comprehension.

This book is in tune with these major changes in social demand and advances in behavioral science and the studies described are representative of the new research tactics that have accompanied these changes. In the old mode of research, findings established in laboratory environments often were extrapolated to complex human learning with relatively little investigation of the limitations and boundary conditions involved. This has now been replaced by research which, in large part, picks its problems and develops its theory from realistic, "ecologically valid" human performance.

What is emerging from research that addresses complex human cognitive performance is a base of knowledge that is relevant to the complexity of educational practice. A reasonable hypothesis to account for the ineffectiveness of many curricular reforms of the past decade is that both the innovations and conclusions about their failures were based upon ignorance of the nature of the cognitive activities involved in acquiring knowledge from text and reasoning with written language. To get beyond this point, knowledge and theory are required about what it is that students do learn when they acquire skill in reading comprehension and the instructional conditions that can be expected to provide such competence. This point of view is the theme of this volume. Current theories and techniques of investigation in cognitive psychology and processes of comprehension are juxtaposed with concerns for curriculum design and instructional practice.

The trends reflected by the conference from which this book derives encourage an interactive mode of work between application, design, and basic science. There is no longer merely the general expectation that discoveries in science will eventually filter into practice. Rather, there is active cooperation and interaction between research and practice that mutually facilitate each other. Hopefully, researchers in cognitive theory, researchers of classroom practices, and curriculum developers eventually will develop a common parlance of instructional theory so that the findings of each are more easily communicated to one another.

Robert Glaser
Learning Research and Development Center
University of Pittsburgh
May 1977

Preface

Reading specialists, students, and professors came from as near as Newark, Delaware, and as far as Paris, France, in the summer of 1975 to a seminar on "The Development of Reading Comprehension" held in Newark. Organized and sponsored by the International Reading Association, the conference was intended to explore basic research and the teaching of reading comprehension. Researchers in cognitive psychology and psycholinguistics and experts in curriculum design in reading gave presentations and reacted to one another's ideas. As the table of contents reveals, each researcher commented on the paper of one curriculum designer and vice versa.

In the history of reading, scientific inquiry and practices of teaching have never been closer together than they are today. From many disciplines, researchers are embracing the challenge of explaining reading comprehension as it occurs in complex, everyday situations. Teachers and other practitioners are attempting to improve their programs in light of the latest research findings, if possible. However, the gap remains between research and practice and between science and service. To close this gap, two points should be widely accepted:

1. Perceptual, cognitive, and language processes that are important for reading comprehension should be instructional goals in educational programs.

2. Characteristics of effective reading programs and teachers should be interrelated and explained in theories of the development of reading comprehension.

This book contains illustrations of these viewpoints. The notion that people read for some purpose, for example, is deeply ingrained in the language experience approach to instruction presented by Stauffer. He believes that discovering a child's purpose for reading and adapting instruction to that purpose are vital to effective teaching. Frase provides an analysis of how purpose influences what we learn and remember from reading—an example of basic research on this problem. Athey shows the theoretical importance of the child's perception of syntactic structure during reading, and how processes of inference occur when a child reads seemingly simple materials. Otto's curriculum incorporates these ideas by including as an instructional objective "detail," which is search for kernel clauses in large, complex sentences. Otto also includes reasoning as a goal of comprehension instruction. He believes that processes of logic and inference should be taught in the reading program to facilitate comprehension.

According to Beck and Wilder, a critical aspect of effective beginning reading programs is an emphasis on decoding printed words to oral language. Wilder reports this as a feature of exemplary programs from a national study and Beck provides a detailed outline of reading instruction for decoding. A theoretical account of why decoding may be important is given by Perfetti. He points out that not only accuracy but speed of decoding are important to enable a person to direct attention to semantic processing and reading comprehension. He proposes that we have a limited capacity for processing information and until decoding can be performed with little effort and attention, reading comprehension is not likely to be highly developed. If his theory is correct, it at least partially accounts for why beginning reading programs that are effective have a substantial decoding component. These are some of the many connections between curriculum design and research on reading comprehension that may be formed from the contributions to this volume.

A note of gratitude is expressed to the seminar faculty (contributors to this volume) who presented their thoughts, engaged in lengthy discussions, and wrote their papers promptly. The workshops were conducted on themes chosen by the participants and were coordinated by Deborah Birkmire, Carol Harding, Ann Pace, Mary Seifert, and Sara Jane Tyler, who acquitted themselves admirably. Special thanks is given to Janice Hiester, who administered the details of the conference and assisted with editing the volume.

JTG

Developmental Parameters of Reading Comprehension

John B. Carroll

There are several sources of confusion in the study of reading comprehension. First is the confusion between reading and language. Despite various qualifications that have been pointed out, and of which I am keenly aware, I still think we must hold to the idea that language is more fundamental than reading. Linguists used to talk about the primacy of speech over writing, but I prefer not to use the term speech in this context, for speech, like writing and reading, is in some sense subsidiary to language. Reading, writing, and speech are ways in which language manifests itself. While the linguists were in many ways correct in stressing the primacy of spoken language over written language, attention to that point overly distracts us from the fact that language, as a basic system of communication, is more fundamental than any particular manifestation of it. A discussion of reading comprehension really has to be a discussion about language comprehension. Let us assume that we are not primarily concerned with the so-called "decoding" aspects of reading—the translation of print into a representation parallel to that of spoken language. We are, however, concerned with the comprehension of that representation. Whatever is read is intended to be comprehended, and comprehension is a problem that goes beyond decoding. It pertains to the comprehension of language, regardless of the form in which it is expressed—speech, writing, or Morse code.

But there is still another source of confusion—the confusion between language and cognition. To comprehend language, in whatever form, is to comprehend the ideas, concepts, propositions, facts, questions, injunctions,

ments, inferences, qualifications, conditions, attitudes, emotions, and anything else that may be expressed in language materials that are spoken or written. So reading comprehension entails cognition processes of knowing, reasoning, and inferencing that are supposed to be evoked by printed texts, oral discussions, and lectures. It also includes affect, if you believe, as I do, that reading comprehension involves the apprehension of affective elements.

Actually, we could go on expanding the sphere of our concerns. Since cognition and affect are only very general terms that pertain to any kind of knowledge, any kind of affect, we can get specific about cognition and affect only when we allow ourselves to deal with any kind of knowledge, any kind of affect, or any specific content of a cognitive process. Teaching reading comprehension has to do with teaching people to understand the literature of any discipline or activity. Reading comprehension has to do with understanding and appreciating any kind of literary product, or the ideas and ideologies of any special interest group. Reading comprehension, we now perceive, is really an enormous topic. It could embrace all knowledge, all science, all of human experience.

Saying this, however, may be more frightening than helpful. We have to draw the line somewhere, and we are obliged to focus our attention on the role of reading in all this. So I will draw the line and say that we can stop short of including all knowledge, as long as we are content to think about reading comprehension in the context of language, cognition, and affect.

Why are these distinctions between reading and language and language and cognition, important for our consideration? Let me illustrate. Several years ago I published an essay on "The Development of Native Language Skills Beyond the Early Years" (Carroll, 1971). In that essay, I presented a graph of the norms of the STEP Reading Test published by Educational Testing Service (1957). The graph gives a striking demonstration of the tremendous variability in "reading ability" among students from the fourth grade to the college sophomore level. While the median performance went steadily upward, even the median at the college sophomore level does not represent an impressive performance, for it is also attained by a few students as early as the ninth grade. And the bottom fifth percentile of the college sophomores was a performance that was similar, it would appear, to the performance of the top 1 percent of the fourth graders!

This test was labeled as a test of reading ability, and a lot of it doubtless had to do with what we would think of as "reading comprehension." But was it really reading comprehension? Was it not language comprehension? Or was it really cognitive ability? To be sure, there was a reading component, perhaps even a decoding component. Maybe some of the low scoring college students performed poorly not because they didn't have the required language comprehension ability and not because they didn't have the required cognitive faculties, but because they couldn't decode the printed material adequately enough to deal with the content. More likely, however, the case was quite the opposite: the low scoring college students performed poorly because they didn't have the requisite language comprehension ability and cognitive ability to deal with the material once decoded. It would be nice if the makers of the STEP Reading Test had provided us with a way of finding out what a low score really means, but unfortunately that is not the case.

Similar remarks could be made about dozens of other tests that purport to measure reading comprehension ability. When New York City reports that a certain percentage of students at a certain grade are "below grade norms" on the Metropolitan Reading Test (or whatever test they may be giving), does this mean that the students are failing in reading ability, or does it mean they are below the expected maturity level in language comprehension or in cognitive ability? I think the latter is more likely than the former, but we have no way of telling.

In a practical way, all this suggests that we may be fooling ourselves or, at least, that we are sorely misguided, if we think we are teaching reading comprehension. Marshall McLuhan is at least partly right in saying that the "Medium is the Massage," for the principal medium whereby schools teach language comprehension, and cognitive ability generally, is the printed word. Yes, the schools do use other means as well—speaking, listening, and discussing; audiovisual materials; and field trips—but one cannot deny the key role of the printed word. That is why the reading specialist finds himself/herself to be the principal medicine man/woman in the business of teaching language and cognitive abilities. That is why the International Reading Association finds itself in the role of a key organization in the general education of our youth. But the confusions between reading and language and between language and cognition, often mislead the reading teacher and the reading specialist into dealing with only a small part of the problem, by thinking that the problem centers in the transaction between the printed word and ideas, whereas the real problem lies in the promotion of language abilities as such. The transaction between print and ideas, which we call "reading," is only incidental to the development of language comprehension and cognitive ability.

Parameters of language development

Developmental parameters of reading comprehension, whatever they are, cannot be meaningful if they concern the reading process alone, or are based on data derived solely from transactions involving print. Developmental parameters of reading comprehension must include developmental parameters of language comprehension that do not involve print, and possibly developmental parameters of cognitive ability that do not involve language.

All this seems obvious, and I find myself rather impatient for, though I have been saying things like this for some, I see little evidence that the idea has caught on in the way people teach reading comprehension or test its attainment. Let me, therefore, be quite explicit about how I think we might establish developmental parameters of reading comprehension.

First, a word is in order about how I am using the term *developmental parameter*. In mathematics, a parameter is a value of some variable that enters into the specification of a mathematical function or distribution, such that different values result in different functions or distributions. In educational and psychological measurement, this notion is applied to using numbers to describe basic characteristics of individual learners; for example, different numbers imply different behaviors, different learning rates, or different rates of growth. The essential task of the educational measurer is to find some way of specifying a small set of numbers or *parameters* that will allow him to describe or predict a large number of behaviors. One such parameter that has been offered is the IQ or intelligence quotient. Perhaps it is one of the parameters that is needed to describe rate of growth in reading comprehension. But in some ways this parameter may not be satisfactory; I would suppose, therefore, that we need to look for other ways of specifying numbers that will describe and predict reading comprehension behavior. These numbers, if obtained for the individual learner, would presumably constitute "developmental parameters of reading comprehension" that would allow us to generalize beyond the particular measuring technique and predict a wide range of outcomes.

The first order of business is to develop ways of clearly distinguishing between reading skill, as such, and language development. This is not a new idea; it is implicit in the notion of a w-o (written-oral) ratio mentioned by Venezky and Calfee (1970) in their model of the reading process, or that has been incorporated into various diagnostic procedures (e.g., those developed by the Committee on Diagnostic Reading Tests [1947-1963]). A particularly interesting use of the idea has been made in the Durrell Listening-Reading Series, which contain parallel tests of listening and reading comprehension (Durrell and Brassard, 1970). If a youngster can't understand a passage when he reads it, can he understand it when it is read aloud to him? Over a whole set of reading passages of varying difficulty, what is the ratio between the amount of understanding he can demonstrate when he reads the passages in printed form and when the passages are presented in spoken form? Presumably, if the ratio is high, the youngster is able to read up to the level of his language comprehension, but if the ratio is low, one may infer that the youngster is having trouble with decoding or some other aspect of his behavior in the presence of printed language. Some sort of ratio between reading and listening skills has been proposed as a criterion of literacy, perhaps even in the adult population: a person is literate to the extent that he can read materials up to the level of his language comprehension.

Right here we might have a good way of indexing *reading* comprehension relative to *language* comprehension. It would seem simple enough to compile a set of passages scaled for comprehension difficulty that could be presented in parallel written and spoken forms. There exist various sets of materials that, with a little further work, might meet the requirements; for example, the McCall and Crabbs (1926-1961) Standard Test Lessons in Reading or the set of passages that Coleman and Miller (1968) have scaled for difficulty by the cloze technique.

There are some technical problems with this approach, but I do not believe they are insurmountable. 1) Ranking the passages for comprehension difficulty assumes that language development is unidimensional. Actually, it must proceed along a number of dimensions that can be at least roughly differentiated—vocabulary, syntax, and style. 2) Quite apart from linguistic variation in complexity, passages can vary in conceptual difficulty. It is possible to talk about simple things in a complex way, or to talk about complex ideas in a simple way. Thus, the technique I propose here has the risk of confusing language comprehension with a more general type of cognitive ability—the ability to reason and to make inferences—precisely one of the confusions I mentioned earlier. To get valid measures of language comprehension as distinct from the comprehension of printed material, we must keep the conceptual difficulty uniformly as low as possible. That may be difficult. 3) The degree to which a passage is appropriate to the general experience and interests of the individual may be difficult to control. An academician with purported good reading and language comprehension might have trouble understanding a passage on crop control, while a crop farmer might have little difficulty which it. 4) There are undoubtedly factors involved in the administration of a pure listening test that are specific to the listening situation and that would interfere with the indexing of pure language comprehension. For example, the rate at which the passage is read; the dialect, tone, and expression of the speaker; the attention span of the hearer; and the hearer's opportunity to think about the passage or to hear it read again are some of these factors. 5) The exact way in which comprehension should be tested is a problem, though this applies with equal force to testing comprehension of printed materials. In the case of a listening test, however, special problems arise in the use of multiple-choice questions, cloze procedure, and the like. If one decides on the use of free-response questions, as I would recommend (Carroll, 1972), how should they be constructed and scored? Should one follow the advice of Bormuth (1970) and develop questions by using some system of syntactic and semantic transformation rules?

It might be interesting to try to produce a W-O Comprehension Scale, where W-O stands for written-oral. Such a scale should be designed to be administered to students and other people from about the second grade up to the college level. It would have two equated components—a printed comprehension scale and an oral comprehension scale such that scores or levels attained on comparable components could be observed and compared. I would discourage the use of a ratio between these levels, for ratios can be deceptive and depend on certain assumptions that might not be easy to satisfy. Actually, the absolute score levels attained on the two components would be of more interest. If our theory of reading comprehension is correct, the score on the printed scale would never be more than the score on the oral portion. In many cases the score on the printed scale might be far less than the score on the oral portion. At any rate, a W-O Comprehension Scale, when fully developed, could be a much-needed device that could be used by teachers and others to index the grosser reading and language comprehension skills. Probably it would have to be administered individually, something like the Stanford-Binet Intelligence Scale, although perhaps at least parts of it could be adapted for group testing, with the use of tape-recordings for the oral portion. Or perhaps if an individual demonstrates a high enough ability to handle printed language, the later parts of the test could rely on the printed medium and be group-administered. The curse of group-administered procedures has been the almost mindless way in which test developers introduce the print medium at some point—e.g., in presenting printed multiple-choice alternatives in a listening comprehension test. There exist ways of avoiding the print medium in a group-administered test—e.g., presenting *pictured* multiple-choice alternatives—but these procedures have often been ignored by test developers. There are lots of reasonably good measures of language development, except that they have too much involvement of the print medium, so that the interpretation of the scores is always clouded with doubts as to how much reading ability as such is involved. (This is true, for example, of many otherwise excellent vocabulary tests.)

Before leaving this idea of a W-O Comprehension Scale, let's see whether we can carry it a bit further. Could we possibly add a cognitive conceptual ability component, thus making it a W-O-C Comprehension Scale? If we could control the conceptual difficulty of the W and O components at a fairly low level, could we develop a graded series of tests or tasks that would index the level of conceptual difficulty that the individual could attain, thus separately from the indices of reading comprehension and language comprehension? The assumption would be that just as one could compare an individual's ability to handle print with his ability to handle language, so one could compare an individual's handling of language with his ability to handle concepts, to reason, to make inferences, etc. A person's ability to handle language would presumably be limited by his ability (or inability) to handle materials of high conceptual difficulty. Yet an individual could have high conceptual or cognitive ability and poor language competence. On the assumption that our language comprehension test is in English, this could be true of the speaker of a foreign languge who has not mastered English. In these days of concern with the teaching of English to children who speak other languages, the need for the testing of conceptual ability, apart from English language competence, becomes more apparent.

I am frankly not sure how we should proceed with the development of a test or scale of cognitive ability that would not involve language. Perhaps it is not even possible. The sort of thing that I have in mind would be some nonlanguage analogue of the Stanford-Binet Intelligence Scale. Let us, however, relax the requirement that the scale not use language, and limit its use to people with at least minimal competence in English. Such a scale would have greater face-validity for the understanding of reading comprehension. We could present a series of language understanding tasks that are graded in terms of the level of complexity of the inferential or reasoning problems that they involve. In fact, a great many of the items on standardized reading and listening comprehension tests are of this character. (This is one reason why reading tests often correlate as highly as they do with verbal intelligence tests [Carroll, 1969].) The tasks would involve the apprehension of simple cause-effect relations, the understanding of the necessities of space and time (e.g., realizing that a person cannot be in two places at once, or that yesterday cannot follow tomorrow), reasoning with syllogisms, analogies, class inclusion and exclusion, and the like—all problems that come up in reading comprehension. They would, however, be administered in oral form, or at least in some way that would not involve print. Like the other components of the W-O-C Comprehension Scale, they would be criterion-referenced in the sense that each level of the scale would be identified with clearly described cognitive tasks. Perhaps a scale of this sort could be put together fairly easily by rummaging around in available reading comprehension tests, tests of factors of cognitive ability, and other sources; but of course a good deal of standardization and tryout would be required.

So there you have it—a proposal for a W-O-C Scale that would define the developmental parameters of reading comprehension and that could be administered by teachers, reading specialists, and others to students or adults to index the relative levels of their ability to a) handle the conceptual and inferential reasoning processes involved in reading, b) handle the language comprehension elements in reading, and c) do these things in the print medium as well as in other media.

A device such as this might, of course, be too unwieldy to give every student. It might be recommended only for use with "problem readers" as a diagnostic device. But even if it were not regularly used with all students, it would be useful as a means for objectively defining the nature of the reading comprehension problem and in indicating what kinds of linguistic and conceptual tasks must be taught if a student is to achieve his maximum potential at a given age. Plotting the progress of students on the three scales as a function of age or grade would give us a clearer idea of rates of development to be expected. The scores would also be infinitely superior to the grade equivalents that are now so prevalently used in assessing reading achievement. And if reading comprehension skills were adequately taught to all students, the three scales of the W-O-C Comprehension Scale would be perfectly correlated (or at least correlated up to the limit of their reliability). That is, every student would, at any point in his school career, achieve at the same level on the three scales. His language comprehension ability would match the level of his cognitive maturity and his ability to handle printed material would match his language comprehension ability. Each component of the W-O-C Scale would have the characteristic of a nearly perfect Guttman scale; i.e., a student would be able to perform all tasks up to a certain level but increasingly fail tasks beyond that level. At least this would be the ideal—how closely it could be achieved in practice could not be ascertained until we try to make such a W-O-C Scale.

It might be found that the kind of scale I am envisaging would be too gross and global—covering too much territory and ignoring the necessary fine details. For purpose of greater precision in diagnosis and in the guidance of teaching it might be useful to have some of the scales broken into, or accompanied by, subscales. We already know enough about language comprehension to set up separate scales for such things as knowledge of vocabulary, knowledge of the grammatical function of words (Carroll, 1970), level of syntactic understanding, and ability to apprehend anaphoric relationships (Bormuth et al., 1970). These aspects of language comprehension are not perfectly correlated and thus may need to be separately gauged. They are, nevertheless, components of language comprehension and thus should correlate highly with the global language comprehension scale.

These subscales could also be produced easily in printed form; in fact, some existing materials (e.g., printed vocabulary tests) might be adapted.

Setting up subscales for cognitive or conceptual ability might not be so easy, since we do not know enough about whether cognitive ability can be divided into separate aspects. At the low end of the scale, certain types of "Piagetian" tasks might be found useful—in an attempt to measure the child's attainment of concrete operations such as seriation and conservation. Further up the scale, tests might be assembled from some of the Thurstone Primary Mental Abilities materials.

Implications for teaching

Suppose the W-O-C Comprehension Scales were already

developed and perfected. What would be the implications for teaching? I have already suggested that the scales would be useful as a way of making more concrete the separate components of the reading comprehension process and of identifying the progressively more difficult kinds of tasks that the reader must master in attaining full competence in reading comprehension. But the scales would be useful in other ways.

First, what about the Cognitive Ability Scale? If a student (or adult) does not reach the highest possible level on this scale, as most students will not, to what extent can the person be helped to acquire the further cognitive abilities needed to attain this high level? The usual assumption is that cognitive ability is something that can increase only with age and biological maturation. That assumption may in fact be correct. The evidence we have on the degree to which intellectual abilities can be promoted through special training is not too encouraging, and any evidence to the contrary is possibly flawed by the fact that some obviously trainable language responses are involved. Nevertheless, the question is still open and will remain so for many years. Anything the reading teacher, or anyone else, can do to promote cognitive skills should of course be encouraged.

In contrast, it seems evident that *language* comprehension skills can be improved by teaching and learning, at least up to the level permitted by cognitive maturity at a given point in the individual's life span, as indexed by the Cognitive Ability Scale of the W-O-C series. One can teach the vocabulary for the concepts that the individual is able to handle, although this may be a slow and difficult process. One can teach strategies of understanding sentences and paragraphs. This teaching should be done with both oral and printed language, since the student needs to learn a new word not only in its spoken form but also in its printed form, so that he can recognize it visually and perhaps even spell it. Teaching strategies of sentence and paragraph comprehension is particularly necessary in the printed language mode because it is in the printed mode that the more difficult comprehension tasks are more likely to occur, and it is in that mode that a sentence or paragraph can be more easily studied as a visual object that can be scanned and rescanned.

Reading teachers must, in fact, consider one of their primary responsibilities to be helping students attain *language* comprehension (quite apart from *reading* comprehension) up to the level of their cognitive abilities. This also is a responsibility of other kinds of teachers—teachers of English, social studies, science—but the reading teacher is in a favorable position to do a great deal in this respect. Teaching language comprehension is a responsibility of the reading teacher even though, with a strict interpretation, it may seem to have nothing to do with reading. Since much of the deficiency that students exhibit in reading comprehension is probably traceable to deficiencies in language comprehension, the reading teacher will have plenty of work to do, even without worrying about the promotion of conceptual and cognitive skills.

Levels attained in language comprehension place limits on levels of attainment in reading comprehension, as we have seen. But undoubtedly many youngsters (and adults as well) fail in reading comprehension not because of deficiencies in language competence, or even cognitive ability, but because of their poor mastery of certain reading skills. Some may be deficient in simple decoding skills, such as the mastery of grapheme-phoneme relationships. But there are other skills that can still be called *decoding*, such as the rapid recognition of whole words; these are particularly critical in the case of words at the more advanced vocabulary levels, for English orthography is not such as to insure that pure phonic skills (or even "guessing from context," which I think is vastly over-rated by some reading experts and teachers) will serve to help in the recognition of such words. Further, decoding skills include strategies for studying word order and word groups in a sentence, trying out different grammatical constructions, and the like. Someone recently told me of the case of a problem reader who was observed while he was reading a little story. He was trying to make sense of the sentence, "Get away from me, bee." He read all the words correctly but complained that the sentence didn't make sense, saying that it would have been somewhat more reasonable if the sentence read "Get away from my bee." Apparently he didn't notice the comma, and failed to recognize that *bee* was to be taken in the vocative case (i.e., that someone was talking to the bee). Certainly he could have understood the sentence if it had been read aloud to him with proper expression. He didn't possess the strategy of responding to cues in the text such as commas, and he didn't understand that the name of a person being addressed is often set off by a comma. Incidentally, my informant commented that apparently today's reading series, in contrast to those of yesteryear, have almost completely dropped the teaching of punctuation as cues to sentence interpretation. If this is true, shame on them! As an experienced reader, I frequently find that commas are wonderful guideposts and sometimes make all the difference in meaning.

In summary

Reading comprehension has to be considered in the light of general language comprehension and in the light of the student's general cognitive maturity. Each of these sets limits on the preceding. To make this idea a little more concrete, imagine a mechanical gadget with three vertical lever controls something like what you find on some hi-fi sets. Each lever can go up or down, or be pushed up or down. Imagine that the three levers are labeled, left to right: Reading Skills, Language Competence, and Cognitive Ability. Now according to my theory, these levers cannot work completely independently. In fact, the one on the right, Cognitive Ability, is not a lever at all, but just an indicator. You can't push it up or down, but as time goes on, it moves slowly upward. But inside our mechanical gadget things are fixed so that you can move the Language Competence lever upward, but only so high as the Cognitive Ability indicator is set. Likewise, things are fixed so that you can move the Reading Skills lever upward, but only so high as the Language Competence lever is set.

These levers correspond to the levels attained by a reading student on our imaginary W-O-C Comprehension scales. The Cognitive Ability lever shows the level attained on the C scale; its level is roughly determined by the student's age and biological maturity, and his ability to profit from his experiences. You can't expect to do much about it, except to make sure that the student has opportunities to develop his abilities. The Language Competence lever indicates the level of the student's comprehension of language. Under normal conditions (that is, when the student has been reared in a language-rich environment) that Language Competence lever tends to move upward with time, along with the Cognitive Ability lever, but sometimes it lags behind seriously. With effort, you can just budge that lever a little higher and higher, but, of course, only as high as the Cognitive Ability lever. Finally, under normal conditions (that is, when the child has had good opportunity to learn to read by good teaching or otherwise) the Reading Skills lever tends to move upward along with the two other levers. There may even be a little play in the mechanism such that the Reading Skills lever can go a little higher than the Language Competence lever—reflecting the fact that some reading skills are independent of language comprehension. (For example, a child might be able to call off words without understanding them very well.) But again, there may be serious lags, lags that can be decreased only by serious effort addressed to the teaching of reading skills.

Thus the levers, and the corresponding levels attained by a student on my proposed W-O-C Comprehension scales, represent the developmental parameters of reading comprehension. Doubtless I have oversimplified matters—perhaps there ought to be many more levers in our mechanical model, with lots more play in them (but still interconnections) corresponding to those subscales I talked about—but in large outline, and as a guide to our thinking, the model has merit. If there is a science-fiction quality to all this, I challenge you to try to turn it into reality.

REFERENCES

Bormuth, J.R. *On the theory of achievement test items.* Chicago: University of Chicago Press, 1970.

Bormuth, J.R.; Manning, J.; Carr, J.; and Pearson, D. Children's comprehension of between- and within-sentence syntactic structures. *Journal of Educational Psychology,* 1970, *61,* 349-357.

Carroll, J.B. From comprehension to inference. In M.P. Douglass (Ed.), *Sign and significance. Thirty-third Yearbook, Claremont Reading Conference.* Claremont, California: Claremont Graduate School, 1969, 39-44.

Carroll, J.B. Comprehension by 3rd, 6th, and 9th graders of words having multiple grammatical functions. Final Report, Project

No. 9-0439, Grant No. OEG-2-9-400439-1059, U.S. Department of Health, Education and Welfare, U.S. Office of Education, December, 1970. Princeton, New Jersey: Educational Testing Service, 1970. [ERIC Document Reproduction Service, Document ED 048 311.]

Carroll, J.B. Development of native language skills beyond the early years. In C.E. Reed (Ed.), *The learning of language.* New York: Appleton-Century-Crofts, 1971, 97-156.

Carroll, J.B. Defining language comprehension: Some speculations. In R.O. Freedle and J.B. Carroll (Eds.), *Language comprehension and the acquisition of knowledge.* Washington, D.C.: V.H. Winston and Sons (New York: Halsted Press), 1972.

Coleman, E.B., and Miller, G.R. A measure of information gained during prose learning. *Reading Research Quarterly,* 1968, *3,* 369-386.

Committee on Diagnostic Reading Tests. *Diagnostic reading tests.* Mountain Home, North Carolina: Committee on Diagnostic Reading Tests, Inc., 1947-1963.

Durrell, D.D., and Brassard, M.B. *Durrell Listening-Reading Series.* New York: Harcourt, Brace and World, 1970.

Educational Testing Service. *Sequential tests of educational progress: Reading.* Princeton, New Jersey: Educational Testing Service, 1957.

McCall, W.A., and Crabbs, L.M. *Standard test lessons in reading.* New York: Teachers College Press, 1926, 1950, 1961.

Venezky, R.L., and Calfee, R.C. The reading competency model. In H. Singer and R.B. Ruddell (Eds.) *Theoretical models and processes of reading.* Newark, Delaware: International Reading Association, 1970, 273-291.

Comments on
Developmental Parameters
of Reading Comprehension

Isabel L. Beck

First, let me say that I consider an opportunity to respond to John Carroll's presentation a very great privilege. His thoughts about reading as contained in his writings, for example, *The Analysis of Reading Instruction: Perspectives from Psychology and Linguistics* (Carroll, 1964) and *The Nature of the Reading Process* (Carroll, 1970), have been seminal to my own work in curriculum development in the beginning reading area.

As I view it, Carroll's paper on Developmental Parameters of Reading Comprehension contains two general themes: the first concerns defining the components of reading comprehension and the second attends to ways of measuring the components and describing their structural relationships. Carroll's notion is that reading comprehension is a multifaceted capability, made up of separate components, each of which plays a significant role in determining overall competence in comprehension. He suggests that reading skills plus language competency plus cognitive ability equals reading comprehension. While this equation is not a particularly new notion in that other theorists have specified these same ingredients, Carroll's arrangement of the facets of reading comprehension is useful.

In his treatment of the multicomponent model, Carroll has compared it, in a very direct manner, to conventional terminology and to some of our current, sometimes fuzzy, and often overly inclusive concepts about reading comprehension. In so doing, he has introduced some important distinctions that must become functional if we are to refine our understanding of reading comprehension and plan interventions that address all its facets directly. Furthermore, Carroll expands upon the distinctions he has introduced in two ways: he includes examples of the subskills to be found in each major component and he attacks in a direct way, the difficult problem of finding satisfactory techniques to measure them. His treatment of the multicomponent model provides the depth and some of the necessary operational detail required to bring theory down to the practical level, enabling important developmental work to get underway.

The aspect of reading comprehension best explicated in Dr. Carroll's paper is the W-O scale, a scale that reflects the relationship of a person's oral language comprehension to his/her comprehension of print. Such a scale, in my opinion, would be an important step in the development of tools that could aid our studies of the comprehension process and, at the same time, provide information to teachers that could be useful in instructional decision making. For example, having a child's score on the W-O scale would be helpful prescriptively as background information on the child's language capabilities to be used in turn for the identification of the next instructional step. In addition, the notion that literacy be defined as the extent to which a person can read materials up to the level of his/her language comprehension appears a far more useful definition of literacy than the search for a minimum grade equivalent for all, in that the score on the O scale would likely be a good gauge of potential reading competence.

Carroll's speculation as to whether it would be possible to add a cognitive or conceptual ability component to the W-O scale, thus resulting in a W-O-C scale, is intriguing. However, I would first like to see efforts directed towards the W-O scale.

Carroll did not explicitly include a *knowledge* component as a major ingredient of reading comprehension. However, he does deal with the importance to comprehension of background information or knowledge about a subject when he suggests that "an academician with purported good reading and language comprehension might have trouble understanding a passage on crop control, while a farmer might have little difficulty with it." The point is that reading comprehension is partly knowledge bound; unfamiliarity with subject matter concepts can cause difficulty in comprehension. Therefore I would be tempted to include knowledge as a major component of reading comprehension. Recognizing lack of relevant experiences and background information as blocks to comprehension is especially important in teaching and in diagnosis of problem readers.

In viewing instructional practice, Carroll notes that reading teachers who deal with only "the transaction between the printed word and ideas are dealing with only a small part of the problem...the real problem lies in the promotion of language abilities *as such* and even the promotion of cognitive abilities *as such*."

From many visits to classrooms, from looking at a variety of reading materials, and from my own experiences as a classroom teacher, it is my strong impression that much of the time spent in "reading comprehension instruction" is indeed spent dealing with "the transaction between print and ideas." A typical reading lesson in the intermediate grades goes something like this: Children read a text, answer written and/or oral questions about the text, and, with the teacher leading the discussion, discuss with their peers ideas contained in the text. While this activity can and often does promote language abilities (e.g., new vocabulary) and cognitive abilities (e.g., inferences from the text are discussed), it is my sense these are secondary rather than primary outcomes. Understanding propositions in printed material is the terminal goal of teaching reading comprehension. Dealing with the goal in terms of discussing the ideas in texts is useful; however, at least equal emphasis should be placed on expanding vocabulary and handling complete syntax. Vocabulary and syntax are the building blocks of language and may be overlooked when they are embedded in a standard "comprehension" activity. Rather, they should be specially attended to in reading instruction. Certainly Carroll's model, including as it does *language competence*, implies this. Increased competence in vocabulary and syntax are transferrable to new texts, whereas the ideas brought to awareness in discussion may not be useful beyond the specific text.

Using information from linguistics, psychology, and psychometrics, Carroll's paper provides a conceptual handle on reading comprehension and outlines some of the technical problems with its measurement; and with all of this, one is struck with the elegant simplicity of his model.

REFERENCES

Carroll, J. B. The nature of the reading process. In H. Singer and R. B. Ruddell (Eds.), *Theoretical models and processes of reading*. Newark, Delaware: International Reading Association, 1970.
Carroll, J. B. The analysis of reading instruction: Perspectives from psychology and linguistics. In E.R. Hilgard and H.G. Richey (Eds.), *Theories of learning and instruction*, Sixty-third Yearbook of the National Society for the Study of Education. Chicago: University of Chicago Press, 1964, 336-353.

Language Comprehension and Fast Decoding: Some Psycholinguistic Prerequisites for Skilled Reading Comprehension

Charles A. Perfetti

To understand the development of reading comprehension it is necessary to understand language comprehension and decoding. The thesis of this paper is that the cognitive part of Reading Comprehension = Language Comprehension + Decoding + X, and, more importantly, that X is small relative to the other two factors. I shall leave factor X to others and focus on language comprehension and decoding. Since both of these factors, especially language comprehension, encompass complex processes, establishing the reasonableness of the equation will not immediately shed light on how reading comprehension develops.

What it might do is to suggest some reduction on the range of misconceptions of reading comprehension. It could cause thinking to focus on language skills and thinking rather than "organization" or "text strategies" as the keys to reading comprehension. Since I've mentioned "thinking," I will admit to a variant of the original equation, viz. Reading Comprehension = Decoding + Thinking. Substituting one ill-defined term for another of course does not help much, except insofar

The research reported herein was supported by the Learning Research and Development Center, supported in part by funds from the National Institute of Education (NIE), United States Department of Health, Education, and Welfare. The opinions expressed do not necessarily reflect the position or policy of NIE and no official endorsement should be inferred. The research reported was carried out with the significant contributions of Susan Goldman, Thomas Hogaboam, and Laura Bell. Susan Alexander and Robert Straub also assisted with parts of the reported research.

as it reminds us that what is crucial in reading comprehension is the interaction of a human mind with a printed page. Reading is thinking constrained by print. Thus, the present view is in the tradition of E.L. Thorndike (1917) and R.L. Thorndike (1973) on reading as reasoning, and it shares with others (J. B. Carroll, 1966 and this volume, and T. G. Sticht, 1972) the assumption that reading is a special case of language. These two traditions are quite compatible when the close connection between language and thinking is acknowledged.

In what follows, I would like to discuss some psycholinguistic processes underlying reading comprehension by referring to my own research in an informal way. I will deal both with decoding and with the "Higher Mental Process" term of the Reading Comprehension Equation (i.e., language comprehension or thinking) by reference to one or two particular aspects of comprehension.

Levels of comprehension

Understanding sentences and bunches of sentences is a matter of degree. That is, it makes sense to speak of levels of comprehension. This idea of levels has been specifically developed in descriptions of sentence processing by Mistler-Lachman (1974) and by Perfetti (in press) and is related to the view of Craik and Lockhart (1972) that memory is best seen as the operation of different processing levels rather than as strictly storage and transfer of information. In an earlier paper (Perfetti, in press) I suggested six levels of sentence processing, but the numbers seem rather arbitrary. For present purposes, I will describe only three levels (see Figure 1). Level I is the lowest level of interest for reading, and it can be characterized as a Surface Level and phonological and acoustic properties salient. Level II is perhaps the most basic comprehension level and can be termed the "semantic-syntactic level." Level III is the interpretive level and differs from Level II primarily in its integrative quality. Thus, it is comprehension of a sentence with respect to something beyond the sentence. This something else can be nonlinguistic or at least nontextual, but it is simplifying to consider it as the linguistic context of the sentence. The levels are descriptive

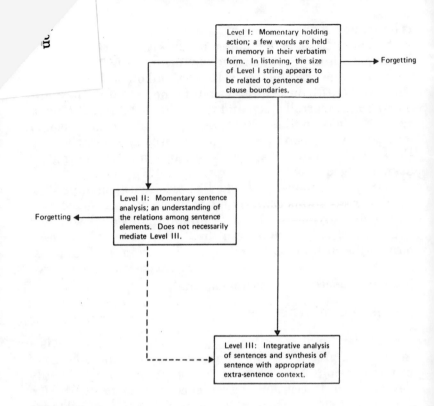

Figure 1. Three descriptive levels of processing.

rather than theoretically interrelated. For example, it seems to me that attention switching is involved in going from Level I to Level II or III but that in going from Level II to Level III it is not. As an illustration of the levels, consider the sentence "The admiral captured the bandit." What do you understand from the sentence? At Level II, your understanding of this sentence can be indicated by some questions transformationally related to the sentence:

1. Who captured the bandit?
2. What did the admiral do?
3. Who(m) did the admiral capture?

Questions of this type require information based on a semantic-syntactic analysis of the sentence and are the kind of "literal questions" that test construction theory is familiar with. Bormuth's theory (1970) of achievement test items is based on the essentially simple transformational relation between these questions and the simple sentence. The knowledge required by Level II in this case can be indicated by some propositionally based form, for example PAST + *captures* (AGENT: *admiral*, RECIPIENT: *bandit*).

What of Level III processing for this sentence? Well, in fact it is impossible unless you know more than is in that sentence. The questions to test Level III cannot be easily specified in the general case because they are not based on the syntax of the single sentence. In the present case, they could include the following:

4. What bandit?
5. Capture how?
6. Why did the admiral capture the bandit?

Thus the information ranges from referential to what is sometimes called inferential. The reader will be able to answer (4) if the previous text has identified a person who is a bandit and he will answer (6) if he is able to relate an earlier proposition in the text to this new one.

The boundary between Levels II and III is thus artificial because it is based on the distinction between a single sentence and bunches of related sentences. But the postulation of these levels does have theoretical and practical consequences. Level II demands basic linguistic competence and Level III demands "thinking" or at least some construction of ideas. One could say Level II is an analysis process, while Level III is a synthesis process based on prior analyses and syntheses. The practical consequences of the distinction can be seen in testing. Some comprehension achievement tests seem mainly to demand Level II processing while others demand substantial Level III processing. For the development of reading comprehension, the question is whether reading skill at Level II normally entails a reading skill appropriate for Level III. Some psychometric approaches to comprehension (e.g., Davis) would seem to suggest some degree of independence between sentence comprehension and paragraph comprehension. To some degree, Level III skills may not inevitably come with Level II skills. However, the chances seem good that little special is needed beyond attention, memory, and some reason for the reader to want to integrate information. (Just in case there are readers who have this characteristic of disposing of sentences after Level II processing, I would like to give them the name "sentence surfers." The parallel with "word barkers" is intentional. Sentence surfers skim along the tops of sentences without getting deeper meaning.)

Mention of "word barking" brings me back to Level I. A reader who can articulate the component words of a sentence but who immediately after reading it cannot answer questions (1) - (3), would be processing at Level I. To the extent that most readers can occasionally exhibit Level I processing, it would seem to be a question of attention. If attention is focused on meaning, Level III, or perhaps II, is engaged. But occasionally attention shifts, to another stimulus, or another thought, which interferes with meaning-conscious processing. But because phonological processing is so over-learned "reading" can continue without comprehension. Attention can also be switched to the sound itself, as with song and poetry. Level I processing is thus normal and characteristic of some reading and listening situations. Whether there are individuals who are *characteristically* Level I processors is another question. I'm inclined to think such individuals are less numerous than is sometimes implied.

With the three levels of processing as a very loose framework, I will now turn to some psycholinguistic principles in reading comprehension that have empirical bases, although some of what I report is fairly tentative. The three psycholinguistic problems to be addressed are decoding, meaning analysis, and memory for discourse. I will attempt to suggest that characteristic levels of comprehension are involved in these processes and that the characteristic level in some cases is not so obvious. Primarily, however, I will try to suggest that decoding and language comprehension are the major ingredients of reading comprehension.

Decoding

Decoding and comprehension achievement

I assume that decoding is an important part of reading comprehension. The remaining part is skill at analyzing language and constructing meanings from language elements. There is probably a residual component connected with the peculiar facts of reading: that it occurs by turning pages, that the reader cannot interrupt the writer to ask for clarification, and that the order of information may be somewhat different. But my hunch is that while such factors are important, they are not so important as decoding and language comprehension.

There are two assumptions that are challenged by this position. One is that comprehension is independent of decoding. The other is that all human beings have the same linguistic competence and hence the same language comprehension skill. Both assumptions are false.

To talk first about decoding and comprehension, the notion that the two are independent may be based on a confusion with the more tenable assumption that decoding is not sufficient for comprehension. It must be true that skilled decoding does not necessarily lead to skilled comprehension. However, I think the reasons for this may be less due to factors like "organization" and more due to factors like vocabulary memory and attention for language.

In order to discuss some aspects of the interdependence between decoding and comprehension, a couple of experiments will be briefly summarized. The first experiment (Perfetti and Hogaboam, 1975) tests the basic requirement of the interdependence hypothesis. Third and fifth graders were separated into two levels of reading comprehension skills, as measured by the reading subtest of the Metropolitan Achievement Test. The measure of decoding was the latency of correct vocalizations of printed words and pseudowords presented one at a time. Figure 2 shows the main results.

Note that not only were skilled comprehenders faster at this decoding task than less skilled comprehenders, but the degree of their superiority increased as the words became less common. For common high-frequency English, the differences were slight, but significant. For pseudowords, which are nonwords that conform to English spelling rules, the average difference between skilled and less skilled was over one second. Since the latency data are only for words produced correctly, we are not dealing with the fact that less skilled readers are less good at decoding. In this case, it is a question of their being

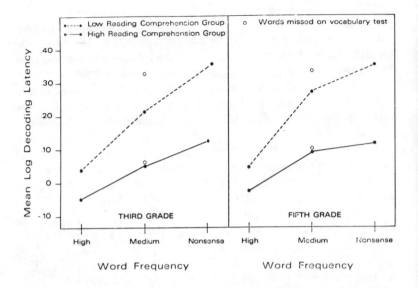

Figure 2. Speed of decoding for skilled and less skilled readers for high and low frequency English words and nonwords.

slower at decoding.

What is the significance of being slower at decoding? To the extent that latency reflects processing time (in this case orthographic-phonetic analysis) being slow reflects the engagement of a limited capacity processor for decoding. Since this same limited capacity processor has to be used to remember words already read and to think about the meaning of what is read, it is possible that slow decoding will in fact lead to poorer comprehension. Thus, the speed of decoding is taken to be an indication of its automaticity. The notion of automaticity has been with researchers of motor skill learning as well as reading researchers for some time. The importance of automaticity for reading and what it might mean in terms of attention to stimulus features has been persuasively stressed by LaBerge and Samuels (1974). With respect to latencies there are some problems. Since time is continuous, are we dealing with degrees of conscious effort or with some fairly sharp distinction between automatic and effortful? It's hard to say at present, but it could turn out to be a matter of degree.

Well and good, one might say, but all you have is a correlation. It is just as reasonable to say that good comprehension leads to fast decoding as the other way around. This is fair enough, and what can be said in response is that there is a conceptualization of the reading process that accommodates the interpretation that fast decoding aids comprehension. This conceptualization is that comprehension during reading involves sharing some limited capacity system among various task components. The less work required by decoding, the more available the system is for other comprehension work.

Factors affecting decoding speed

I would like to turn now to some further studies in decoding that aim at separating quantitative from qualitative factors in decoding speed. In briefly summarizing this research, a possible problem concerned with the measure of decoding can be taken care of. The problem is the possible objection to vocalization latencies as measures of decoding. After all, vocalizing is an unnatural act during skilled reading. In fact, the study that I will summarize does seem to suggest that the measure of decoding does matter somewhat. However, the use of a second decoding measure does not affect the main results that skilled comprehenders are faster decoders than poor comprehenders and that their advantage increases with nonwords. The second measure we used was the latencies of correct responses in a same-different task. The child's task was to press a button when two word strings were the same. Following a procedure of Comber and Hogie (1974), we separated the letter-strings maximally on the presentation slide to encourage the child to decode the top string and compare it with the bottom string. Without further details of this measure, the main point concerns some word experiences that the children had and their effects on decoding speeds. Since the two decoding measures produced similar results, I will use the data for vocalization latencies.

The object was to provide certain systematic experiences with words for the child and observe the effects of these experiences on decoding speed. The rationale is that when a reader encounters a given word, there are roughly four categories for his prior experience with the word: 1) A word he has never seen nor heard. 2) A word he has heard but never seen, and he does not know what the word means. 3) Same as (2), except he does know the meaning from his oral language vocabulary. 4) A word he has heard *and* seen, but he does not know the meaning. 5) Same as (4), except he does know the meaning. For purposes of the study, we wanted to provide the relevant word experiences for the child. Therefore, most of the words in these 5 categories are extremely rare words (*nabob*) that resemble pseudowords. In fact the rare words resemble paralogs so strongly that it is difficult to convince adults otherwise, except with a dictionary. So additionally we have categories (6) and (7) which are medium and high frequency English words, respectively. An example of (6) is *model*, and an example of (7) is *money*. Note that in principle (6) and (7) should be somewhat like (5), the difference being that during the experiment, the child does not have any experience with (6) and (7). We provide experience with (5) to simulate (6) and (7).

The nature of the experience is simple. For (1), there is no experience and the child's first encounter of the word is in the decoding speed test. For (2) and (3), the child hears the experimenter say a word and then says it himself. The frequency of hearings and sayings is about 20 spread over three days. In (3), but not (2), the experimenter in addition to saying the word tells an elaborate story about the word's meaning. The meanings were made up by the experimenter to refer to concrete objects. The important point about the meaning experience is that it was not simply a paired-associates procedure (e.g., *Nekoz* means *ball)*. We provided a rich conceptualization for a word which was to have meaning. For example, a *polef* was a type of banana, distinguished by its color, which was red. It was the major crop of a certain South Pacific island, and residents of the island depended on it for food and other things. Moreover, the child was brought to a criterion based on two tests. He had to produce the word given the meaning by the experimenter, and he had to produce the meaning given the word. Because we wanted to control for frequency of exposure to the word, the frequency of a given child's oral-only experience (2) was made roughly the same as his oral + meaning experience (3).

In the case of (4) and (5), the child had *decoding* experience ("visual" is really too weak a term) in addition to

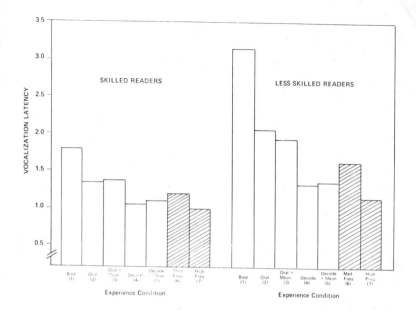

Figure 3. Effect of four types of word experience on decoding speed (measured by vocalization latencies) of skilled and less skilled readers.

hearing the word. After hearing the word, he would see it and say it. The difference between (4) and (5) was one of meaning experience and is completely parallel to the oral cases (2) and (3).

In summary, we have isolated three types of single word experiences: oral, decoding, and meaning. Over all conditions the number of word exposures and the number of productions by the child were equalized. We tested fourth grade children, matched by pairs on IQ, who were separated as skilled and less skilled comprehenders as before.

The results can be stated more briefly than the procedure. As can be seen from Figure 3, both skill groups were aided a good deal by oral experience. And both groups were aided by decoding experience. Two points are of major interest: 1) Meaning did not matter. Oral plus meaning was no better than oral alone, and oral plus decoding plus meaning was no better than oral plus decoding. 2) The two groups of readers were affected by the word experiences in the same way. Thus, the possibility that skilled readers have learned to benefit more than less skilled readers from certain experiences is ruled out. Less skilled readers begin at a large disadvantage for words never seen nor heard, but improve with experience to the same extent as skilled readers.

Finally, there are two minor points. One is that decoding speed for high frequency English words was not faster than speed for words given oral + decoding experience. We seem to have approximated the effect of high frequency in the course of a few days. The second point concerns the long-term effect of our word experience. We tested each child again after two months. The effects were still there. They appeared to be somewhat attenuated, but clearly were still there.

An experiment recently completed suggests further clarification of how decoding speed is related to single word experiences (Perfetti and Hogaboam, 1975). Skilled and less skilled readers either heard and said or decoded (read and said) pseudowords a predetermined number of times, varying from zero to 18 spread over three days. In the decoding speed test that followed, skilled readers were faster for all values of the frequency variable. Of interest is the fact that skilled readers benefited greatly from just a minimum amount of aural exposure, one per day, while a greater frequency was needed for the less skilled readers to show any gains in decoding speed. In so far as this procedure simulates the establishment of an oral language unit for decoding, this result suggests for the less skilled reader either less stability in the development of a phonetic representation or less well developed print-to-sound correspondences.

In the case of decoding and comprehension, we have the following general picture. The basic skills of decoding are better developed in skilled comprehenders than less skilled comprehenders. What is "basic" about them is that they are observed for never-seen words. Some difference in sub-word unitizing must be involved. The skill of recognizing letter sequences and unitizing them may be the basic skill. There seems to be little role of meaning in decoding, although this conclusion does not necessarily generalize to reading text. It also appears not to be true that decoding is dependent on meaning only for less skilled readers but not for skilled readers. I suggested earlier that unskilled readers, because they have less automated decoding skill, may rely more on meaning to identify words (Perfetti and Hogaboam, 1975). The possibility is that unskilled readers have a whole-word sight store that they can use but they slow down when a letter string doesn't match this store. I'm more inclined now to conclude that this isn't true except for a very small set of words.

Decoding and levels of comprehension

In terms of levels of comprehension, decoding at first glance may seem to be strictly Level I processing. While for a few rare cases converting print into language may occur as meaningless activity, it is sensible to suppose that sound without meaning will occur only when the reader does not know the meaning of the word or when his decoding of it fails to match his oral language representation.

In the normal case, my assumption is that access of meaning automatically accompanies decoding. If this is so, it means that differences in reading comprehension skill are not due to differences in accessing meanings. An empirical prediction from this decoding model is that skilled readers should be no faster than less skilled readers at determining whether a given word belongs to a given semantic category (e.g., food, animal). The differences should occur mainly in determining "what the word is" rather than "what it means." This is not to say that there will be no semantic differences related to comprehension skill. Indeed, vocabulary is one of the major factors. The hypothesis is that if a common salient semantic category is known to a reader he will access it rapidly even if he is unskilled in reading comprehension.

There are data consistent with this hypothesis in a study in which children attempted to name pictures of common objects while ignoring words that were printed on the pictures (Golinkoff and Rosinski, 1975). In one condition, the printed words interferred with naming the pictures because they belonged to the same semantic category; e.g., the word *pig* on a picture of a cow. By comparison with control conditions, Golinkoff and Rosinski found large interference effects in these stimuli as measured by the time to name all the pictures. Most important for the present argument is that skilled and less skilled readers did not differ in magnitude of interference. This seems to suggest that accessing the meanings of the printed words was "automatic," or at least compelling, for both skilled and less skilled readers. My suggestion is that the salient categorical features, although not the entire range of semantic attributes, come "free" with decoding.

Language comprehension

Two assumptions are challenged by the present thesis. The first assumption is that of independence between decoding and comprehension. The second is that all persons have the same linguistic competence and hence the same language comprehension skill. This second assumption seems to be based on a confusion between the potential of linguistic competence and actualization of linguistic performance. To say all persons have the same linguistic competence is a rationalistic assumption. To ask about language comprehension is to go well beyond this assumption in the involvement of memory, attention, and sequential patterning. (Note the obvious factor of vocabulary is omitted. It is a different claim to say that there are differences in language comprehension if one means only that there are differences in knowledge of word meanings.)

The suggestion being made here is that there are significant individual differences in the comprehension of spoken language that go beyond vocabulary (which, in fact, accounts for much of the total difference) and is reflected in reading comprehension. This position is in general agreement with that of Sticht (1972) and Carroll (1966), who seem to have concluded that oral language comprehension and reading comprehension are closely related. I will exemplify the significance of language comprehension by summarizing the logic and results of a recent experiment carried out with the help of Susan Goldman and Laura Bell.

The assumption we make reflects certain notions of the operation of memory during the comprehension of discourse owing to Jarvella (1971) and to Bever and his colleagues, Fodor and Garrett (1974). In order to comprehend spoken discourse, a kind of three-ring circus must be coordinated. The three rings may be thought of as roughly analogous to the three levels of processing, although I wouldn't want to push this too

Perfetti

far. The three levels of processing may go on practically simultaneously, which means that they operate with rapid attention shifts among storing the incoming sentence or sentence fragment in a verbatim form (Level I), completing a semantic analysis of the most recent discourse segment (Level II) and integrating the semantic analysis with the up-till-now representation of the discourse (Level III). Again, these three components occur without strain during listening for most persons and the rapid switching among levels is not normally available to self-observation.

To some extent, Levels II and III processing depend on Level I processing. There is reduced opportunity to complete a semantic analysis of a sentence or to integrate the result of that analysis with the previous discourse if the just heard segment of discourse is too rapidly forgotten. On the other hand, it is adaptive to forget the words after a certain point. Otherwise, on the assumption that all three levels of processing share the same limited capacity to *some* extent, Levels II and III processing would be more difficult. The point at which it seems adaptive to forget the words recently heard appears to be the end of a sentence (Jarvella, 1971). Up to that point, it is helpful to remember the sequence of words or phrases verbatim so that the unheard portion of the sentence (e.g., the verb) can be related to the first part of the sentence.

This Level I processing is thus a kind of memory, which may provide source of individual difference in comprehension. This is so because, as suggested, the higher levels II and III seem to partly depend on it and because it itself appears to be a complex skill. It seems to depend on an analysis of word meanings (it cannot be assumed that a string of 6 or 7 words is ordinarily stored in memory without meanings) and on syntactic (sequential) operations on the word string.

With this latter factor, we touch on two memory components of reading that have been fairly widely noted. This is that short-term memory capacity and sequencing abilities are factors contributing to reading difficulty. It has been found that digit-span performance correlates positively with reading achievement (e.g., Guthrie et al., 1972), although some studies fail to find such a relationship (e.g., Valtin, 1973). In the case of sequencing, which appears to be necessary for digit-span performance, Baaker (1972) has made an argument for the importance of a generalized sequencing ability related to reading. The roles of short-term memory "capacity" and sequencing appear to be complex, and I can offer only a suggestion toward clarification.

The basis for the suggestion is two experiments carried out with third and fifth grade children distinguished as skilled and less skilled in reading comprehension, as measured by the reading subtest of the Metropolitan Achievement Test. Across reader groups the children were matched on IQ. The first experiment tested the children on a probe-digit memory task. This differs from a digit-span test in that only one digit is produced on each test and what varies is the number of digits intervening between the occurrence and the target digit in the string and the end of the string. For example, if the child hears the string 8, 5, 7, 6, 3, 5, 2, 4, 9, 3, 7. The correct digit is 6. (The last digit heard is the probe and is marked by a tone.)

The results of this experiment of interest for the present purpose is that there were no differences in memory performance between the two skill groups. This task seems to be a meaningful estimate of short-term memory capacity free of sequential response problems. Since this result has been replicated on a new population, the conclusion seems reasonable that so long as IQ is controlled, there are no STM capacity differences with this task.

The second experiment was analogous to the first in that it involved a probe memory task. The same subjects heard passages through earphones and were interrupted with unpredictable tests in which a word from a just-heard section of discourse was repeated. The child's task was to give the word that had followed it. Sometimes this probe word was from the sentence just heard. Other times, it was from the final clause of the previous sentence. The just-heard sentence sometimes had two clauses and sometimes was a shorter one-clause sentence. When it was a two clause sentence, the probe was sometimes from the first clause and sometimes from the second.

The results were that the skilled readers were significantly and substantially better in performance than the less skilled readers. Only for the single clause shorter sentence did the less-skilled readers do as well as the skilled. For the single clause sentence, in which the probe was for what the listener had heard about 5 or 6 words back performance was high for most children (about 90 percent recall). However, if that last clause was not the whole sentence, performance for less skilled readers dropped off. Similarly, for the first clause of a two clause sentence and for the final clause of the previous sentence, the less skilled readers did not recall the word following the probe as well as the skilled readers.

Since the measure here is *verbatim* recall, could it be just that less skilled readers were paraphrasing more? When paraphrases are added, the differences between groups are even larger. Skilled readers are remembering more words *and* more meanings. Furthermore, when the skilled readers produced a paraphrase nine times out of ten it was for a word from the previous sentence or from the first clause of a two clause sentence. In other words, it was seldom for the most recently heard clause. By contrast, less skilled readers were just as likely to paraphrase from the most recently heard clause as from a previous clause. This is confirmation of the conclusion from the verbatim results. Skilled readers hold a string of words in memory in verbatim form. Less skilled readers do this less well, except for a single clause sentence.

Well, could it be vocabulary? I think not since we composed the passages based on third grader readers. The group differences were just as large for fifth graders as for third graders. A possibility which cannot be ruled out is that less skilled comprehenders are having trouble with Level II and Level III comprehension. For example, they may be working on integration of the previous sentence with the prior discourse when the test sentence should be attended to. One could say, perhaps, that organizational skills are implicated, rather than a strictly Level I process. The search for an adequate explanation will require more work. The most supportable and general statement at present is that there are significant differences in Level I language memory that provides a basis for differences in comprehension skill. It does not seem to depend on short-term memory "capacity," but rather is a function of memory perhaps unique to linguistically structured input.

At the moment, it is difficult to be more definite concerning the properties of this *linguistic memory*. As a starting point, we may speculate that its salient property is its sensitivity to temporal structure. Temporal structure is a general notion, and two refining possibilities might be suggested. A string of digits (5-4-2-7-5) has a temporal structure, but it is wholly arbitrary. By contrast, linguistic input has inherent structure. The sequencing of words is constrained by co-occurrence rules of syntax and by semantic constraints. Certainly individual differences either in memory for temporal order or in memory for linguistic structure might be expected to develop and serve as the basis for the observed differences in discourse memory. It seems to me that the parallel in our research between the probe digit task, in which we found no reader difference, and the discourse memory, in which we did find a difference, weighs perhaps a little in favor of looking for a strictly linguistic basis for the memory mechanism. It is not unreasonable to imagine that we are dealing with individual differences in the efficiency with which linguistic input is encoded and integrated. "Keeping things straight" at Level I becomes difficult because words are analyzed too slowly, or attention switching between Level I and Level III is poorly-timed, etc. One possibility is that loss of Level I information is largely a result of pressure from Level III (and/or Level II) processing demands which are ineffectively handled. For example, Level III processing will create such pressure to the extent that a reference system for the discourse has not been effectively established. An effective reference system allows the reader to focus on new information and relate it to old, as opposed to treating each element as new. One direct implication of this hypothesis is that for unskilled comprehenders, Level I memory should decrease with increasing distance into the discourse. This is so because the discourse will increasingly rely on information provided earlier. Thus, temporal observations in memory for discourse should help in understanding how the levels of comprehension interact.

While a more definite explanation is not possible at this time, what is possible perhaps is to clearly state the implication of a memory for language difference. It provides a basis for the hypothesis that reading comprehension depends on language comprehension. In a recent dissertation, Berger (1975) found that differences between IQ matched skilled and less-skilled readers were as large for listening comprehension as for reading comprehension. Furthermore, the differences were as large when measured by literal questions as when measured by paraphrased recall. Since answering literal questions (i.e., verbatim from the passage) presumably requires less organization than paraphrase recall, this finding would seem to argue against "organization" as a major factor in comprehension differences. Under the present hypothesis, I would expect to find the differences observed in a test given after a passage is read or heard to be largely present *during* the time it's being read or heard. Specifically, information is being lost by unskilled comprehenders beyond the immediate clause or sentence.

Before concluding this part of the discussion, I would like to briefly cite an additional piece of evidence that seems to support the importance of general language comprehension in reading comprehension. We have recently carried out a simple study of syntax comprehension with third grade children. As usual, the children differ in reading comprehension skill, but are matched on IQ. A distinguishing feature of this study is that it is very simple in two critical aspects. One is that it required no verbal response from the child. The second is that it involved no vocabulary knowledge beyond the words *square, circle, red, green,* and *yellow.* Thus two simplifying factors which comprehension research often cannot have were present here. The child simply had to touch an object, a square or a circle of a given color. We used varied syntactic structures ranging from something basic like "Touch the red circle" to the double-embedded "Touch the one under the one under the red circle." In all, eight syntactic structures were tested for each child under controlled oral conditions and reading conditions. For present purposes, I will neglect the syntactic structures and summarize the error data for the two reader groups for the two conditions. Children less skilled in reading comprehension as a group had an error rate of 21 percent in the oral task and 29 percent in the reading task. Skilled readers had error rates of 9 percent in the oral and 15 percent in the reading task. Thus, the group differences were about 12 percent for oral and 14 percent for reading. Again, as in the Berger study I cited, we have a case in which comprehension differences occur for an oral task to the same extent as for a reading task. And here we have a simple situation of fixed vocabulary, no verbal output, and no long-term memory or "organization" is required.

Decoding and linguistic memory

Having considered decoding and linguistic memory separately, I will conclude with a brief speculation on how they fit together. The object of reading and listening normally, but not always, is to achieve Level III comprehension. Semantic analyses are combined and integrated in constructing a changing representation of information. Level III comprehension occurs as a function of many factors, two of which are 1) the availability in memory of a Level I string, i.e., immediate linguistic memory, and 2) the availability of working memory to perform the comprehension work on stored strings and retrievable prior meanings. Decoding that is not more or less automatic slows down comprehension work and so does the unavailability of just-heard sentences.

Memory and decoding will interact during reading, and the nature of this interaction is perhaps not obvious. The highly skilled reader will tend to short-cut the phonological representation of words because he is skilled at decoding. Perhaps linguistic memory is less good in this case to the extent that it depends on word sounds. On the other hand, memory for words several words back ought to be fairly good for the skilled reader. This is because his rapid decoding permits him to be combining the beginning and end of a sentence (Level II - Comprehension) thus making both parts more available. The less skilled reader is not automatically decoding the end of the sentence and there may be two consequences of this: The first part is slipping away because decoding operations on the end of the sentence are using working memory. However, the end of the sentence is quite available as linguistic memory because slow decoding has (perhaps) increased the acoustic consciousness of the last few words.

In a study currently underway, children are interrupted by a memory probe that occurs during reading every few pages or so. Children read some passages silently and some orally. A paradoxical result is that children who are less skilled comprehenders and also the slowest decoders among our sample (these are independent measures) are as good as children who are skilled comprehenders and fast decoders at remembering a word they have just read three words back. In fact, in silent reading they seem to be better than skilled readers at remembering a just-read word. The reason appears to be that skilled readers—remember these are readers who are at once skilled in comprehension and fast in decoding—develop a briefer Level I trace in the silent reading condition. They are reading for meaning. In our experiment, these highly skilled readers also read faster under silent conditions than under oral, while there is little difference for the unskilled reader. His slow decoding is adversely affecting him whether he reads aloud or silently.

Now to return to the ability to remember a word recently read. If we ask whether the child has remembered a word only a little farther back, 6 words instead of 3, we get a very different picture. At 6 words, a case in which the word to be remembered is more likely to be from the previous sentence, the unskilled reader is no longer as good or better than the skilled reader. Now, for both a silently read or an orally read passage, the less skilled comprehender is recalling about 26 percent less than he did after 3 words. By contrast, the recall of the skilled reader is just as good as it was after 3 words and about 16 percent better than the less skilled reader.

This is just what might be expected according to the present view on the interaction between decoding and memory. Slow decoding makes the decoded word more available in memory through its phonological representation. This high availability lasts for only a few words, however, because the other consequence of slow decoding is to place demands on the same memory that must hold on to a Level I representation of words. The earlier part of the sentence and the previous sentence thus are more likely to be lost after a few words for the unskilled reader.

Conclusion

This view of reading comprehension needs much work to fill in the many gaps. The explanations of the comprehension phenomena are still sketchy and, perhaps more important, it is not obvious how these comprehension skills develop nor how to instruct them. While I do believe that the three levels I have described make up a useful framework for comprehension, additional work is needed to apply it to the development problem. Level III is certainly the kind of goal we want in reading comprehension and I would not necessarily suggest that drill and practice at Level I would be a good idea. On the other hand, I hope that I have suggested an important intermediate comprehension function served by Level I. It serves at least as a holding action during brief periods that information is needed more or less verbatim in order to carry out higher levels of comprehension.

In all of this has been an emphasis on language comprehension functions and a strong suggestion that speeded decoding is intimately tied with skilled comprehension. The position that most (not all) of reading comprehension is decoding plus language comprehension is reasonable and perhaps true. If so, it may provide a focus for thinking about how reading comprehension can be optimally developed with respect to individual differences that exist in these two major components.

REFERENCES

Baaker, D.J. *Temporal order in disturbed reading.* Rotterdam University Press, 1972.

Berger, N. An investigation of linguistic competence and organizational processes in good and poor readers. Unpublished doctoral dissertation, University of Pittsburgh, 1975.

Bormuth, J.R. *On the theory of achievement test items.* Chicago: University of Chicago Press, 1970.

Carroll, J.B. Factors of verbal achievement. In A. Anastasi (Ed.), *Testing problems in perspective.* American Council on Education, 1966, 406-413.

Coomber, J.E., and Hogie, D.W. Perceptual and decoding factors in reading disability. Paper presented at the meeting of the American Educational Research Association, Chicago, 1974.

Craik, F., and Lockhart, V. Levels of processing: A framework for memory research, *Journal of Verbal Learning and Verbal Behavior,* 1972, *11,* 671-685.

Fodor, J.A.; Bever, T.G.; and Garrett, M.F. *The psychology of language: An introduction to psycholinguistics and generative grammar.* New York: McGraw-Hill, 1974.

Golinkoff, R.M., and Rosinski, R.R. The access of printed word meanings by children and adults. Paper presented at meeting of Society for Research in Child Development, Denver, 1975.

Guthrie, J. T.; Goldberg, H. K.; and Finucci, J. Independence of Abilities in Disabled Readers. *Journal of Reading Behavior*, 1972, 4(2), 129-138.

Jarvella, R.J. Syntactic processing of connected speech. *Journal of Verbal Learning and Verbal Behavior*, 1971, *10*, 409-416.

LaBerge, D., and Samuels, S.J. Toward a theory of automatic information processing in reading. *Cognitive Psychology*, 1974, *6*, 293-323.

Mistler-Lachman, J.L. Depth of sentence comprehension and sentence memory. *Journal of Verbal Learning and Verbal Behavior*, 1974, *13*, 98-106.

Perfetti, C.A. Levels of sentence comprehension. *Bulletin de Psychologie*, in press.

Perfetti, C.A., and Hogaboam, T. The effects of "word experience" on decoding speeds of skilled and unskilled readers. Paper presented at the annual meeting of the Psychonomic Society, Denver, 1975.

Perfetti, C.A., and Hogaboam, T. The relationship between single word decoding and reading comprehension skill. *Journal of Educational Psychology*, 1975, *67*, 461-469.

Sticht, T.G. Learning by listening. In J.B. Carroll and R.O. Freedle (Eds.), *Language comprehension and the acquisition of knowledge*. New York: John Wiley & Sons, 1972.

Thorndike, E.L. Reading as reasoning: A study of mistakes in paragraph reading. *Journal of Educational Psychology*, 1917, *8*, 323-332.

Thorndike, R.L. Reading as reasoning. *Reading Research Quarterly*, 1973, *9*, 135-147.

Valtin, R. Report of research on dyslexia in children. Paper presented at International Reading Association, Denver, 1973. (ERIC document ED 079 713)

Purpose in Reading

Lawrence T. Frase

Introduction
The importance of goals

The subject of this paper is mental activity. Similar concepts to what I have in mind are attention or perhaps even active responding. The point that I want to emphasize is that purpose in reading gives rise to unique perceptions, memories, and understandings. These outcomes vary with different purposes. Furthermore, purpose is something that can be communicated from teacher to student. By modifying purpose, by directing reading activities, the teacher influences learning.

The fate of contemporary cognitive approaches to reading is, in part, to rediscover in a more precise way what has been discovered before. The distinction between the nominal and effective stimulus is a case in point. As John Dewey (1925) put it,

> It is usual in current psychology to assert or assume that qualities observed are those of the stimulus. This assumption puts the cart before the horse; qualities which are observed are those attendant upon response to stimuli. We are observantly aware (in distinction from inferentially aware) only of what has been done; we can perceive what is already there, what has happened. By description, a stimulus is not an object of perception, for stimulus is correlative to response, and is undetermined except as response occurs. I am not questioning as a fact of *knowledge* that certain things *are* the stimuli of visual and auditory perception. I am pointing out that we are aware of the stimuli only in terms of our response to them and of the consequences of this response.

My interpretation of Dewey's statement is that our awareness of sensory qualities can only be understood as an outcome of the mental operations that we bring to bear upon objects presented to our senses. So it is with reading; the unique perceptions, memories, and understandings that occur as a consequence of reading depend upon the responses that the reader makes to the printed word and the consequence of those responses. In this paper, I'll review some studies that show how goals, or purpose, modify responses to written materials.

A fundamental response, upon which further knowledge must rest, is the encoding of words or propositions (Frase, 1975). By encoding, I mean the translation of symbols into some meaningful internal representation. In some respects, it is odd that much current work in cognition is devoted to higher level semantic processes when we have not yet clearly established the necessary and sufficient conditions for insuring the complete meaningful encoding of text.

Aside from encoding, higher level activities might include rehearsing and relating encoded items to previous learning. That learning outcomes are the consequence of just so much rehearsal, semantic integration, and so on, we are not able to say from our experiments. What we have learned, however, is that the focus and form of the reader's goal limits the range, stability, and transferability of his memories. We've tried to objectify the focus and form of the reader's goals by asking subjects to perform clearly defined experimental tasks. In most cases, we have given the reader problems that have a well defined relation to a written document. In other experiments, we have recorded subjects' verbalizations while they engage in tutorial sessions. Learning outcomes could then be related to the focus of the subject's activities. Perhaps a review of some of these studies will elicit fruitful thoughts about attentional processes in both researchers and practitioners alike. Before talking about research, however, I would like to offer one caveat. This has to do with the possibility that purpose in reading may lead a reader to stray from, as well as move toward, desirable learning outcomes.

Learning goals—positive and negative learning outcomes

I find it useful to think of human behavior as purposeful activity, whether conscious or guided by habits whose purpose has long since receded from awareness. To put it in behavioral terms, we know that human action is controlled by environmental stimuli, but the stimuli that provide the occasion for responses, and the responses that are made, are often optional in the sense that their influence is subject to internalized but potentially self-modifiable standards of performance. In the absence of instructor or experimenter imposed learning goals, reading is still goal-directed activity. In some cases, a reader has no cue to what may or may not be content relevant to some later behavioral demand (for example, a test). The task may be to learn everything, and what cognitive operations might be useful for learning may be unspecified. In other cases, a reader may be constrained to relate text contents to specific semantic categories, to learn portions of a passage in a certain sequence, and so on. The experimenter's or instructor's model of how reading activities map onto appropriate learning outcomes can suggest whether such goals will have positive *or* negative learning effects. This is the point. There is no reason why goal-directed reading should have positive effects for all learning outcomes (see Rothkopf, 1970). There are many ways in which explicit learning aids (such as questions or objectives) can have limited consequences. Understanding the reasons for negative effects (suppression of learning) can provide important clues to processing activities and the conditions which control them (Frase, 1968).

Research shows that there are certain activities, for instance, activities that involve limited encoding and inappropriate content expectations, that not only restrict the meaningful processing of text, but that result in the formation of incorrect associations, or unclear ideas. Hence, knowing when and why goals suppress learning can aid in the development of more effective learning aids. In some cases, negative learning outcomes might be desirable, for instance, to suppress the acquisition of content that might interfere with learning more important content. In other cases, the discovery of the stimulus conditions that elicit inefficient reading activities, such as partial encoding of propositions, can suggest rules for the construction of learning aids that do achieve desirable effects. Therefore, negative learning effects of, for instance, adjunct questions, should be taken as an occasion for sharpening our understanding of the conditions that might improve learning and not as a general criticism of the usefulness of such techniques in practice.

In the remainder of this paper I would like to discuss studies that relate learning outcomes to the focus and form of reading activities. My assumption is that goal-directed reading has at least two components: a) contents and b) operations. By content, I mean the environmental stimuli that may become the focus of attention. By operations, I mean the processing activities that a reader brings to bear on those contents. In the following section, I want to indicate three conditions and some of their characteristics that may provide a focus for a reader's attention. These conditions may be experimenter imposed, self imposed, or they may arise from an interaction of a text and the reader's goal.

Content focus
Experimenter imposed focus

Let us begin with a simple experiment, the object of which was to determine if learning is related to the precision and directness with which the reader's goal maps onto text information (Frase and Kreitzberg, 1975).

The experimental situation was as follows. One hundred and thirty college undergraduates were told to learn the information in certain sentences of a text. The text was a 588-word biographical passage about Nathaniel Bowditch, a great American navigator-mathematician.

The learning directions (or goals) given to subjects were intended to establish a performance set, the efficiency of which we expected to vary across experimental groups. The precision of reference was varied by identifying the relevant (to be learned) sentences by the first few words of the sentences or by identifying them by topics. For instance, one text sentence was, "French, Spanish, Latin, Greek, and German were among the two dozen or more languages and dialects he studied during his life." A *Word* direction told the subjects to learn the information in the sentence that began "French, Spanish, Latin...." A *Topical* direction told subjects to learn the information in the sentence that deals with the topic, "The number of foreign tongues that Nathaniel studied." In a later recall posttest, this information would be tested by the question, "How many languages and dialects did Nathaniel finally master?" Each direction was intended to identify just one sentence. In a separate study we found that judges were able to reliably identify the sentences referred to by the topics. Given a single topic, the mean proportion of correct identifications was .90 and the mean proportion incorrect identification (false positives) was .07.

I have referred to the distinction between word and topical reference as a "precision" variable. The assumption is that for word directions, the subject need only match words in the text with words in the direction. For topical directions, the subject must transform content in order to determine that a sentence matches the direction. Topical directions, because they require additional transformations, seem less precise. Yet it is possible to argue that topical directions require meaningful processing of sentences, and that such operations contribute to learning. One purpose of the present study was to determine if this were true.

The directness of reference was varied by phrasing the directions in a negative or positive form. The description of the sentences to be learned were given in a list, so that a general *positive* direction could state, "Learn the information in all of the sentences...." A *negative* direction stated, "Learn the information in all of the sentences *except* ...." In short, for the negative directions subjects had to identify the sentences that they did not have to learn. This indirect reference might insure processing of the sentences that did not have to be learned, but do such activities contribute significantly to learning?

The two factors of precision and directness were varied in the experiment. There were four experimental groups of 24 subjects each; *topical-positive* directions; *topical-negative; word-positive;* and *word-negative* directions. A control group of 34 subjects was directed simply to learn the text. With these groups it was possible to explore the effects of different learning directions on the recall of relevant (to be learned) and incidental information.

The experiment was conducted in class. A printed booklet containing instructions, learning directions and the reading passages was given to subjects. They were permitted to look at the learning directions along with the text. Ten minutes were allowed for study and after one hour of class activities, subjects were given a 54 item short answer recall test.

Let us consider first the recall of relevant text information. Mean proportion correct responses for the control group was .50. Word-positive and word-negative groups averaged .67 and .49, respectively. Topical-positive and topical-negative groups averaged .55 and .53, respectively. Dunnett's test showed that only the word-positive group was significantly higher than the control group ($p < .05$). Thus, only the availability of direct and precise cues to what should be learned resulted in improved performance.

The recall of incidental information also revealed significant effects for the word condition. Mean proportion correct for the word-positive and negative groups were .39 and .19, respectively. For the topical-positive and negative groups the means were .47 and .45, respectively. The word-negative group was significantly lower ($p < .05$) than all other groups, which did not differ among each other. The significant suppression of incidental learning for the word-negative group can be interpreted as a shift in learning activities away from sentences that subjects had been directed not to learn.

Furthermore, the data offer no support for the notion that topical reference would elevate incidental learning. The word-positive group was not significantly lower on incidental recall than the topical groups. In summary, both positive and negative learning outcomes were obtained on sentences containing words that matched exactly the words used in the learning directions. These results support the idea of two components to goal directed reading, content and operation. For the word groups, specific words in the text provide the occasion for certain operations. In the case of positive directions, these cues signal the reader to engage in activities that have positive learning outcomes. No direct cues are available for where not to study. Hence, relevant learning was elevated above control group performance, but incidental learning was not suppressed. For negative directions, however, word cues signal where not to study, but no direct cues are available for where to study. Hence, incidental learning was suppressed, but relevant learning was not elevated. For positive directions text cues are directly available to turn learning activities on, but not off. For negative directions, cues are directly available to turn learning behaviors off, but not on.

The present study is not an isolated instance of the effectiveness of precise reference in cuing learning activities. For instance, Rothkopf and Kaplan (1972) found that relevant information was learned better when content was referred to in specific rather than general terms. In the Rothkopf and Kaplan study, general objectives directed subjects to learn the characteristics of type faces. Specific objectives enumerated the names of the type faces that were to be learned.

To this point I have been discussing the effects of specifying the cues in a text that should provide the occasion for appropriate learning activities. But is specificity sufficient, or do human limitations constrain the effects of externally imposed goals? Research on the effects of questions inserted in text bears on this point. In several experiments (see Anderson and Biddle, 1975), questions have inserted before, concurrent with, or after text. After reading, subjects are tested on retention of the question relevant material. In a strong majority of such studies, retention of question relevant content was higher for subjects who were exposed to the questions than for subjects who studied without the questions. But the research also shows that the effects of questions are diminished when they are placed some distance from the relevant text content (Boyd, 1973; Eischens et al., 1972; Frase et al., 1970; Rickards and DiVesta, 1974). Questions, like other text content, fade from memory, and in so doing lose their ability to focus learning activities.

Let us turn, now, to the effects of a reader's own questioning activities on what is learned from a text.

Self imposed focus

Stable predispositions to respond are likely to modify learning behaviors, unstable ones are not. If so, then, even without experimenter-imposed directions about what to learn, what a reader remembers should be related to the content upon which his attention focuses. In recent experiments (Frase and Schwartz, 1975) we obtained data on subjects' attentional focus by having them verbalize or write out their own questions as they learned a text. Again, we used the Bowditch biographical passage and a prompted recall test. Rather than a detailed description of these studies let me summarize them briefly.

In one experiment, 48 high school students cooperated in a tutorial setting. At different times a subject asked questions, answered questions, or merely studied. The subjects were yoked, that is, when one subject asked questions his partner had to answer. Tape recordings of these sessions allowed us to identify which test items were related to the subjects' questions. One prediction was that recall would be higher for question-relevant content than for incidental content.

We also were interested in whether a questioner would recall more incidental information than an answerer. We hypothesized that constructing questions would involve encoding all of the text information to make decisions about what is and is not question-worthy information. For the answerer, question content may provide cues that permit limited encoding of the text. For instance, a key word might be used to search the text for the answer to a question. Therefore, we predicted an interaction between recall for relevant and incidental information and whether a subject was answering or asking questions.

The results confirmed the first hypothesis. Proportion correct recall for question relevant information was .67 when answering, .70 when questioning. Recall averaged .50 when subjects only studied the text ($p < .001$). Recall for question incidental information was .49 when answering questions and .52 when constructing questions. Neither of these two means differ significantly from the study alone condition. Thus, positive learning outcomes were confined to information that subjects had explicitly focused upon in their questioning or answering.

There were no suppression effects, thus we did not confirm our second hypothesis that answering questions might suppress incidental learning, although a slight trend in that direction can be seen. It should be emphasized, however, that subjects were told before reading that they would be tested over all of the content.

In a second study, we had 64 college students work alone,

either writing out questions or simply studying. The proportion correct recall for question related information was .72, for incidental information the proportion was .55. Study alone scores averaged .53. This study confirms the results of the previous experiment in a non-tutorial situation. In this experiment, subjects were also instructed to vary the number and difficulty of the questions constructed. Although characteristics of subjects' questions changed as a consequence of these task demands, the level of incidental learning was not significantly affected.

The question of what an appropriate control condition is in experiments such as these is a difficult one. From a practical standpoint, one would like to know when learning achievement differs from achievement when readers study alone. From the standpoint of understanding the learning process, however, this may be an unwise comparison since it is unclear what factors are being pitted against each other. For instance, in the two previous studies subjects expected to be tested later over all of the text, hence the processes brought to bear on question incidental information probably included operations that subjects performed on question relevant content. When subjects "study," we do not know precisely what they are doing. One reason why we have done research on telling subjects what to learn is that we can determine the effects of defined goal characteristics on learning outcomes.

Text imposed focus

Another source of content focus arises from an interaction between the readers purpose and document characteristics. For instance, one organization of information may require that the reader perform different operations on the content than another organization would. One illustrative experiment will indicate what I mean.

In this study (Frase and Silbiger, 1970), college undergraduates were told the attributes of a planet. Their task was to determine as rapidly as possible what the name of the planet was (if it existed) by reading a text. In fact, none of the planets described in the text satisfied the criteria given to the subjects. The subjects were not told that they would be tested at a later time, hence this was an incidental learning task.

The text described 15 planets, each with five attributes (such as the number of moons a planet had, the kind of life it supported, and so on). Each sentence of the text contained one planet name and one of its attributes. The sentences in the text were ordered in four different ways, so that a subject would have to search the text for either zero, three, nine or eighteen related sentences. In the zero condition, for instance, each paragraph completely described one planet. The problem could be solved by disregarding the planet names and scanning the attributes. For the other conditions, attributes of a planet were described in other portions of the text. In terms of the reader's goal, these passages were not well organized.

We assumed that subjects would enter a planet name briefly into memory in order to locate the other attributes of the planet. After having evaluated all attributes of a planet, a decision could be made whether that planet was the one that the subject was searching for. Our hypothesis was that goal relevant names would be encoded (and rehearsed) in accordance with their relevance to the solution of the problem and the demands of information integration that the different text organizations imposed.

We were able to categorize three classes of names in relation to the role that they would play in controlling search. *Criterions* names were those which had to be entered briefly into memory in order to search out related information in other portions of the text. *Compared* names were those in other sentences which allow the reader to reject irrelevant sentences (sentences that did not contain attribute information that the subject was searching for), but which would have to be encoded briefly to make a decision that a sentence was not relevant. Finally, *irrelevant* names were those which could be disregarded because sentences about the planet were grouped together. When the sentences were grouped together only the attributes had to be scanned, according to our task analysis.

Recognition tests for names of the planets were administered immediately after reading and after one month. The results were similar for the immediate and delayed tests. Mean proportion delayed recognition for the criterion names was .68. For compared names the mean was .58. This difference, which could be calculated only for the conditions in which search was required, was significant at the .001 level. Furthermore, delayed recognition for the groups that did not have to search (the zero condition) averaged .34, which was significantly below the average for compared names (.58) in the three, nine, and eighteen sentence search groups.

These findings are consistent with the hypothesis that memory for items is a function of whether those items enter into subject's goal directed activities, and that the processes of encoding and rehearsal are modified by an interaction between the reader's purpose and the characteristics of the text that he encounters. Not only the range of items that had to be encoded was reflected in memory (both criterion and compared names were well retained), but the names that were subject to longer representation in short-term memory (the criterion names) were retained best of all. Organization thus elicited three levels of processing; one of incomplete or very temporary encoding, one of moderate temporal duration, and another level of longer duration that resulted in the most stable learning outcomes.

Let me now summarize this discussion of content focus.

Summary of content focus. I have indicated three sources of focus for a reader's attention; from others, from within himself, and from an interaction between his purpose and text characteristics. The illustrative data that I've cited indicate that learning outcomes are strongly related to the properties of the goals given to readers and to their own focus of attention.

Results also suggest that goals might fail because they imprecisely or indirectly define what should be learned. Studies also show that goals are not likely to affect performance if they have not themselves achieved stable representation in memory. Content focus, regardless of its source, is likely to be associated with positive learning outcomes.

One might think that telling a reader what to learn would be a simple instructional manipulation, but it turns out to be a complex affair.

I would like, now, to turn to some goal defined operations that contribute to learning. These include semantic, sequential and review operations which comprise the form of processing activities.

Operations

Semantic operations

The experiment just described did not involve variations in the reader's semantic criterion for evaluating words in the text. Decisions about the relatedness of information in sentences could be based upon a direct match between the names in sentences and the name for which the subject was searching. Ordinary reading activities probably involve more subtle fluctuations in attention. Aside from shifts in the focus of content and the rehearsal of an item in the mind, the responses that a reader makes to words in a text may involve relatively superficial or deep processing of its semantic attributes.

In the study above, only surface features of the planet names had to be encoded. But suppose that the names had some previously learned meanings, i.e., properties that are orderable on a semantic dimension. For instance, a name might represent a particular type of animal with known properties that the subject could elaborate to a greater or lesser degree. One hypothesis is that when subjects elaborate the specific properties of items, a rich semantic network is elicited, and this network provides multiple contexts for subsequent retrieval. If the subject's attention to semantic features (or meanings) of words were to vary, then the consequence of this fluctuation would be to make some items more or less accessible to recall at a later time.

Consider the following experiment in terms of the way in which reading interfaces with previously learned meanings of words. Adults are asked to determine if each word in a list of words is a member of a particular semantic category. The list of words includes such things as *beans, tomatoes, oranges,* and so on. In one condition, subjects check off the *foods* (a general category); in another condition they check off the *fruits* (a specific category). After engaging in this task on one or more lists of words, subjects are given a surprise recall test.

I encourage you to try this task with the following set of words. First, scan the list for living things.

gorilla
barracuda
process

whale
minnow
mouse
grasshopper
herring
elephant
sardine
inspiration
porpoise
lion
kitten
spider
giraffe
shark

Now, go through the list again, scanning it for large creatures. A more specific search might entail a search for sea creatures that pose a threat to human life.

Experiments show that for a 16-18 word list, the average recall for the general search is .36; for the specific search, it is .52 ($p < .01$). Several studies have been conducted with lists of words (Frase and Kammann, 1974) and with prose stories describing animals that vary on dimensions of size, harmlessness, and whether they are sea or land animals (see Frase, 1975). In all cases the findings have been the same. Processing written words for specific semantic properties results in greater recall than processing for general properties.

Improvements in recall are apparently due to specificity of encoding, and not simply to retrieval phenomenon. It might be claimed, for instance, that knowing the specific categories helps one to guess the words on a later recall test. But the experiments have shown that recall is not improved when subjects are told just before recall what categories of words were on the list.

The implication is that not only the focus of attention (restriction of the class of relevant stimuli) affects learning, but the form of attention is an important factor in recall. In fact, our studies show that recall increases, to some asymptote, as the size of the target category of words becomes smaller. The critical factor appears to be the semantic criterion against which all the words are evaluated, rather than simply the total number of positive identifications that a subject makes. The concept of attention, merely as some content focus, is insufficient to account for the effects of these finer semantic variations in processing. It does not capture the critical distinction among different behaviors in which a reader might engage while "paying attention."

It should also be noted that in these studies we have not found significant differences in the time that it takes to complete the task when searching for general as opposed to specific categories of words. Total time spent in the task appears to be a less significant variable than the operations that the subject engages in during that time.

There are many other studies that might be cited to support the importance of the form of processing activities. Unfortunately, few studies have systematically investigated the effects of elaborating the properties of complex propositions. Anderson and Hidde (1971) found that if subjects rated the pronounceability of sentences, they remembered less than if they rated the imagery of the sentences. McKenzie (1971) studied the effects of inference quizzes on eighth-grade students' ability to draw other inferences. Students who had seen inference quizzes over a period of eight weeks were better able to draw inferences about the original text than students who had seen only factual quizzes. These effects were not due to greater knowledge of the question relevant information by the inference subjects.

But the process of meaningful elaboration is not confined to reading. It involves thinking in general. To confine it to reading would be to underestimate the complexity of what is involved in meaningful reading. For instance, consider elaboration in another context. Sometimes, in public places, we watch men, women, and children pass before us. At times our thoughts go no further. But sometimes attention is directed to manners of speech, features of a face, or to a person's attire. Torn clothing and shoes in poor repair become occasions for conjectures about the circumstances of a person's life. Comparing our own clothing, which is not torn, nor our shoes in disrepair, may raise questions about social justice. These elaborations leave their own residues of knowledge that go beyond the minimal perception of reality. But all too soon, and too easily, one slips back into the mere seeing of men, women, and children.

So with reading, it is an easier matter to respond to the superficial, yet research shows that it is possible to encourage students to go beyond it (see Rohwer, 1971; Wittrock, 1974).

But not all reading activities have positive consequences. I would like now, to discuss the ways in which the sequential characteristics of a reader's goal can interfere with learning.

Sequential operations and expectancies

I will describe one study in which we varied the sequence of information contained in the directions given about what to learn from a text. The findings suggest that the sequential properties of complex learning instructions can inhibit learning if they do not match the sequence of information that the reader encounters in a text.

The present study arose from research on the organization of text sentences. Several experiments have explored the learning of texts generated from a matrix in which the names and attributes of things are conceived as superordinate items, and the attribute values are subordinate items. Table 1 shows one text matrix. Each cell of the matrix represents a sentence of the text; for example, "The Shark has a fore and aft sail plan." These sentences can be grouped in various ways. The sentences might be ordered *randomly*. They might also be ordered in a systematic way, by grouping them according to the ships' *names*. The sequence 1, 2, 3, 4, 5, etc. (see numbers of sentences in Table 1) results in grouping the attributes of each ship together. Alternatively, the sentences might be grouped according to the *attributes*. The sequence 1, 5, 9, 13, 2, etc. results in placing all of the speeds, sail plans, and so on together in the text. Several studies (Frase, 1969; Friedman and Greitzer, 1972; Myers, Pezdek, and Coulson, 1973; Perlmutter and Royer, 1973; Schultz and DiVesta, 1972) have shown that systematic grouping produces better recall than the random arrangement of sentences.

But our interest was in the effect of matches between the sequence of information represented in the reader's mind (through the learning directions) and the sequence of information in the text. Ninety-six college undergraduates participated in this experiment. They were instructed to learn

Table 1.   Matrix of Names, Attributes, and Attribute Values

| Name of Ship | Attribute | | | |
	Sail plan	Hull	Design	Speed (knots)
Shark	1. fore and aft	2. wood	3. brigantine	4. 14
Squid	5. gaff rigged	6. fiberglass	7. schooner	8. 18
Ray	9. square	10. steel	11. bark	12. 20
Swordfish	13. marconi	14. cement	15. sloop	16. 12

all of the information in the text, but the directions focused upon the vessels first, or upon the attributes first. For instance, the directions to "Learn the sailing vessels' attributes." or to "Learn the Shark, Squid, Ray and Swordfish sail plan, hull construction, design and speed " mentions the sailing vessels first. The direction to "Learn the attributes of the sailing vessels." or to "Learn the sail plan, hull construction, design and speed of the Shark, Squid Ray and Swordfish." mentions the attributes first. For present purposes, we need only consider the two variables relating to the sequence of information in the learning directions (names *first* or *second)* and the sequence of information in the text (sentences organized by *names* or by *attributes*), although there were several other variables in this study (Frase, 1973).

The students were given three trials of three minutes each to learn the passage. After each trial, a free recall test was given. Subjects wrote out whatever they could recall from the text. Correct recall consisted of associating the names with the correct values of each attribute.

Consider two different models of how a subject might perform this task. One model assumes that subjects attempt to learn the information as they encounter it in the text. On this view, the different forms of learning directions, which refer to all of the information in the text, should have no effect upon performance. The other hypothesis is that subjects do not know what the text contains, and that the learning instructions provide a context that controls the way in which subjects respond to the intersentence relations that they encounter. On the latter view, the form of the directions should interact with the form of the text.

But here, several possibilities for processing offer

themselves. Consider, for instance, the condition in which subjects have seen a complete list of attributes first, followed by a list of names. This would be the attribute first condition. Assume, further, that the text sentences are organized by names. In this organization, each paragraph would contain the complete list of attributes for each ship. This list of four attributes matches the first four elements in the learning direction. In the attribute organized passage, however, the first four sentences refer to only one attribute. If the sequence of information in the direction determines some critical aspect of reading activities (input expectancies) than learning might be retarded when the directions mention the attributes first and the passages are organized by attributes.

Several specific models might be used to describe how performance is affected. At present, we are unable to precisely describe these performances, however the data on confusions in recall justify the conclusion that the sequence of items in the learning directions affects recall.

A confusion in recall consists of incorrectly associating the name of a ship with an attribute value. The mean number of confusions for the attribute first directions was 1.1 under the name organized passage; 2.7 under the attribute organized passage. The mean number of confusions for the name first direction was 1.7 for the name organized passage; 1.6 for the attribute organized passage. This interaction was significant at the .025 level. The data suggest, therefore, that learning is affected, not only by the range of content and level of semantic processing, but by subtle sequential expectancies that govern reading activities. (See, also, Gagné and Rothkopf, 1975).

In the final section on operations, I would like to consider briefly the effects of review upon recall.

Review operations

There have been many studies on the effects of posttests and review on the retention of text information. Experimental studies have been conducted from the early 1900s to the present and many reviews are available. Therefore, I see no point in describing specific studies on this topic. Anderson and Biddle (1975) summarize the research showing that posttests consistently facilitate performance on relevant text information, and sometimes on incidental text information.

Anderson and Biddle found, in their own research, that post-tests are most effective when they repeat verbatim (rather than paraphrase) text information. Precise reference (matches) to contents in memory may thus be an important condition for the effective use of post-reading adjunct aids. The facilitative effects of review have also been obtained with instructional objectives (Kaplan and Simmons, 1974).

Although the act of retrieval may have special significance for retention, if we wish to learn about the effects of certain stimulus controls on memory, it may be important to study these controls in an encoding, rather than retrieval, context. Many of the studies on review have to do with relatively long-term memory constraints. Often they seek to alter the retention of incompletely learned content, or content that may have faded from memory. For instance, Surber, Anderson, and Stevens (1975) presented lists of verbatim or paraphrase learning objectives to subjects in order to guide text study. The objectives were given before reading. Although the objectives improved retention over a read-only control group, the paraphrase and verbatim objectives did not differ in their effects. On the basis of these results, one might not expect paraphrase posttest questions to result in better retention than verbatim posttest questions (Anderson and Biddle, 1975), although theoretically they could entail more processing of content in memory.

By studying the effects of different learning operations on text content, as opposed to memory content, we may be able to make useful conjectures about the effects of those operations in a retrieval context. The point is, if we are interested in studying the process of comprehension then it might be well to minimize the effects of long-term memory on subjects' performance (Carroll, 1972).

This is not to say that characteristics of memory, such as the internalized organization of learned information, should not be considered part of the comprehension processes. Subjects have more or less difficulty "comprehending" test items, depending upon the way in which memory is organized. For instance, on the encoding side, we know that a reader must search a text when asked a question that involves combining information that is widely dispersed in the text. Less search is required when the information is contiguous in the text than when it is dispersed. Assume that a reader stores text information in memory in a way that preserves the sequence or grouping of text information. Organization might then influence the speed and accuracy of different memory searches.

In one study (Frase, 1973), subjects learned sentences that were grouped according to the names or attributes of ships (as previously explained). All subjects were required to learn the text until they had achieved perfect recall. Then they were given a test that required integrating the information that had been learned. If the subject had learned "The Squid had a green mainmast." and "The Squid had a red jigger." an integration item might ask, "What was the color if the mainmast of the ship with a red jigger?" Results showed that subjects' ability to answer the integration questions depended upon whether the information to be combined was near or far in the text (distance varied with the text organization). This study suggests how input grouping operations might affect later retrieval. A reader's organizational abilities no doubt should be considered a component of comprehension.

The thrust of this paper has been to suggest that we need to learn more about the conditions that affect how information initially gets from the printed page into different forms of representation in the mind. After we understand this process, we may be in a better positon to understand what occurs when subjects engage in higher level activities associated with retrieval.

Summary of operations. I have indicated three kinds of operations that affect learning outcomes; the semantic operations that a reader performs on text, the sequential nature of the content represented in his goal, and the retrieval and review operations that he must perform.

The discussion of semantic operations was intended to emphasize that not only the focus of attention affects what is learned, but the form of attention alters the stability of items in memory. Paying attention to the deeper semantic properties of a text has greater payoff than paying attention to its superficial properties. A reader may devote much time to study, but if that time is devoted to surface characteristics of the message, he is not likely to learn much.

The discussion of the effects of sequence on subjects' goal directed reading suggests that the order of information in the reader's goal and the order of information in a text can alter the formation of correct associations. In short, the structure of information that the reader has internalized about what he is to read guides reading performance. Mismatches can result in deterioration of learning. The sequence factor appears to involve matching events just as the semantic factor does. Sequence involves the match between serial lists of information in the head and the serial order of text inputs. Semantic factors entail matches (and elaborations) between the reader's memory (semantic properties) and text elements. Sequence may relate to subjects' search activities during reading. These latter activities are perhaps not at a very deep semantic level, however they nonetheless contribute to learning.

Conclusion

In this paper I have provided a brief framework for thinking about purpose in reading. Purpose has two components; *content focus* and *form.* Content focus may be externally imposed, it may arise from the reader's own predispositions, or it may arise as a consequence of an interaction between the reader's goal and the properties of the text being read.

Items upon which attention is focused are often well remembered, but learning outcomes are determined by the form of those operations, not only by the content. For instance, sequential mismatches between the reader's goal and what he reads may intefere with learning, and the semantic criterion that guides reading may entail deep or superficial operations.

Although I have necessarily been selective and sketchy in describing this research, the studies suggest that the human response to written materials can be a very precise affair. Comprehension and learning depend upon specific contingencies between text contents, the responses that a reader makes to the printed word, and the consequences of those responses. What a reader learns depends upon the precision and directness of his goal. Research on these contingencies may eventually provide better tools for giving purpose to reading.

What does this all mean for reading comprehension? I believe that a new and more precise perspective on the concept of purpose in reading is called for. I've attempted to provide this perspective by tying purpose to attention, attention to contents and operations, and contents and operations to learning outcomes. Of course, the studies that I have described clarify the outcomes of only a few reading operations. But they do reveal the power of purpose as a precise executive in the acquisition of knowledge. Purpose sets the stage for responses which determine the contents of memory, and consequently whatever knowledge may be generated from those contents.

Elsewhere (Frase, 1975), I have described a model of processing that elaborates this conception of purpose at greater length. The model is divided into four levels: a) goal orientation, b) encoding, c) rehearsal and integration of text information, and d) retrieval and relation of text information to previously learned knowledge. An assumption of the model is that the actions of encoding, rehearsal and retrieval are modifiable by alterations in goal orientation.

If this is true, then it may be possible to instruct readers about how to alter their own goals in appropriate directions. Such self-control is a desirable aim of education.

REFERENCES

Anderson, R.C., and Biddle, W.B. On asking people questions about what they are reading. In G. Bower (Ed.), *Psychology of learning and motivation* (Vol. 9). New York: Academic Press, 1975.

Anderson, R.C., and Hidde, J.L. Imagery and sentence learning. *Journal of Educational Psychology,* 1971, *62,* 526-530.

Boyd, W.M. Repeating questions in prose learning. *Journal of Educational Psychology,* 1973, *64,* 31-38.

Carroll, J.B. Defining language comprehension: Some speculations. In J.B. Carroll and R.O. Freedle (Eds.), *Language comprehension and the acquisition of knowledge.* Washington: V.H. Winston and Sons, 1972.

Dewey, J. *Experience and nature.* Chicago: Open Court Publishing Company, 1925.

Eischens, R.R.; Gaite, A.J.H.; and Kumar, V.K. Prose learning: Effects of question position and informational load interactions on low signal value information. *Journal of Psychology,* 1972 *81,* 7-12.

Frase, L.T. Some unpredicted effects of different questions upon learning from connected discourse. *Journal of Educational Psychology,* 1968, *59,* 197-201.

Frase, L.T. Paragraph organization of written materials: The influence of conceptual clustering upon the level and organization of recall. *Journal of Educational Psychology* 1969, *63,* 394-401.

Frase, L.T. Integration of written text. *Journal of Educational Psychology,* 1973, *65,* 252-261.

Frase, L.T. Prose processing. In G. Bower (Ed.) *Psychology of learning and motivation* (Vol. 9). New York: Academic Press, 1975.

Frase, L.T., and Kammann, R. Effects of search criterion upon unanticipated free recall of categorically related words. *Memory and Cognition,* 1974, *2,* 181-184.

Frase, L.T., and Kreitzberg, V.S. Effect of topical and indirect learning directions on prose recall. *Journal of Educational Psychology,* 1975, *67,* 320-324.

Frase, L.T.; Patrick, E.; and Schumer, H. Effect of question position and frequency upon learning from text under different levels of incentive. *Journal of Educational Psychology,* 1970, *61,* 52-57.

Frase, L.T., and Silbiger, F. Some adaptive consequences of searching for information in a text. *American Educational Research Journal,* 1970, *7,* 553-560.

Frase, L.T., and Schwartz, B.J. Effect of question production and answering on prose recall. *Journal of Educational Psychology,* 1975, *67,* 628-635.

Friedman, M.P., and Greitzer, F.L. Organization and study time in learning from reading. *Journal of Educational Psychology,* 1972, *63,* 609-616.

Gagné, E.D., and Rothkopf, E.Z. Text organization and learning goals. *Journal of Educational Psychology,* 1975, *67,* 445-450.

Kaplan, R., and Simmons, F.G. Effects of instructional objectives used as orienting stimuli or as summary/review upon prose learning. *Journal of Educational Psychology,* 1974, *66,* 614-622.

McKenzie, G.R. Facilitating inferential thinking with weekly quizzes. Paper presented at the meeting of the American Educational Research Association, New York, February, 1971.

Myers, J.L.; Pezdek, K.; and Coulson, D. Effects of prose organization upon recall. *Journal of Educational Psychology,* 1973, *65,* 313-320.

Perlmutter, J., and Royer, J.M. Organization of prose materials: Stimulus, storage, and retrieval. *Canadian Journal of Psychology,* 1973, *27,* 200-209.

Rickards, J.P., and DiVesta, F.J. Type and frequency of questions in processing textual materials. *Journal of Educational Psychology,* 1974, *66,* 354-362.

Rohwer, Jr., W.D. Learning, race, and school success. *Review of Educational Research,* 1971, *41,* 191-210.

Rothkopf, E.Z. The concept of mathemagenic behaviors. *Review of Educational Research,* 1970, *40,* 325-336.

Rothkopf, E.Z., and Kaplan, R. Exploration of the effect of density and specificity of instructional objectives on learning from text. *Journal of Educational Psychology,* 1972, *63,* 295-302.

Schultz, C.B., and DiVesta, F.J. Effects of passage organization and note taking on the selection of clustering strategies and on recall of textual materials. *Journal of Educational Psychology,* 1972, *63,* 244-252.

Surber, J.R.; Anderson, R.C.; and Stevens, K.V. Instructional objectives and learning from text: A cautionary note. Paper presented at the American Educational Research Association Annual Meeting, Washington, D.C., March, 1975.

Wittrock, M.C. Learning as a generative process. *Educational Psychologist,* 1974, *11,* 87-95.

Comments on
Purpose in Reading

Cheryl Hansen

It has been reported that teachers use a predominance of recall types of questions to assess children's understanding of stories (Guzak, 1968; Bartolome, 1969). They seldom attempt to extend student thinking, and comprehension questions often call primarily for low level memory responses. In addition, the questions included in basal teacher guides at all grade levels consist mainly of workbooks and readers' literal questions (Cooke, 1970). The type of question we ask children is directly related to the level of response we receive. Therefore, if we wish to produce better comprehenders, we must begin by becoming better questioners.

Frase's paper is directly relevant to this issue. His work suggests that two components should be considered in evaluating the effect of questions upon subsequent comprehension. Frase labels these components contents and operations.

Content focus refers to the environmental stimuli which affect a reader's subsequent comprehension. Frase considers three variables which can influence comprehension including: experimentor, self, and text imposed focusing. Four findings were discussed in this section. First, direct precise cues significantly improve recall performance. Second, tutorial questioning results in significantly better recall than studying alone. Third, writing out answers as a study aid during reading promotes recall. Fourth, the organization of text material influences subsequent ability to comprehend; criterion names are retained better than compared names, while both criterion and compared are retained better than irrelevant names.

Frase states that learning outcomes are strongly related to the properties of the goals given to readers and their own focus of attention. These results suggest that the stimuli, whether cues externally or internally derived or the organization of the material, do affect learning. Obviously, one would expect poor comprehension if a child did not pay attention to what he read, or merely glanced over the material. There is some question, however, whether goals strongly influence the comprehension of young children.

Purpose setting and prereading questions have been investigated in a variety of studies. Three studies which sought to investigate the role of purpose setting with elementary aged children generally produced non-significant results. When children were given a purpose for their reading, their comprehension was no better than when they were merely instructed to read a passage (Farley, 1972; Pettit, 1970). One exception is a study by Grant and Hall (1967) in which students of differing abilities were divided into two groups which were either given thought provokers before reading or merely required to read a story. These thought provokers were similar to what Frase called "topical references." Grant and Hall reported significant gains for students given prereading thought provokers; however, the results varied for each ability group. Significant gains in comprehension were found only for children of average ability. Thought provokers had no effect on the performance of high ability children and, interestingly enough, adverse effects on the comprehension performance of students of low reading ability.

These studies, in light of Frase's comments, suggest that general purpose setting organizers may affect subsequent recall differentially, according to the ability level of the subjects or perhaps there is a relationship between purpose setting and difficulty of the passage. In accordance with Frase, these studies suggest that general topical references before reading, such as "learn about the characteristics and history of dirigibles," seldom facilitate comprehension. An alternative to this type of purpose setter would be to provide students with specific information to search for in their reading. What could be more specific than providing students the opportunity to preview or preread their comprehension questions.

One might imagine that prereading would lead to improved comprehension. Frase indicates that direct cues aid recall. However, this procedure resulted in non-significant differences in comprehension by Bloomer and Heitzman

(1965), with eighth graders; Noakes (1969), using fifth grade students; and Goudey (1970), who studied the effects of pre-reading questions upon the comprehension performance of fourth grade youngsters. The "positive learning outcomes" associated with direct focusing on critical components of content reported by Frase were not supported by this data.

The disparities observed between the finding of Frase and the studies I have just cited may be due to the ages of the subjects, the precision of the measures, or the differences in the content of the tasks. Further research will be necessary to discern whether content focus is a determining variable in the ability to comprehend and, if so, the relationship between these two variables.

Goal directed reading according to Frase also includes consideration of the operations which are entailed. Operations is the term applied to the processing activities of the reader. While I would not deny that some sort of mediation does occur between the stimuli and a response, the form and characteristics involved in this mediation are unclear. Frase suggests that three types of operations occur: semantic, sequential, and review.

According to Frase, processing for specific semantic properties results in greater recall than processing for general properties. To use his example, persons recall words categorized as *fruit* better than those categoriezed as *food*. A wealth of paired-associate literature on memory supports this finding. The implication for teachers is to be specific about what you want children to remember.

Frase suggests that there is a relationship between the sequential nature of operations and expectancies. Systematic grouping of sentences produces better recall than random arrangements. Therefore, mediation and subsequent recall appear to be facilitated when materials are organized logically rather than haphazardly. Frase also reports an interaction between the sequence of learning directions and the sequence of information in the text. The finding reminds us once again of the complexity of that concept we glibly refer to as comprehension, and the delicacy with which it must be handled to prevent confusions for the learner.

The third way in which operations influence comprehension relates directly to the mediation between stimuli and response. This area is called review operations by Frase. He suggests that the characteristics of memory should be considered part of the comprehension process. The organization of a person's memory may influence comprehension. Research in the field of memory indicates that it is influenced by the rehearsal and retrieval strategies of the subject. This is a potentially exciting and useful area of investigation, yet Frase provides little beyond whetting our appetite. Unfortunately, research on this subject is complicated by the fact that we cannot see what goes on inside the brain but must be content with the weak shadows of observable response.

One very important comment which should not be overlooked in Frase's paper is his idea (which has been suggested by others) that we should focus children's attention on whether their reading makes sense to them rather than merely requiring that they read accurately. Motivators, such as "This is the exciting tale of two crickets in a field." should be replaced by cues to learn why the crickets make noise, or how Noah's flood affected the crickets' later marriage. Precise cues should help readers focus their attention on relevant stimuli within the story. Perhaps an extension of this strategy would be to develop ways to provide precise cues which would facilitate higher level comprehension including inference, synthesis, and translation.

In a year long study of children in grades one through six, King et al. (1967), found that teachers' questions were directly related to the level of student responses they received. Developmental trends in the level of responding were also noted: pupils in grades 5 and 6 generally gave higher level responses than pupils in grades 1 and 2. These findings suggest that pupils' responses are affected by the type and frequency of teacher questioning, and the level of responses made may be influenced by improved teacher questioning strategies.

The relationships of the organization of material to subsequent comprehension is a matter which deserves further investigation. Frase's seminal work should provide direction for these inquiries. Until such research is available, practitioners should be cautioned to become familiar with the material they expect children to read and to pay close attention to the relationship between their questions and the organization of the material. Sets of materials and questioning paradigms could be developed to teach children how to integrate information from different parts of material. The result would be better critical readers.

A second area of interest sparked by Frase relates to study strategies. His data suggest that certain methods of study, such as tutoring and writing answers while reading, enhance subsequent recall performance. The SQ3R (Robinson, 1961) and PQ4R (Preview, question, read, reflect, recite, and review) are examples of study strategies which should be learned and practiced by readers to improve their recall performance. There should be no doubt as to the value of repetition and recall in learning textual material.

Perhaps most importantly, Frase reminds us that we should always focus children's attention on reading for meaning rather than merely decoding words. Through continually asking "does it make sense," the child will be able to learn that reading entails communication rather than verbally identifying symbols. "Making sense" is the primary purpose in reading.

The research presented by Frase should be extended to determine whether his model will hold for young children who are just learning how to read. I would be especially interested in seeing a replication of his study on direct cues with young children. The generalizeability of his research would be enhanced by such replications. A second need would be to engage in intervention research with poor readers. While it is interesting and informative to learn how purpose affects learning outcomes with adults, we might gain further insight into this subject through the development of teaching techniques that facilitate purpose setting for those children who have failed to acquire proficiency in reading.

Results of these studies might help us teach children the important skill of setting purposes during reading.

REFERENCES

Bartolome, P.I. Teachers' objectives and questions in primary reading. *The Reading Teacher.* 1969, *23,* 27-33.
Bloomer, R.H., and Heitzman, A.J. Pretesting and efficiency of para-

graph reading. *Journal of Reading*, 1965, *8*, 219-223.

Cooke, D.A. An analysis of reading comprehension questions in basal reading series according to the Barrett Taxonomy. Unpublished doctoral dissertation, Cornell University, 1970.

Farley, F.H. Children's learning from discourse: Advanced organizer, text sequence, and arousal effects on literal and inferential comprehension. Technical Report No. 265, Wisconsin University, 1972.

Goudey, C.E. Reading—directed or not? *The Elementary School Journal* 1970, *70*, 245-247.

Grant, E.B., and Hall, M. The effect of purposeful reading on comprehension at differing levels of difficulty. Paper presented at the International Reading Association Convention, Seattle, Washington, 1967.

Guzak, F.J. Questioning strategies of elementary teachers in relation to comprehension. Paper presented at International Reading Association Convention, Boston, Massachusetts, 1968.

King, M.; Wolf, W.; Huck, C.; Ellinger, B.; and Gansneder, B. Observations of teacher pupil verbal behavior during critical reading lessons. Unpublished manuscript, Ohio State University, Columbus, 1967.

Noakes, A.M. The effects of conditions of pre-questioning upon comprehension of fiction and non-fiction selections with fifth grade children. Unpublished doctoral dissertation, University of Delaware, 1969.

Pettit, N.T.B. Effects of reading for a given purpose on literal and influential comprehension. Unpublished doctoral dissertation, University of Missouri, Columbia, 1970.

Syntax, Semantics, and Reading

Irene Athey

Those aspects of linguistics which are most relevant to reading are phonology, syntax, and semantics. While the importance of phonology is seen most clearly in the decoding process, syntax and semantics are fundamental to both the productive and receptive aspects of comprehension, of which reading is one. Consequently, this paper will address the basic question, "What do we know about the English-speaking person's understanding of syntactic and semantic conventions, and how does this understanding affect that person's ability to read with comprehension?" In the course of answering these broad questions, we shall have occasion to consider a number of corollary questions, such as how children develop their understanding of syntactic and semantic rules, the relationship between syntax and semantics, and others.

Syntax and reading

It should be stated at the outset that our knowledge about syntax far exceeds our knowledge about semantics. The theory of transformational grammar which emerged in the late 1950s has led to an enormous amount of research on the syntactic structures of sentences and the transformational rules which enable a native speaker to apprehend their meaning. Interest in the semantic context of utterances is much more recent—having emerged in the last five years or so—but the importance of this aspect of linguistic communication is becoming more and more apparent in the literature, and may indeed supersede the earlier preoccupation with syntax. As Wolfram (1975) has declared, "The Chomskyian revolution is over."

Transformational theory was built on a number of philosophical assumptions, most notably the notion of innate structures which predetermine the sequence and timing of linguistic development in the young child. Empirical support for this notion has been seen in the rapid growth of language, a phenomenon which could not occur, it is argued, if language learning followed the same course as other types of learning that depend primarily on experience. So remarkable is this phenomenon of rapid growth that the adult speech which serves as input for the child's language acquisition is seen as a completely inadequate model, since it is a random, haphazard sample, incapable of instructing the child in grammar (McNeill, 1966). Hence, the need arises to posit the existence of a Language Acquisition Device (LAD) possessing various innate properties such as the ability to distinguish speech sounds from other sounds, to organize linguistic events into classes, and to construct a simple and coherent linguistic system from the surrounding corpus of linguistic data (Wardhaugh, 1971). Of course, other forms of evidence such as linguistic universals, case histories, etc., have been adduced to bolster the theoretical structure of Chomskyian lingustics. Still, the fact that virtually all the syntatic constructions found in adult speech are found in the speech of a normal six-year-old is seen as pivotal to the thesis. Moreover, since the argument has been further extended to imply that language development, being truly complete before reading instruction begins, can have little influence on the process of learning to read (Wardhaugh, 1971), it is worthwhile to examine this "fact" in more detail.

Notice in the first place that it refers to speech production. Apparently young children by age six talk pretty much the way adults do. But this need not mean that their linguistic development is complete. An alternative explanation might be that adults do not in everyday speech use the full range of syntactic structures they are capable of comprehending. They tend to speak in short sentences, or even to leave their sentences unfinished, and to eschew embedding and other sophisticated structures, even though they comprehend them perfectly. They rely heavily on the context and on nonlinguistic modes of communicating. We may have been misled by these facts into supposing the syntactic development of children to be much more precocious than it really is.

We are now compiling evidence that the development of syntax is a much more protracted process than was assumed by the theory of transformational grammar, and that experience does play a role in its acquisition after all. In fact, there seems to be a hierarchy of difficulty for processing certain types of syntactic structure, which follows the kind of sequence we find in other types of learning, e.g., from the simple to the complex, from the familiar to the unfamiliar, from the concrete to the abstract, from the positive to the negative instance. All this we find in concept learning, problem solving, and other forms of higher mental activity.

Consider, for example, the use of the conjunction *and*. Although speakers of all ages use this construction, they do so in different ways. Conjunctions appear in children's language as early as 3 or 4 (Miller, 1973). Menyuk (1972) notes that children entering kindergarten use *and* freely to join short sentences together, but the sentences so joined would not be considered appropriate for this operation by adult standards. In fact, there are implicit rules governing the combination of sentences in this manner, rules which the child must induce from the examples he hears around him. Lakoff (1971) has suggested that sentences may be conjoined if they share a common topic based on the identity of certain elements, or on presuppositions which permit one to infer a relationship between the elements. However, this relationship is not the same in all such sentences. There is a hierarchy of appropriate uses. At the bottom of the hierarchy, the presence of common elements would seem to be the minimum necessary condition, but the relationships become increasingly intricate and diversified as we proceed up the hierarchy.

Consider the following sentences:

1. *It was growing darker and the rain was coming down heavily*. No intrinsic relationship exists between the two component sentences. It may grow darker without rain or rain without grow darker. The "similarity" of the elements (no pun intended) is that they contribute to the description of a gloomy evening and do, in fact, often occur together.

2. *He dreamed about growing up and becoming a famous scientist*. Here the relationship is the "similar element" of dreaming common to the two sentences. There is no inherent, necessary relationship between the *content* of the two sentences (one can grow up without be-

coming a famous scientist), but there is a relation of temporal sequence combined with "appropriateness." A sentence such as "He dreamed of growing up and eating a delicious supper that evening" would be inappropriate.

3. *Jim is tall and John is short.* The relationship is one of opposition within a given context, e.g., comparing brothers or friends.

4. *He said he would come and I believed him.* The relationship is not exactly causal, but reflects a social convention that we believe what someone says, unless and until we have sufficient grounds for not believing.

5. *The dog bared its teeth and Billy ran in terror.* Here the relationship is clearly causal.

These sentences represent a few of the ways in which *and* may be used to imply a relationship between two (or more) sentences which is not explicitly stated, but which children must learn to infer. It seems that there is more to learning the permissible uses of this conjunction than appears at first sight. We should not be surprised, therefore, by findings such as those of Hutson and Shub (1974), showing a developmental trend from a largely random use of the conjunction at grade one, to adherence to the rule of similar elements at grade four, envolving to the use of more complex rules at grade ten.

A study by Stoodt (1972) at the fourth grade confirmed that *and* is among the easiest conjunctions to comprehend (the others being *how, for,* and *as*). The most difficult were *when, so, but, or, where, while, that,* and *if*. Intelligence was found to be highly related to understanding conjunctions.

Linguists have familiarized us with the notion that passive and negative concepts or propositions are, in general, more difficult to process than simple active affirmatives. For instance, children find it more difficult to identify an object which is round and *not* red than one which is round and red (Neimark and Slotnick, 1970). Similarly, *but* is harder to understand or use than *and,* because it implies negation (Katz and Brent, 1968). In fact, the negative connotation and opposition of ideas implied in the use of *but* seems to be quite difficult even for some children of elementary school age when confronted with a sentence such as "One cannot always be a hero,_____ one can always be a man." This particular sentence is an item on the Minkus Completion subtest of the Stanford-Binet and is placed at age 12. Terman remarks in passing that "such connective words . . . are rather highly abstract" (Terman and Merrill, 1937). Hutson and Shub, in the study previously cited, found as expected that children did seem to infer a simple rule (or at least behave as if they were inferring some such rule) that "clauses which have a similar position on a dimension are joined with *and*; clauses which have contrasting positions on a dimension are joined with *but*" (pp. 9-10). Deviations from this simple rule were greater for sentences calling for *but* than for those calling for *and*, suggesting that the former does indeed involve more complex relationships and hence is more difficult. The developmental trend did not level off, however, with convergence to this simple rule. Beyond a certain point, there was a new divergence toward a more complex rule, suggesting that children are becoming aware of more and more of the kind of elaborations we discussed in connection with the conjunction *and*.

Carol Chomsky (1972) has pointed out that other syntactic errors arise from the fact that particular constructions have a suppressed noun phrase or verb phrase which the reader must generate correctly if he is to understand the meaning of the sentence. Thus, in the sentence "The doll is easy to see," the person doing the seeing is unspecified. The only thing we are sure about is that it is *not* the doll. But that is precisely the error that elementary school children make. They overgeneralize the rule which they have inferred from experience that the subject is the person or thing who is performing the action indicated by the verb. Chomsky found five structures (easy, promise, ask, and, although) which evoked this type of confusion.

Another possible type of error is suggested by what Downing (1969) calls "cognitive confusion." He cites Vernon as saying that poor readers do not understand why sequences of printed letters correspond to particular phonetic sounds, and indeed seem to be almost indifferent to the order of letters in a word. Would it be stretching the analogy too far to suggest that some poor readers may not understand that sequences of words correspond to particular meanings and are either indifferent to the order of words, or are simply unable to integrate a sequence of words to produce a coherent unit of thought? Denner (1970) found that even children who could express themselves fluently in conversation had difficulty integrating a series of symbolic forms to produce a sentence such as "Walk around the teacher" or "Jump over the block," although they understood the symbols when they were presented separately.

Bormuth and his colleagues (1970) have investigated the understanding of syntactic structures in a much more comprehensive way than any of the researchers previously cited. They found an unexpectedly low level of performance among fourth grade students on many of the sentence structures which, on the face of it, seem both basic and simple.

Table 1 shows the percentage of students responding correctly to questions testing each sentence structure. These questions were mostly of the wh-type (who, what, when, where, by whom, etc.) and were posed on materials scaled for reading difficulty, so that the vocabulary and syntactic complexity of the material were held to a minimum. Bormuth concluded that "the major categories of structures may be hierarchically related, as shown by the fact that they differed in difficulty," and that "this ordering of difficulty [is] the same as one would derive from linguistic theory" (p. 356). If such a hierarchy is borne out by further studies, it could have many implications for the teaching of reading. For we can infer that, if students cannot respond correctly to such simple questions, they are not comprehending as much of the printed material as teachers would like to believe.

Such findings are not too surprising, perhaps, if we reflect on the arbitrary nature of our syntactic rules. To take a simple example: Why do we insert the indefinite article in an expression such as "What a fool!" Neither French nor Spanish includes the "a", whereas to leave it out in English turns the expression into a question: "What fool?" Similarly, whether or not a preposition follows a verb, and what this preposition is, can make a profound difference to the meaning of the verb. "To search" someone means something quite different from "to search *for*" someone. Other languages have their own conventions which are equally arbitrary. In Spanish, for example, "querer una cocinera" means "to need a cook," whereas "querer a una cocinera" means "to love a cook." Examples like these crowd in upon us when we are learning a foreign language, but as adults we do have the syntactic system of our own

Table 1. Percentage of Students Responding Correctly to Questions Testing Each of the Sentence Structures.

Structure	% Correct
Comparative, unequal	88.3
(Joe runs *faster than* Bill.)	
Nominal compound, noun + verb + preposition + noun	87.9
(*Hammer blow*, a blow struck with a hammer.	
Nominalization, possessive + verb + ing	87.0
(*His going* came as a surprise.)	
Prenominal adjective	85.5
(The *tall* boy is Joe.)	
Subordinate sentence, causal	83.3
(We came because we smelled lunch being served.)	
Relative clause, with deletion	80.9
(The man *working in the yard* is the owner.)	
Nominalization, verb + ing	80.6
(*Finding him* was easy.)	
Adjectival prepositional phrase	80.0
(The man *with the hat* manufactures cans.)	
Subordinate sentence, after	79.8
(*After we entered*, the play began.)	
Nominalization, factive	78.9
(The *fact that he came* surprised us.)	
Subordinate sentence, although	77.3
(*Although it rained recently*, the ground remains parched.)	
Nominal compounds, verb + ing	77.3
(*Washing machine,* The machine is for washing clothes.)	
Subordinate sentence, purposive	76.3
(*In order to make certain*, we asked a second time.)	
Relative clause, appositive	73.7
(Mr. Joseph, *who is our mailman*, retired.)	
Nominal compound, someone operates	71.7
(*Elevator operator*, Someone operates an elevator.)	
Subordinate sentence, conditional	70.5
(If we don't hurry, we'll miss the show.)	
Nominal compound, noun + preposition + noun	69.8
(*Ranger station*, a station for rangers)	
Nominalization, for-to	69.6
(*For us to find him* was difficult.)	
Nominal compound, preposition + noun	67.4
(*Potato dumpling,* The dumpling is made from potatoes.)	
Relative clause, without deletion	67.0
(The man *who has been working in the yard* is the owner.)	
Adjective compliment	66.2
(He is *clever* to go.)	
Subordinate sentence, before	65.1
(*Before we arrived*, people had already been seated.)	
Subordinate sentence, tense shift if clause	61.4
(*If you had some money*, you would buy some.)	
Subordinate sentence, simultaneous	56.1
(As *we entered*, the curtain rose.)	
Comparative, equal	28.1
(Joe runs *as fast as* Bill.)	

language to use as a base of reference. We can remember this or that construction because it is the same as that of English, or is different in a particular way which strikes us. Children do not have such a reference system, but must evolve their own. Even young children appreciate the fact that there *are* rules governing the way sentences are put together, just as they understand that things may be categorized under a certain label; and just as they overgeneralize on the use of the label, they extend the syntactic rules they perceive to cover inappropriate instances. In this way, we find young children uttering such expressions as—Where Daddy went?" and "Two foots." It would be interesting to see whether older children of seven or eight make the same kind of errors of overgeneralization with respect to the rules they find difficult.

We do not have many studies like Chomsky's at the elementary level, which test hypotheses about the psychological processes underlying the syntactic errors made by children. As we saw, Bormuth's investigations uncovered the extent and proportion of such errors. It would be instructive to go beyond his percentages, and analyze the nature of the incorrect responses to try to discover what is going on in the child's head when he makes the errors. If we knew this, we would then be in a better position to know what the child is understanding when he reads sentences using the various constructions in question—just as we now know that when he reads "The doll is easy to see," he thinks it is the doll who is seeing.

Some of the most familiar and apparently easy structures may, indeed, be among the most difficult to comprehend, as Chomsky demonstrates. This fact has led us to the realization that syntactic development does not consist of a series of structures which evolve in a programmed sequence, unrelated to the development of meanings. Some psycholinguists have hypothesized, for example, that there is a hierarchy of difficulty, in which a simple active, affirmative sentence such as "The boy throws the ball" would be the baseline, followed by negative, passive, and passive negative transformations, in that order. If we measure the difficulty level in terms of the time it takes for the individual to process the sentence, we find this to be substantially true. However, there are important exceptions to this general rule. If the *meaning* of the sentence is positive, even though the surface structure is negative, the sentence is relatively easy. In other words, we seem to respond, in some cases, directly to the meaning, while ignoring the syntactic structure of the sentence. As we know, a child does not respond to the question, "Shouldn't you be in bed?" by considering the pros and cons of the issue, or by assuming that the questioner is looking for a negative answer. What he has learned is the convention that when we ask a question in the affirmative (*Did you go?*) we have no previous assumptions and are seeking information; but when we ask the same question in negative form *(Didn't you go?)* we are expressing surprise, or the violation of some expectation.

Our language packs many hidden items which may or may not be obvious to the receiver of a message. Donaldson and Wales (1970) have pointed out that many words in our lexicon are really relational, e.g., when we say a person is tall, we mean tall against some implicit standard, or tall for his age; and, of course, all comparative and superlative, expressions such as *more, less, too much* of something, *not enough* of something, *to the right of, different from,* and many others do involve a relational concept. Piaget and his followers have demonstrated that young children have difficulty in handling certain relationships, especially when they involve two or more simultaneous comparisons. If the child is still working out the precise meaning of these common relational terms, we must conclude that his reading of printed text containing such terms is correspondingly imprecise.

Notice that there is an assumption throughout this discussion that the meanings conveyed by certain syntactic structures are more or less stable, and that the child's task is to move closer and closer to "the correct meaning." Such an assumption is only partially true. The meanings attached to particular structures may be like the meanings attached to concepts. There is a core of common meaning (in the case of a concept, the definition or denotative aspects of the concept) which makes it possible for us to communicate intelligibly about the object. Beyond the definitional aspects, however, is the vast web of connotative meanings, including the peripheral, the subjective, the personal, all of which make the word or phrase much more interesting than its simple definition. So a particular syntactic structure may come to have a different meaning in a subculture or in a different part of the country. Most speakers of English for example, use *rather* to mean *quite* or *somewhat* (in fact, this is the dictionary definition); but in certain parts of the country it is used as a synonym for *very* (Rystrom, 1975). Examples like this one spring readily to mind. In other words, the "correctness" of certain structures in the English language may vary, depending on the community of speakers. A person who is accustomed to using the American construction *Do you have (*or *I don't have)* soon finds it to be unacceptable in England, where the "correct" construction is *Have you* (or *Have you got,* for emphasis) and I haven't (or *I haven't got)*. I am not speaking here of so-called black dialects or nonstandard English, but of different usages among speakers of standard English.

While it is true that there are certain constructions which we are willing to label "correct" or "incorrect" without much hesitation, correctness is not an all-or-none concept, but a matter of degree. In other words, while two syntactic structures may be "correct," one is *more* correct for any one of a variety of reasons. Perhaps one structure is more familiar, or has a slightly different implication; perhaps it is more appropriate to the context in which it is used, or to the affective tone one wishes to convey. In brief, one cannot divorce the correct use of a syntactic structure from the meaning of the particular situation in which it is embedded. A skillful reader exploits cues in the surface structure to help recover the underlying meanings, including their affective dimensions (Fodor and Garrett, 1967). All this is to say that we cannot profitably study syntactic development apart from the development of semantics, because syntactic structures are learned in relation to the way they trigger meanings.

It would clearly be advantageous for both teachers and psychologists to have a scale of syntactic development. Piaget has given us a model to follow by postulating the various stages and substages which can be detected in the development of particular concepts such as "life" or "justice." As his hypotheses have been substantiated, there have been sporadic efforts to scale the Piagetian tasks and assemble them into tests of cognitive functioning.

The transition from preoperational to concrete-operational thought which occurs as the result of decentration is a major aspect of Piaget's theory. Since this process typically occurs between the ages of five and seven, or even later, most of the experimentation and test construction has been concerned with this period. By contrast, the belief that syntactic development is essentially complete by the age of four has focused attention on the growth of language in the very young child, while the language of the elementary school child has been relatively neglected. We have nothing to correspond at this level to the major studies of early language development which came out of Harvard, California, and Maryland in the 1960s. As a result of these studies, it is possible to show rather precisely the sequence of specific syntactic structures as they emerge in the child's speech, and to develop and test hypotheses about the deep structures represented in one- and two-word utterances. When we turn to the elementary school years, we do not find the same frenzy of activity. There have been a few landmark studies attempting to establish the sequential nature of syntactic usage.

Templin's finding (1957) that the proportion of verbs used was about the same in three-year-olds as in older children has led other investigators to conclude that the distribution of parts of speech is not a satisfactory measure of language development. Sentence length has proved equally inadequate, because shortening a sentence sometimes indicates greater syntactic maturity. For example, younger children are more liable to say, "That one's blue and that one's blue," rather than "*They* are blue" or "*Both* are blue" (Donaldson and Wales, 1970). Equally unsatisfactory as a measure is the length of clause. However, the subordination ratio, i.e., the proportion of predicates in dependent, subordinate clauses as compared with the number of predicates in independent main clauses, has been found to increase substantially in older children's writing (LaBrant, 1933).

Harrell (1957) tabulated the total number of movable adverb clauses, relative adjective clauses, noun clauses, and other types of subordinate clauses used at each grade. The only type showing significant growth was the relative adjective clause, which was found to increase fourfold from grades four to twelve and even beyond.

In a 1965 study of children's writing in grades four, eight, and twelve and also that of skilled adults, Hunt introduced a new measure called the T-unit. He defined the unit as "one main clause plus any subordinate clause or non-clausal structure that is attached to or embedded in it . . . . The T-unit is minimal and terminable. Any complex or simple sentence would be one T-unit, but any compound or compound-complex sentence would consist of two or more T-units" (Hunt, 1965: 4). With this concept as an intermediary structure between clause and sentence, Hunt found that, as children mature from grades four to twelve, they use more 1) words per T-unit, 2) words per clause, 3) clauses per T-unit, and 4) words per sentence—these measures being in decreasing order as indices of syntactic maturity (Hunt, 1965: 6). Words per sentence is the least adequate because it reflects the fact that, as children mature, the number of T-units per sentence actually declines, even though there are more words in each T-unit. Older writers, especially skilled adults, use a much larger number of sentence-combining, sentence-embedding transformations per T-unit and per clause.

Using general linguistic theory as a guide, Hunt (1965) tabulated the phrase structure rules and transformations which produce the basic sentence patterns and found that fourth-graders use virtually all of them. He also found that those transformations which expand nominal structures are particularly indicative of maturity. O'Donnell et al. (1967) also found that "the mean length of T-unit has special claim to consideration as a simple, objective, valid indicator of development of syntactic control" both in speech and writing. They also report the relationship between the number of sentence-combining transformations and length of T-units to be "impressive."

Hunt's later study (1970) was designed to demonstrate that as school children mature mentally, they tend to embed more of their elementary sentences. The fact that they do so, and that they transform in different ways at different age levels suggests that this is a psychological phenomenon, showing the effect on surface structure of the processes represented in the transformations from deep structure. In other words, as the mind matures, it is able to organize information more intricately, and so can produce and receive more intricately organized sentences. As Miller (1956: 93) has pointed out:

> Since the memory span is a fixed number of chunks, we can increase the number of bits of information that it contains simply by building larger and larger chunks, each chunk containing more information than before....In the jargon of communication theory, this process would be called recoding. The input is given in a code that contains many chunks with few bits per chunk. The operator recodes the input into another code that contains fewer chunks with more bits per chunk.

Hunt maintains that psycholinguistic research should address the question of whether the multiple embedding characteristic of older writers does indeed make it easier for information to be processed.

Loban's classic longitudinal study (1963) of elementary school children's language also used a unit very much like the T-unit, which he called a "communication unit," the main difference being that a communication unit need not contain a full clause, but could consist of brief answers to questions or qualifying phrases such as "on the other hand." Like Hunt, Loban found an increase in length of the communication unit with maturity.

Chomsky's study (1972) of the acquisition of syntax in children from five to ten has already been referred to, and is mentioned again here for the purpose of noting that it differs from the others in certain important respects. The others have been concerned primarily with children's productions in speech and writing, and we should perhaps be cautious in drawing conclusions from their findings about children's comprehension of the constructions they encounter in print. Moreover, Chomsky's study tests comprehension of a few specific structures, and arranges them in a sequential hierarchy, whereas the others simply report more global tendencies which increase with age. At this point, more research like the Chomsky study needs to be extended to the many types of structures such as Bormuth investigated, in order to uncover the psychological processes which result in errors of comprehension. Such data would be extremely useful to the teacher in alerting her to the possibilities of errors whenever such structures occur in the course of reading.

Why is syntax so important to reading? It may have something to do with the fact that, as Throndike (1917) pointed out many years ago, reading is largely a process of the correct selection and synthesis of key elements in the sentence. Some years later, Gibbons (1941) tested this hypothesis by means of a "disarranged phrase test," and found a correlation of .89 at the third grade level between the ability to see relationships among parts of a sentence and the ability to understand the sentence, even after intelligence was partialled out. The syntax of the sentence may be the best single cue for the student as to what these key elements are, and as to how the author intended them to be related. In a recent study, Siler (1973-74) found that syntactic violations of prose had a more deleterious effect on the oral reading performance of second and fourth graders than semantic violations, and almost as much effect as syntactic and semantic violations combined. In fact, sentences which were violated syntactically were also violated semantically, though the reverse was not the case. Siler cites a number of other studies (Epstein, 1962; Maclay and Sleator, 1960; Prentice, 1966) to support his contention, while evidence to the contrary (Danks, 1969; Marks and Miller, 1965) he finds less compelling. Additionally, Siler points to the need to develop semantic taxonomies comparable in sophistication to those developed for syntax.

Further evidence of the importance of syntactic cues for comprehension may be seen in the fact that the ability to use such cues differentiates between good and poor readers. When children are unfamiliar with the syntactic patterns they find in text, they are likely to substitute structures with which they are familiar (MacKinnon, 1959), and good readers do a better job of substituting appropriate structures than poor readers (Goodman, 1970; Weber, 1970). Rewriting such passages using patterns of language structure which occur frequently in children's speech therefore aids compehension, even if the vocabulary difficulty, sentence length, and subject matter content remain the same (Ruddell, 1965; Tatham, 1968). Even at the high school level, there is a moderate correlation between awareness of the structural relationships of words in sentences and reading comprehension (O'Donnell, 1961; Rinne, 1967).

On the other hand, syntactic patterns which are too easy may also affect reading comprehension adversely. Smith (1972-73, 1974) found that eighth grade students recoded both *more* complex and *less* complex material into structures appropriate to their own level of syntactic maturity. Peltz (1973-74) made a similar finding at the tenth grade level, and concluded that "attempts to simplify vocabulary may result in the creation of structures which inadvertently embed concepts in a manner which may result in syntactic structures and, concomitantly, a semantic conceptual load which are out of the learner's realm of expectation and experience" (p. 620). An alternative explanation might be that when a child is able to process a complex syntactic structure, the redundancy inherent in a simpler structure interferes in some way with comprehension, perhaps by taking up space in memory storage which could be used for additional information. Indeed, the tendency to redundancy at earlier levels of development has been documented in the example cited by Donaldson and Wales (1970). Other writers (e.g., O'Donnell, Griffin, and Norris, 1967) have also observed the tendency to substitute shorter noun modifications such as "The man wearing a coat" for relative clauses ("The man who was wearing a coat").

In general, then, we can accept the proposition that reading comprehension is related both to children's understanding of syntax in written text and to the level of syntactic complexity exhibited in their oral or written language production. The question arises as to whether the relationship is the same and, if not, which is the better predictor of reading comprehension—comprehension of syntax or the production of certain syntactic structures in spontaneous language. The question is somewhat complicated by the fact that the two abilities do not develop at the same rate, nor is either one uniformly in advance of the other. In the very young child, comprehension of what he hears seems to be clearly superior to his productions, at any given age. Similarly, oral expression seems to be superior to written expression in transformational complexity at third grade. However, at grades five and seven, the reverse is true (O'Donnell, Griffin, and Norris, 1967). Harrell (1957) also found that by the intermediate grades, more subordinate clauses and adverb and adjective clauses were used in writing than in speaking. Such discrepancies are not surprising if we remember Piaget's conceptualization of language and thought as two systems which, though inter-related, evolve somewhat independently, so that at any one stage of development we may see thought outstripping language, or language running ahead of thought (Piaget, 1968).

We need not conclude that we should confine our inquiries to comprehension, ignoring production, but simply that we should keep in mind which of these variables is more developed at the age under discussion.

Semantics and reading

As previously noted, Thorndike (1917) many years ago viewed the understanding of paragraphs as a process of reasoning depending upon selection of the right elements and synthesis of these elements in the right relationships. How does the good reader know what these "right elements" and "right relationships" are in any given passage? A knowledge of the meaning of the key words in the passage is obviously important. But Robert Thorndike (1973-74) has recently suggested that even this skill is highly dependent on reasoning. Goodman (1970) has pointed out that good readers can deal more successfully with words in context than with the same words in isolation, whereas this ability is lacking in poor readers. According to Kress (1955), good readers are also superior on the ability to draw inferences from relevant cues and to shift their set when a solution is not readily forthcoming. The initiative and persistence displayed by good readers in attempting to wrest meaning from the printed page (or perhaps we should say "imbue it with meaning") suggests that they have built up a strong expectation that the pieces of this semantic puzzle can be made to fit together to yield information which is meaningful and interesting. Such expectations are built on prior experience of lawfulness and meaning. Entwisle (1971) has written about the effects of "control beliefs" on the general expectancy for success in school, especially in relation to social class. There are apparently large social-class and ethnic differences in problem-solving strategies, such as generating and testing hypotheses, identifying and verbalizing the crucial elements in a problem, and deferring solution until the evidence is in. Entwisle sees these strategies as particularly relevant to reading, and notes that they are inculcated in the middle-class home before the child is expected to confront the problem of reading.

We see, then, why a child equipped with these strategies will be more likely to engage in the "psycholinguistic guessing game" with the expectation of success. Perhaps one of the first things a good reader does is to establish the dimensions of the subject with which he will be dealing in the paragraph, article, or volume. Rystrom (1975) has referred to this process as "establishing the matrix."

> Reading is a matrixing event between the reader and the text; the matrix is a framework, or latticework, in which there is a substantial percentage of unfilled squares, which can be thought of as information gaps. In the processes of reading, the reader produces a small framework of meaning based upon the information on the page and his own stored information. If there is a match, he continues, slowly expanding the grid outward, sometimes by adding information from his own experiences, at others by filling the grid with information provided by the author (p. 5).

In this terminology the good reader uses all possible clues, such as the title and opening sentences of the passage, to establish the parameters of the matrix, and begins simultaneously to fill the squares from his own experience and from what the author has to say.[1] He operates on his knowledge of the probabilities of certain events occuring—physical, social, and linguistic events. Bever (1970) has shown that sentences are better understood if they refer to probable rather than rare events. Strohner and Nelson (1974) have shown the importance of nonverbal context, event probability, and syntactic structure for young children's understanding of spoken language. We may hypothesize that in reading, where the nonverbal dimension is missing, extra reliance is placed on the other two. If the child understands the correspondence between event probabilities in the external world and those portrayed in text,

---

[1] If this interpretation is correct, the concept of reading as "information gain" (from the passage) is only half of what constitutes comprehension.

we can expect that his ability to use correspondence will improve with age. In an interesting paper entitled "IQ is and is not related to reading," Singer (1972) demonstrates that, if the reading task is kept constant from first to fourth grade, the correlation between reading and IQ diminishes. Beyond fourth grade, when reading is measured by a norm-referenced test, the correlation steadily increases. He suggests that the reason for this phenomenon may be that up to the fourth grade most students are learning primarily decoding techniques. As more and more children achieve mastery of these techniques, the correlation naturally declines. On the other hand, beyond fourth grade intellectual skills and previous experience become increasingly important. Through the elementary school years, children are learning not only the behavior of objects (including human objects in the world around them) but also the social conventions, and what is implied by both speaker and hearer in dialogue. Wolfram (1975) reported on a study in which he asked children and adults their age, followed by the question, "How come?" Adults either looked at him suspiciously or treated the latter question as a joke. Occasionally the question was seen as legitimate if the circumstancs were unusual, such as a discrepancy between the person's looks or behavior and his age. Children, on the other hand, treated the question as legitimate, and gave criterion-based responses such as "Because I'm in kindergarten" or "because I've had five birthdays." In other words, young children have not yet learned that there are some questions which require neither a causal nor a logical explanation because no such explanation exists (i.e., they are meaningless questions on the order of "Why is the moon?"). Nor have they learned the convention that we do not ask questions about the obvious, questions to which we and everyone else knows the answer, partly because they have not yet determined what information is obvious and what is not. Moreover, even when a reader does know the appropriate uses of language outside reading, there may be a conflict between this knowledge and what is assumed by the author. The conflict with real life may be inherent in the style of the passage, or in the reasoning (explicit and implicit) employed by the author.

Assuredly, this means that children should learn as early

Athey

as possible to establish a relation between reading and language usage, and should be encouraged to expect books to match their knowledge of the real world (Wolfram, 1975). It also implies that those responsible for preparing or administering reading materials should be aware not only of the child's syntactic development but of the cognitive level of his understanding of events around him. Piaget has pointed the direction in terms of the child's understanding at different developmental stages of concepts of the physical world (causality, probability, space, time, etc.), and others (Furth, 1975) are expanding this research to social institutions (government, law, roles and functions, money, etc.).

Conclusions and implications

1. *Syntax*. Research such as that of Hunt and others has successfully demonstrated the growth of syntactic usage with age, and has isolated the criteria which provide the best indicators of syntactic maturity. We have some studies (Bormuth, Chomsky, Hutson, and Shub) which have investigated the development of specific structures, but we need more. Above all, we need to apply what is known from these studies to the teaching of reading.

Interestingly enough, Chomsky cautions against using the results of her study for practical purposes such as diagnostic or teaching procedures, because her choice of those particular syntactic structures for study was highly arbitrary. On the other hand, as more and more structures are studied, it would seem reasonable for teachers to use the results to assist students in their understanding of text, if not for specific teaching of the structures themselves. One could imagine, for example, that within a single structure, some sentences may be more difficult than others. "The doll is easy to see" would be more difficult than "The block is easy to see," because (conceivably) the doll could see, whereas the block could not. Sentences like the latter would draw the child's attention to the fact that there are occasions on which the subject of the sentence cannot possibly be the agent of the action. Moreover, one could demonstrate to children the elliptical nature of the sentence by expanding it in various ways such as "The doll is easy for me to see (for Jim, for everybody, etc.)." Chomsky's conclusion that "our findings with regard to complexity of structure should not be interpreted to mean that because a child does not know a particular construction therefore we should attempt to teach it to him" (p. 32) would be acceptable, *if* we could assume that the child would not meet that construction in the teacher's instructions to him, or in the textbooks and primers he was supposed to master. On the other hand, one may agree with her general conclusion that "perhaps the best thing we might do for him in terms of encouraging this learning could be to make more of it possible, by exposing him to a rich variety of language inputs in interesting, stimulating situations" (p. 33). But even in classrooms where this type of language teaching is favored, the teacher who is aware of the particular interpretations children may be deriving from certain syntactic structures can be on the alert to clarify, introduce new examples, or otherwise exploit the "teachable moment."

Hunt draws somewhat different implications from his work, namely that a sequential curriculum on syntactic maturity covering many grades should be undertaken, and that perhaps a variety of curricula should be available to facilitate syntactic maturity. One cannot quarrel with his further conclusion that teachers of writing should be trained in at least the rudiments of transformational theory. Perhaps this training should be extended to include teachers of reading as well. In fact, both reading and writing are improved when the meaning relations between the structural elements of sentences are emphasized (Ruddell, 1970; Baele, 1968).

As far as research endeavors in this area are concerned, we are beginning to question the use of a transformational grammar model as the basis for a psychological model. Pearson (1974-75) recently conducted a series of experiments to test counter hypotheses derived from the deep structure model and the chunking model, and found that the results systematically favored the latter. Basically, this means that the hypothetical memory storage units are large components such as complete sentences, rather than atomistic deep structure components such as "tall man" and "short girl" which must be synthesized if comprehension is to occur. Bransford and Franks (1971) have demonstrated the superiority of the chunking explanation with adult subjects, thereby emphasizing the primacy of semantic over syntactic factors influent readers. On the other hand, the deep structure model may be more appropriate where the material to be understood is so difficult that it can only be handled in small segments. Although Thorndike's (1917) original study suggests a synthetic model which would be at variance with Pearson's conclusion, it should be remembered that Thorndike was analyzing *errors* in comprehension, which suggests that the material in question was too difficult for the subjects under study.

If a different model is indeed appropriate for easy and difficult material, this would have different implications for the sentence components to be emphasized by teachers at different stages of reading, or at the same stage of reading with easy and difficult materials.

2. *Semantics.* Syntax helps the reader to comprehend because his understanding of sentence structure helps him to narrow down the possibilities of what is to come in subsequent parts of the text (Miller, Heise, and Lichten, 1951). He can use this help, however, only to the extent that he comprehends the objects and events described and their relationships to one another, and only if he understands written language as a vehicle for transmitting information about real life. Any experience which facilitates the match between reading and real life, and promotes verbalization of the child's understanding and insights, will thus contribute to his reading development. The language experience approach to learning need not be confined to early reading, for children of all ages are faced with the problem of relating reading to their experience, albeit at different levels.

If children are encouraged to think about their experience and concurrently, to anticipate that what they read will correspond to what they know, they will become adept at what we have called "filling in the squares of the matrix." They will show initiative and persistence, and be willing to take risks in looking for ways to build the matrix, in the confident belief that what they learn will not only be consonant with their experience but will add to it. If Frank Smith's hypothesis (1971) is correct that good readers bypass many of the words and process what they read directly into their own meaning structures, this ability must come about as the result of using many of the above strategies. Children should therefore be encouraged from the beginning to paraphrase what they read, to relate it to what they know, and to evaluate it in terms of its meaning for them, as they do in the perception of speech (Powers and Gowie, 1975). This is Piaget's notion of assimilation, and it is especially important in terms of remembering what they read. Memory is based on semantic properties rather than syntactic forms (Blount and Johnson, 1973; Sachs, 1967). We cannot begin too early to convey to children the message that reading is a communication system as inherently rational and informative as spoken language.

3. *Readability*. This brings us to the final point in reference to the implications of syntactic and semantic development for reading, and that concerns the readability level of materials and how it is to be matched against the level of the students for whom the material is designed. Typically, the best way to do this with the tools currently available is to administer an achievement test as a rough indicator of the student's level, and use a readability formula as an index of the difficulty of the material, and then match the two. Since both measures are inadequate to the task, we need to seek ways of improving both phases of the diagnosis.

A measure of syntactic development in addition to, or even as a replacement for, the IQ test might improve the prediction of reading significantly because, as we have seen, syntactic cues are important in deriving meaning from a sentence.

As far as readability is concerned, most formulas currently available use two indices, the number of "difficult" words in the passage and the average sentence length. Yet Hunt found the number of words per sentence to be the least satisfactory of his measures of syntactic maturity. In recognition of this fact, there have been sporadic efforts in recent years to develop readability formulas which do incorporate some index of the syntactic complexity of sentences in the passage under consideration. For example, Granowsky and Botel (1974) have developed a device for the identification of syntactic structures that affect readability, though the instrument is "a directional effort still requiring further validation" (p. 33). Endicott (1973) also has a proposed scale for syntactic complexity based on the T-unit of

Athey

Hunt. This measure yields a complexity ratio derived from the number of transformations imposed on a basic one-morpheme-per-word sentence.

Since reading is itself a complex phenomenon, it should come as no surprise that the factors affecting readability are themselves many and complex. In a comprehensive study, Bormuth (1966) used correlational and multiple regression analysis to determine the predictive power of over 100 structural variables, with cloze test as the criterion of passage difficulty. He found a number of new variables, among which was a measure of sentence complexity based on Yngve's (1960, 1962) word depth analysis. He concluded that "mean word depth evidently measures a form of sentence complexity which is somewhat independent of the lengths of independent clauses and, to a lesser extent, of the length of sentences" (p. 122). It has also been shown that nominalizations of active verbs ("His explanation" vs. "He explained" [Coleman, 1965]); the use of idioms (Edwards, 1974), especially those not found in mainstream native speech; and the complex use of auxiliaries (Minkoff, 1974) have a significant effect on reading comprehension. Learning these many conventions used in mature writing is a long-term process, calling for explicit instruction by all teachers, not only reading teachers.

Formulas which recognize the semantic features in language are likely to emerge even more slowly than those taking account of syntactic structures. As a result of Piaget's work, we do know much more than we did fifty years ago about the child's concepts of the world around him, but when we consider the vast number of concepts and their interrelationships to be acquired, we see that much more research is needed. Moreover, we have done little about applying what we do know in this area to the task of matching reading materials to the child's level of *understanding* (as opposed to vocabulary). For example, it would seem important, below a certain level of syntactic maturity, to cast materials in such a way that they do not place an undue inferential burden on the reader, by implying rather than stating relationships or other semantic features. Pearson (1974-75) has illustrated the difficulty children may encounter in inferring causal relationships from two juxtaposed sentences in which the relationship is unstated. He concludes that "the possible implications for social science and science content, where the intent is often to present *new* causal relations, are quite serious" (p. 190). In view of Piaget's finding, we may look for the same kinds of difficulty with respect to the understanding of other relationships he has studied in children.

Reading is an activity in which the highest human abilities—perceptual, intellectual, and linguistic—interact and support one another in pursuit of a single goal, the processing and assimilation of written information. If at times we are overwhelmed by the complexity of the subject, we should also be encouraged by the fact that we are coming closer to understanding the nature of reading comprehension, even though progress takes place in a piecemeal fashion. Although there are still many pieces missing in the puzzle, it is a satisfying experience to see each new piece fall into place. There is much work to be done, but the need is pressing and the direction has been set. We can surely expect much exciting research in this area in the next few years.

REFERENCES

Baele, E.R. The effect of primary reading programs emphasizing language structure as related to meaning upon children's written language achievement at the third grade level. Unpublished doctoral dissertation, University of California at Berkeley, 1968.

Bever, T.G. The cognitive basis for linguistic structures. In J.R. Hayes (Ed.), *Cognition and the Development of Language.* New York: Wiley, 1970, 279-352.

Blount, H.P., and Johnson, R.E. Grammatical structure and the recall of sentences in prose. *American Educational Research Journal,* 1973, *10,* 163-168.

Bormuth, J.R. Readability: a new approach. *Reading Research Quarterly,* 1966, *1,* 79-132.

Bormuth, J.R.; Carr, J.; Manning, J.; and Pearson, P.D. Children's comprehension of between- and within-sentence syntactic structures. *Journal of Educational Psychology,* 1970, *61,* (5), 349-357.

Bransford, J., and Franks, J. The abstraction of linguistic ideas. *Cognitive Psychology,* 1971, *2,* (10), 331-350.

Chomsky, C. Stages in language development and reading exposure *Harvard Educational Review*, 1972, *42*, (1), 1-33.

Coleman, E.B. Learning of prose written in four grammatical transformations. *Journal of Applied Psychology*, 1965, *49* (10), 332-341.

Danks, J.H. Grammaticalness and meaningfulness in the comprehension of sentences. *Journal of Verbal Learning and Verbal Behavior*, 1969, *8*, 687-696.

Denner, B. Representational and syntactic competence of problem readers. *Child Development*, 1970, *41*, 881-887.

Donaldson, M., and Wales, R.J. On the acquisition of some relational terms. In J.R. Hayes (Ed.), *Cognition and the Development of Language*. New York: Wiley, 1970, 235-268.

Downing, J. The perception of linguistic structures in learning to read. *British Journal of Educational Psychology*, 1969, *39*, (3), 267-271.

Edwards, P. Idioms and reading comprehension. *Journal of Reading Behavior*, 1974, *6* (3), 287-293.

Endicott, A.L. A proposed scale for syntactic complexity. *Research in the Teaching of English*, 1973, 7 (1), 5-12.

Entwisle, D.R. Implications of language socialization for reading models and for learning to read. *Reading Research Quarterly*, 1971, 7 (1), 111-167.

Epstein, W.A. A further study of the influence of syntactical structure on learning. *American Journal of Psychology*, 1962, *75*, 121-126.

Fodor, J., and Garrett, M. Some syntactic determinants of sentential complexity. *Perception and Psychophysics*, 1967, *2* (7), 289-296.

Furth, H.G. Children's understanding of social institutions. Paper presented at the Jean Piaget Society Meeting, 1975.

Gibbons, H.D. Reading and sentence elements. *Elementary English Review*, 1941, *18*, 42-46.

Goodman, K.S. Reading: a psycholinguistic guessing game. In H. Singer and R.B. Ruddell (Eds.), *Theoretical Models and Processes of Reading*. Newark, Delaware: International Reading Association, 1970, 259-271.

Granowsky, A., and Botel, M. Background for a new syntactic complexity formula. *Reading Teacher*, 1974, *28* (1), 31-35.

Harrell, L.E., Jr. An inter-comparison of the quality and rate of the development of the oral and written language in children. *Monograph of the Society for Research in Child Development*, 1957, No. 22.

Hunt, K.W. *Grammatical Structures Written at Three Grade Levels*, National Council of Teachers of English, Report No. 3. Champaign, Illinois: National Council of Teachers of English, 1965.

Hunt, K.W. *Syntactic Maturity in School Children and Adults*. Monograph of the Society for Research in Child Development, 1970, *35* (1), No. 134.

Hutson, B.A., and Shub, J. Developmental study of factors involved in choice of conjunctions. Paper presented at the American Educational Research Association Conference, Chicago, 1974.

Katz, E.W., and Brent, S.B. Understanding connectives. *Journal of Verbal Learning and Verbal Behavior,* 1968, *7,* 501-509.

Kress, R.A. An investigation of the relationship between concept formation and achievement in reading. Unpublished doctoral dissertation, Temple University, 1955.

LaBrant, L. A study of certain language developments in grades 4-12 inclusive. *Genetic Psychology Monographs,* 1933, *14,* 387-491.

Lakoff, R. Ifs, ands, and buts about conjunctions. In G.J. Fillmore and D.T. Langendoen (Eds.), *Studies in Linguistic Semantics.* New York: Holt, Rinehart and Winston, 1971.

Loban, W.D. *The Language of Elementary School Children.* Champaign, Illinois: National Council of Teachers of English, 1963.

MacKinnon, A.R. *How Do Children Learn to Read?* Vancouver, British Columbia: Clapp Clark, 1959.

Maclay, H., and Sleator, M. Responses to language: judgments of grammaticality. *International Journal of American Linguistics,* 1960, *26,* 275-282.

Marks, L.E., and Miller, G.A. The role of semantic and syntactic constraints in the memorization of English sentences. *Journal of Verbal Learning and Verbal Behavior,* 1965, *3,* 1-5.

McNeill, D. Developmental psycholinguistics, In F. Smith and G.A. Miller (Eds.), *The Genesis of Language: A Psycholinguistic Perspective.* Cambridge, Massachusetts: M.I.T. Press, 1966, 15-84.

Menyuk, P. Language development: universal aspects and individual variation. Paper presented at the International Reading Association Conference, Detroit, 1972.

Miller, G.A. The magic number seven plus or minus two. *Psychological Review,* 1956, *63,* 81-97.

Miller, G.A.; Heise, G.A.; and Lichten, W. The intelligibility of speech as a function of the context of the test material. *Journal of Experimental Psychology,* 1951, *41,* 329-335.

Miller, W. The acquistion of grammatical rules by children. In C.A. Ferguson and D.I. Slobin (Eds.), *Studies of child language Development.* New York: Holt, Rinehart, and Winston, 1973, 380-391.

Minkoff, H. Speech is speech, and prose is prose and (n)ever the twain.... Paper presented at the New York State English Council Meeting, 1974.

Neimark, E.D., and Slotnick, M.S. Development of the understanding of logical connectives. *Journal of Educational Psychology,* 1970, *61,* 451-460.

O'Donnell, R.C. The relationship between awareness of structural relationships in English and ability in reading comprehension.

Unpublished doctoral dissertation, George Peabody College for Teachers, 1961.

O'Donnell, R.C.; Griffin, W.J.; and Norris, R.C. *Syntax of Kindergarten and Elementary School Children: A Transformational Analysis.* Champaign, Illinois: National Council of Teachers of English, 1967.

Pearson, P.D. The effects of grammatical complexity on children's comprehension, recall, and conception of certain semantic relations. *Reading Research Quarterly,* 1974-75, *10* (2), 155-192.

Peltz, F.K. The effect upon comprehension of repatterning based on students' writing patterns. *Reading Research Quarterly,* 1973-74, *9* (4), 603-621.

Piaget, J. Language and thought from the genetic point of view. In J. Piaget (Ed.), *Six Psychological Studies.* New York: Vintage Books, 1968, 88-99.

Powers, J.E., and Gowie, C.J. The passive transformation on its own. Paper presented at the Society for Research in Child Development Conference, 1975.

Prentice, J.L. Semantics and syntax in word learning. *Journal of Verbal Learning and Verbal Behavior,* 1966, *5,* 279-284.

Rinne, C.H., Ill. Improvement in reading comprehension through increased awareness of written syntactic patterns. Unpublished doctoral dissertation, Stanford University, 1967.

Ruddell, R. B. Effect of the similarity of oral and written patterns of language structure on reading comprehension. *Elementary English,* 1965, *42,* 403-410.

Ruddell, R. B. Language acquisition and the reading process. In H. Singer and R. B. Ruddell (Eds.), *Theoretical Models and Processes of Reading.* Newark, Delaware: International Reading Association, 1970, 1-19.

Rystrom, R. Reflections on meaning. Paper presented at the Preconvention Institute on *Reading Comprehension and Syntax,* International Reading Association Conference, 1975.

Sachs, J. Recognition memory for syntactic and semantic aspects of connected discourse. *Perception and Psychophysics,* 1967, *2* 437-442.

Siler, E. R. The effects of syntactic and semantic constraints on the oral reading performance of second and fourth graders. *Reading Research Quarterly,* 1973-74, *9* (4), 583-602.

Singer, H. IQ is and is not related to reading. Paper presented at the Preconvention Institute on *Intelligence and Reading,* International Reading Association, 1972.

Smith, F. *Understanding Reading: A Psycholinguistic Analysis of Reading and Learning to Read.* New York: Holt, Rinehart, and Winston, 1971.

Smith, W. L. The controlled instrument procedure for studying the effect of syntactic sophistication on reading: a second study. *Journal of Reading Behavior,* 1972-73, *5* (4), 242-251.

Smith, W. L. Syntactic recoding of passages written at three levels of complexity. *Journal of Experimental Education*, 1974, *43*(2), 66-72

Stoodt, B. D. The relationship between understanding grammatical conjunctions and reading comprehension. *Elementary English*, 1972, *49*(4), 502-504.

Strohner, H., and Nelson, K. E. The young child's development of sentence comprehension: influence of event probability, nonverbal context, syntactic form, and strategies. *Child Development*, 1974, *45*, 567-576.

Tatham, S. M. Reading comprehension of materials written with select oral language patterns: a study at grades two and four. Unpublished doctoral dissertation, University of Wisconsin, 1968.

Templin, M. C. *Certain Language Skills in Children: Their development and Interrelationships.* Institute of Child Welfare Monograph Series, No. 26. Minneapolis: University of Minnesota Press, 1957.

Terman, L. M., and Merrill, M. A. *Measuring Intelligence.* Cambridge, Massachusetts: Houghton-Mifflin, 1937, 271.

Thorndike, E. L. Reading as reasoning: a study of mistakes in paragraph reading. *Journal of Educational Psychology*, 1917, *8*, 323-332.

Thorndike, R.L. Reading as reasoning. *Reading Research Quarterly*, 1973-74, *9* (2), 135-147.

Wardhaugh, R. Theories of language acquistition in relation to beginning reading instruction. *Reading Research Quarterly*, 1971, *7*(1), 168-202.

Weber, R. First graders' use of grammatical context in reading. In H. Levin and J. P. Williams (Eds.), *Basic Studies on Reading.* New York: Basic Books, 1970, 147-163.

Wolfram, W. Extended notions of grammar and comprehension. Paper presented at the Preconvention Institute on *Reading Comprehension and Syntax*, International Reading Association Conference, 1975.

Yngve, V. H. A model and hypothesis for language structure. Proceedings of the American Philosophical Association, 1960, *404*, 444-446.

Yngve, V. H. Computer programs for translation. *Scientific American*, 1962, *206*(6), 68-76.

Comments on
Syntax, Semantics, and Reading

Karlyn Kamm

Language acquistion and learning to read

In her discussion regarding the nature of language acquisition, one of the points Athey addresses concerns the mounting
evidence that "... the development of syntax is a much more
protracted process than was assumed by the theory of transformational grammar. . . . In fact, there seems to be a hierarchy
of difficulty for processing certain types of syntactic
structure, which follows the kind of sequence we find in other
types of learning, e.g., from the simple to the complex, from the
familiar to the unfamiliar, from the concrete to the abstract,
from the positive to the negative instance." These findings can
be made relevant to classroom instruction in reading comprehension. In the past many reading researchers have ignored
the differences between the nature of language acquisition and
the nature of learning to read, (Samuels, 1976). Thus, subsequent attempts to practically relate findings in the study of
language to reading instruction were unsuccessful. But if
reading researchers acknowledge the differences between
language and reading acquisition, and also recognize the
necessity of a subskill approach to the complex task of learning
to read, then perhaps such findings about the difficulties in
processing syntactical structures can indeed be appropriately
interpreted and ultimately applied to enhance classroom
reading instruction in comprehension.

A need for a scale of syntactic development

A related issue which Athey discusses concerns the need
for a scale of syntactic development for both teachers and

researchers. This point is well taken. The development of such a scale does have the potential for widespread implications for more effective classroom instruction. To have any impact on the direction reading instruction takes, however, the scale would have to meet two basic criteria: 1) it would have to be written so that teachers untrained in linguistic development could easily grasp the sequences of ideas and be able to incorporate them into all aspects of their reading instruction; and 2) the scale would have to be used and recognized by teachers and publishers of materials as a basis on which to judge difficulty of material—so that more appropriate matches could be made between the print on the page and the reading level of the learner.

Setting the direction

One of the points Athey makes in her conclusion is that although there is much work to be done, the direction has been set—that there will be exciting research in the area of children's language in the years ahead. The practitioner, when he surveys the current status of the research in this field, would have to disagree that the direction has been set. Thus far we have done a lot of observing and have written innumerable descriptions of what we see; and this has value in that we learn what happens naturally. But the results of our efforts have not yet been taught. We need to interpret the findings in terms of relevance to reading comprehension instruction, and then develop a system that will assist teachers in managing comprehension instruction. The thrust of our effort should focus on the *teaching* aspect. We should be wondering what can be learned more efficiently and then, ultimately, which techniques might be employed to most effectively accomplish our goal of getting children to understand what they read. Only by concentrating our attention and energies on a pragmatic-empirical approach can we ever bridge the traditional gap between the realities of the classroom and the inputs and demands of the researchers.

REFERENCE

Samuels, S. J. Hierarchical subskills in the reading acquisition process. In J.T. Guthrie (Ed.), *Aspects of reading acquisition,* Baltimore: The Johns Hopkins University Press, 1976.

The Development of Child Language Research

Lois Hood

Before the 1960s, language development research consisted primarily of anecdotal diary studies, records kept by an interested linguist or psychologist-parent on his or her own child (e.g., Bloch, 1921, 1924; Chao, 1951; Guillaume, 1927; Gregoire, 1937; Leopold, 1939-1949; Stern and Stern, 1907), and "count studies," gross normative measures such as size of vocabulary or number of sentence types on large numbers of children (see McCarthy, 1954, for an extensive review of these studies). The studies of Brown (1957) and Berko (1958) marked the beginning of in-depth inquiry into the rule systems underlying child language. In the fifteen or so years since then, the field of child language research has flourished and expanded in several directions, while the basic purpose underlying the research has remained the same.

In general, research in language development has attempted to describe the systematic nature of child language in terms of rule systems and strategies that underlie linguistic behaviors. At the same time, however, the focus of language development research has undergone great changes, most notably in the kinds of linguistic behaviors studied and the kinds of explanations postulated. More specifically, the focus of study has changed from just looking at the form of language to the present attempt to study language as three interrelated components: 1) content—the meaning that is coded in an utterance; 2) form—the ways in which the content is expressed, including syntactic, lexical, and phonological aspects of an utterance; and 3) use—the function of an utterance within a communicative setting. This change in what is studied has necessitated changes in the kinds of rules and strategies that can be postulated as underlying the language behaviors. One can no longer simply write rules of grammar; it is also necessary to account for the systematicity in the meaning and use of language. The result of these changes has been a much richer, more varied, more complicated, and hopefully more fruitful field of study. In this paper, I will discuss both the continuity of purpose and change in focus in child language research and describe several recent studies to illustrate the present state of the field.

Syntactic development

The first major change in the research design was in the kinds of linguistic knowledge studied. At first, in the early 1960s, child language studies were concerned with syntactic development, and examined the form of child utterances without regard to meaning or context. The important finding of these studies was that early syntax was systematic (Braine, 1963; Brown and Bellugi, 1964; Brown and Fraser, 1963; Miller and Ervin, 1964). Rules were written that could account for word order in child sentences and that could predict certain facets of syntactic acquisition.

For example, Braine (1963) observed a phenomenon of early syntax which has come to be called "pivot grammar." Braine's subjects were observed to use a small number of words the pivots, such as "no," "more," "there," in fixed position, with a much larger class of words, the "open" class. Two rules, $Pivot_1$+Open (for example, "more car," "more sing") and Open + $Pivot_2$(for example, "hot in there," "milk in there"), could account for the majority of early syntactic constructions. Brown and Fraser (1963) described a somewhat different aspect of early child sentences. They observed that most sentences of two-year-old children contained "contentives" (mostly nouns, verbs, and adjectives) but lacked "functors" (prepositions, articles, and morphological endings). Since such sentences, for example, "read book," and "where go," presumably contain only the essentials of the message, Brown and Fraser referred to them as telegraphic. Another aspect of telegraphic speech Brown and Fraser observed was the frequent use of a small group of words which occurred with a larger group of less frequently used words.

These two findings, pivot grammar and telegraphic speech, have been observed in many children since the first reports and appear to be well-established facts of child grammar. However, they are facts that relate to a very limited part of language development. First, both pivot grammar and telegraphic speech refer to distributional phenomena only; certain classes of words appear in certain positions. Secondly, they refer only to the syntactic property of the language, and only a small part of it at that; the meanings of these early sentences and the functions they serve for the child have not been considered. And finally, pivot grammar and telegraphic speech are descriptive terms only that refer to the product of speaking rather than to any underlying process. They do not and did not intend to explain child language.

Thus, the early grammars of child sentences that were written did little more than describe the phenomena. When researchers attempted to *explain* the facts of early syntax, it became clear that the child's underlying knowledge had to include more than a grammar that could generate strings of words in a systematic way. This led more or less directly to two changes in focus of research: 1) in terms of the component of language described, the emphasis shifted to the semantics or meaning of child sentences; and 2) in terms of the kinds of explanations given, the emphasis on semantics led to a search for the correlates of meaning in cognitive development.

Semantic development

With the realization that what children were talking about was important, the semantics of child language became the prime focus of study. Studies of children learning English and certain other languages (Bloom, 1970, 1973; Bowerman, 1973; Brown, 1973; Schlesinger, 1971; and Slobin, 1971) have resulted in a consensus about the semantics of early sentences. Children learn that objects exist, cease to exist, and recur; that objects can be acted upon and located in space; that people do things to objects or are otherwise associated with objects.

The emphasis on semantics was so great, in fact, that some researchers began to ignore the importance of syntax. Schlesinger (1971) and Bowerman (1973) suggested that children have learned semantic relationships and not grammar when they put two and three words together; that early language learning is semantic rather than syntactic. But this claim—that children are learning only semantics—is as limiting as the similar claim for syntax in the early 1960s. By isolating either syntax or semantics, one ignores the interdependence of the two. The meaning relations among words are influenced by the syntactic relations among them, for example, their order relative to one another. Similarly, the syntactic relations influence the meaning relations. Semantics and syntax are inseparable and both must be considered in any description or explanation of a language. The next phase in the study of child language emphasized this interaction, as researchers began to study the child's semantic-syntactic development.

For example, Bloom, Lightbown, and Hood (1975) identified more than 20 categories of semantic-syntactic relationships in multi-word utterances from four children in the period from mostly single words to mean length of utterance of approximately 2.5. The major categories, those that were most frequent and showed developmental change, were seven categories of verb relations and possession. Some examples are: Action-on Affected-Object—"open drawer," Locative Action—"put in box," Possession—"my book." All four children showed the same sequence in the emergence of semantic-syntactic categories, and the results were generally consistent with reports from comparable studies (for example, Brown, 1973).

Pragmatics

Use (or pragmatics) is also an integral part of language. Both the form and the content of what someone says influence and are influenced by the communicative function of what has been said before and will be said subsequently. Thus, the pragmatics of child language has come to the forefront. Although it has always been obvious that children don't learn to talk in a vacuum, that adults and other children are constantly talking to and with them, it has not been until very recently that the explicit study of language use has gained importance in child language. Researchers are now attempting to delineate the systematic ways in which the child uses language, to trace the developments within the child's language as communication, and to describe the underlying

Hood

conversational competence of the child. For example, Bates (1971) examined conversations between adults and children in terms of answering rates and the number of statements, questions and commands. Garvey (1975a) compared direct, indirect, and inferred requests in peer exchanges, and Keenan (1974a) described the uses of repetition in peer communication (see also, Garvey, 1975b; Garvey and Hogan, 1973; Shatz, 1974).

Although pragmatics is receiving considerable attention at the moment, it often unfortunately has been to the exclusion of other aspects of language. However, there are a few studies in child language that have begun to study language behavior as a complex interaction of form (syntax), content (semantics), and use (pragmatics). For example, in a study of adult-child discourse, Bloom, Rocissano, and Hood (1975) described the speech of two to three year olds in terms of such variables as whether the child was responding to an adult utterance or not and, if so, what semantic, syntactic, and/or pragmatic aspects of the adult's utterance were taken into account by the child in formulating his own utterance. Keenan (1974b) described exchanges—mostly routines such as rhymes—between twin boys at about age 2.9, in terms of how each utterance related to what preceded and followed it. Corsaro (1975) examined the sociolinguistic interaction of two boys with their parents, adult friends, and peers, from the time the children were two and a half to three and a half years old.

The reasons for the gradual broadening of the aspects of language that have been studied are many. However, two developments within other related fields come to mind as being most influential. First, developments within linguistic theory, most notably the turning from syntactic structure to emphasis on semantic structure in generative grammar, led to a corresponding shift away from syntax in child language. Second, the field of sociolinguistics, with its emphasis on language as communication, influenced child language research in its recent attention to pragmatics.

Cognitive and linguistic development

The changes in the components of language that researchers have attempted to account for have led to changes in the kinds of accounts that have been offered. From the beginning, various kinds of explanations were given in terms of systematic rules or strategies that underlie linguistic behavior, but the orientation of the structures and strategies that have been postulated has changed. When researchers were concerned only with syntactic development, for example, general syntactic rules based in linguistics were considered adequate. However, with the recognition that children were talking about what they were experiencing and with the realization of the interdependence of syntax and semantics, it has become clear that something more than linguistic rules is necessary. Thus, one general trend has been the turning away from theoretical accounts based solely on linguistic formalism and the concurrent turning toward a theory incorporating aspects of cognitive development.

Studies of very early language development have drawn upon Piaget's description of sensorimotor intelligence. For example, Bloom (1973) in a study of single-word utterances, has emphasized the relationship between landmarks in the sensorimotor stage and early language development. She has hypothesized that before the child has attained object permanence his use of nouns is very fluid. Certain nouns are used for a short time with a particular meaning. They then are overextended, drop out, appear again with a different meaning, etc. It is only when the child has a firm concept of the permanence of objects, at about 18 months, that he acquires a large and stable vocabulary of nouns. More generally, the well accepted observation that very young children talk in the "here and now," about what they are seeing and doing, has been linked to stages of sensorimotor intelligence and Piaget's notion of action-schema.

Explanations of language development at a slightly later stage have incorporated perceptual and other nonlinguistic factors. For example, Bever (1970) and Slobin (1971) have proposed non-linguistic strategies to explain the child's expression and understanding of basic grammatical relations, such as Subject-Verb-Object. Clark (1973) has explained the child's comprehension of certain locative relations, such as those expressed by the prepositions "in," "on," and "under," in terms of perceptual strategies.

Individual differences

Second trend

A second and more recent trend has been the gradual expansion from a strictly developmental and sequential outlook, that is, looking *across* stages in language acquisition, toward an explanation that also takes into account variation among children *within* a given stage. Examples of the earlier viewpoint, looking across stages, are the strategies by Bever (1970), Clark (1973), and Slobin (1971), which were offered in order to explain change in linguistic behavior as a function of development. They postulated rules that children follow for proceeding from one level of development to another, and such strategies, in effect, represent stages in development.

Stage

In contrast, there have been a few recent studies which have expanded the notion of strategy to explain variation observed among different children at the *same* level of development. Three recent studies (Bloom, Hood, and Lightbown, 1974; Bloom, Lightbown, and Hood, 1975; Hood, 1975) found evidence of strategy differences in the speech of children at the same level of semantic-syntactic development. The first study (Bloom, Hood, and Lightbown, 1974) explored the role of imitation in language development. This study examined spontaneous imitation, where the child happens to repeat all or part of what an adult previously says, as opposed to elicited imitation, where the child is specifically asked to repeat. Longitudinal, observational language data from six children, from the time they were approximately one and a half to two years old, were examined to determine the extent to which children imitated, what kinds of things they imitated, and the possible functions such imitation might serve. In terms of strategy differences, it was found, first, that the children differed from each other in the amount they imitated (the proportion of speech that was imitative ranged from .04 to .42). Second, for those children who did imitate, the function varied. For example, one child consistently imitated utterances that contained specific words that were relatively new to him, and imitation seemed to function in his lexical learning. Two other children consistently imitated new semantic-syntactic structures, and imitation appeared to function in their semantic-syntactic learning. However, regardless of what the children were imitating, or even if they imitated at all, they

strate- gies

were all talking about the same kinds of things at the same general level of development.

A further study of four of the same children (Bloom, Lightbown, and Hood, 1975) revealed that when they began to use syntax the children had two alternative strategies to express certain notions of action and possession. Two of the children used a pronominal strategy—they said things like "fix it," "broke it," "put here," "my book." The two other children used a categorization strategy—they said things like "fix train," "read book," "cup table," "Kathryn slipper." However, by the time mean length of utterance reached 2.75, each child gave evidence of having incorporated the alternative strategy, and all four children used both from this point on. Again, as in the earlier study, the children were at the same level of language development and were talking about the same kinds of things; they just had alternative ways of expressing these same notions. Finally, in a study of the development of the expression of causal relations, Hood (1975) found differential use of clause orders and causal conjunctions in the causal statements of two to three year old children, even though the meanings of the causal statements were similar.

In somewhat different areas of language development, strategy differences in children at the same stage of development have been found. Clark and Sengul (1974), in a study on the comprehension of deictic verbs, reported different strategies in children at the same stage of development. Finally, Ferguson, Peizer, and Weeks (1973) have described inter-subject variation in phonological development.

This interest in individual variation has led to a different orientation in terms of the kinds of evidence considered adequate and the kinds of conclusions drawn. In the past, the emphasis was on accounting for similarities among children at the same stage of development and differences among children at different stages. This led to the presentation of evidence that a particular rule did or did not underlie a particular linguistic behavior, or that children at a particular stage did or did not use a particular strategy. With the recent interest in individual variation, however, evidence of a probabilistic nature is gaining acceptance. In other words, a few recent studies have drawn conclusions that a particular rule can account for a particular behavior some proportion of the time, while another rule may account for the same behavior in the same child or in different children some other proportion of the time.

An illustration of this can be found in a recent study that attempted to account for the varying length of early child sentences (Bloom, Miller, and Hood, 1975). The basic question probed in that study was: why do children continue to use two-constituent sentences, such as "read book," at the same time they are also using three-constituent sentences, such as "Mommy read book." Bloom, Miller, and Hood (1975) isolated three basic factors that could account for the variation in sentence length: a lexical access factor (whether the verb used in the utterance was "old" or "new"); a complexity factor (whether there was added grammatical complexity to the basic constituents of the utterance); and a discourse interaction factor (whether the utterance in question was preceded or followed by a longer or shorter utterance). In addition, there was a performance factor, to account for the remaining nonsystematic variation. It was found that no one factor could differentiate between the two- and three-constituent sentences either at the same time or developmentally. Rather, some proportion of the variation in sentence length could be accounted for by one factor, some by another, some by a combination of factors, etc. The use of probability factors to account for linguistic variation comes from the work of sociolinguists (Cedergren and Sankoff, 1974; Labov, 1969) and has only recently been applied to child language (Bloom, Miller, and Hood, 1975; Brown, 1973; Suppes, 1970).

To summarize, the approach to child language research has expanded in several directions over the past fifteen years. Most notably, there has been a broadening of the focus of linguistic knowledge with the result that language is now studied as consisting of three interrelated components: form, content, and use. In order to account for systematic developments within these components, it was necessary to broaden the theoretical perspective in at least two ways. First, it is now assumed that underlying the child's linguistic behavior is both linguistic and cognitive knowledge and, second, it has been recognized that the existence of individual variation must be accounted for as well as developmental variation.

It was my intention in presenting this brief review of the development of child language research to accomplish two goals: first, to present an overview of the kinds of questions we are seeking to answer and to describe what we are beginning to know about language development; and, second, to illustrate the theoretical and methodological changes within the field that have both influenced and been influenced by what we have come to know about child language.

REFERENCES

Bates, E. The development of conversation skill in 2, 3, and 4 year olds. Unpublished master's thesis, University of Chicago, 1971.

Berko, J. The child's learning of English morphology. *Word*, 1958, *14*, 50-117.

Bever, T. The cognitive basis of linguistic structure. In J. Hayes (Ed.), *Cognition and the Development of Language*. New York: John Wiley & Sons, 1970.

Bloch, O. Premiers stades du langage de l'enfant. *Journal de Psychologie*, 1921, *18*, 693-712.

Bloch, O. Le phrase dans le langage de l'enfant. *Journal de Psychologie*, 1924, *21*, 18-43.

Bloom, L. *Language Development: Form and Function in Emerging Grammars*. Cambridge, Massachusetts: M.I.T. Press, 1970.

Bloom, L. *One Word at a Time: The Use of Single-word Utterances before Syntax*. The Hague: Mouton, 1973.

Bloom, L.; Hood, L.; and Lightbown, P. Imitation in Language Development: If, when, and why. *Cognitive Psychology*, 1974, *6*, 380-420.

Bloom, L.; Lightbown, P.; and Hood, L. Structure and variation in child language. *Monograph of the Society for Research in Child Development*, 1975, *2*.

Bloom, L.; Miller, P.; and Hood, L. Variation and reduction as aspects of competence in language development. In A. Pick (Ed.), *The 1974 Symposium on Child Psychology*. Minnesota: University of Minnesota Press, 1975, 3-56.

Bloom, L.; Rocissano, L.; and Hood, L. Adult-child discourse: Interactions between information processing and linguistic knowledge. Manuscript submitted for publication. Teachers College, Columbia University, 1975.

Bowerman, M. *Learning to Talk: A Cross-linguistic Study of Early Syntactic Development with Special Reference to Finnish*. Cambridge, England: Cambridge University Press, 1973.

Braine, M. The ontogeny of English phrase structure: The first phase. *Language*, 1963, *39*, 1-13.

Brown, R. Linguistic determinism and the parts of speech. *Journal of*

    Abnormal Social Psychology, 1957, *55*, 1-5.

Brown, R. *A First Language, the Early Stages*. Cambridge, Massachusetts: Harvard University Press, 1973.

Brown, R., and Bellugi, U. Three processes in the child's acquisition of syntax. *Harvard Educational Review*, 1964, *34*, 133-151.

Brown, R., and Fraser, C. The acquisition of syntax. In C. N. Cofer and B. Musgrave (Eds.), *Verbal Behavior and Verbal Learning: Problems and Processes*. New York: McGraw Hill, 1963.

Cedergren, H., and Sankoff, G. Variable rules: Performance as a statistical reflection of competence. *Language*, 1974, *50*, 333-355.

Chao, Y. R. The Cantian idiolect: An analysis of the Chinese spoken by a twenty-eight month old child. *Semitic Philogy*, University of California Publications, 1951, *11*, 27-44.

Clark, E. V. Non-linguistic strategies and the acquisition of word meanings. *Cognition*, 1973, *2*, 161-182.

Clark, E. V., and Sengul, C. Deictic contrasts in language acquisition. Paper presented at the Annual Meeting of the Linguistic Society of America, New York, December, 1974.

Corsaro, W. A. Sociolinguistic patterns in adult-child interaction. Unpublished manuscript, Indiana University, 1975.

Ferguson, C. A.; Peizer, D.; and Weeks, T. Model-and-replica phonological grammar of a child's first words. *Lingua*, 1973, *31*, 35-65.

Garvey, C. Requests and responses in children's speech. *Journal of Child Language,* 1975a, *2*, 41-63.

Garvey, C. Contingent queries. Unpublished manuscript, Johns Hopkins, 1975b.

Garvey, C., and Hogan, R. Social speech and social interaction: Egocentrism revisited. *Child Development*, 1973, *44*, 562-568.

Gregoire, A. L'apprentissage du langage. Vol. 1, *Les deux premières années*. Paris: Droz, 1937.

Guillaume, P. Les débuts de la phrase dans le langage de l'enfant. *Journal de Psychologie*, 1927, *24*, 1-25.

Hood, L. The development of the expression of causal relations. Paper presented at the Annual Meeting of the Eastern Psychological Association, New York, April, 1975.

Keenan, E. O. Again and again: The pragmatics of imitation in child language. Paper presented at the Annual Meeting of the American Anthropological Association, Mexico City, 1974a.

Keenan, E. O. Conversational competence in children. *Journal of Child Language*, 1974b, *1*, 163-183.

Labov, W. Contraction, deletion, and inherent variability of the English copula. *Language*, 1969, *45*, 715-762.

Leopold, W. F. *Speech Development of a Bilingual Child*. Evanston, Illinois: Northwestern University, (4 volumes), 1939-1949.

McCarthy, D. Language development. In L. Carmichael (Ed.), *Manual of Child Psychology*. New York: John Wiley & Sons, 1954.

Miller, W., and Ervin, S. The development of grammar in child language. In U. Bellugi and R. Brown (Eds.), The acquisition of language. *Monograph of the Society for Research in Child Development*, 1964, *29*.

Schlesinger, I. M. Production of utterances and language acquisition. In D. Slobin (Ed.), *The Ontogenesis of Language: Some Facts and Several Theories*. New York: Academic Press, 1971.

Shatz, M. The comprehension of indirect directives: Can two-year-olds shut the door? Paper presented at the summer meeting of the Linguistic Society of America, Amherst, Massachusetts, 1974.

Slobin, D. I. Developmental psycholinguistics. In W. D. Dingwall (Ed.), *A Survey of Linguistic Science*. College Park, Maryland: University of Maryland Press, 1971.

Slobin, D. I. Cognitive prerequisites for the acquisition of grammar. In C. A. Ferguson and D. I. Slobin (Eds.), *Studies of Child Language Development*. New York: Holt, Rinehart, and Winston, 1973, 175-208.

Stern, C., and Stern, W. *Die Kindersprache*. Leipzia: Barth, 1907.

Suppes, P. Probabilistic grammars for natural languages. *Synthese*, 1970, *22*, 95-116.

Comprehension During the Acquisition of Decoding Skills

Isabel L. Beck

The distinction between a code-emphasis and a meaning-emphasis in beginning reading programs was proposed and used by Chall (1967) to describe differences in the extent to which existing curricula stressed one aspect or the other. This distinction proved very useful in conceptualizing the existing situation in beginning reading instruction, and it enabled Chall to document the important finding that a code-emphasis produces better results than a meaning-emphasis. However, it may also have created the serious misunderstanding that a reading program that emphasizes phonics must automatically decrease attention to meaning. This is not necessarily so. A reading program can be well designed in its phonics component *and* also be well designed in its meaning component. In deed, it is a thesis of this paper that phonics and meaning should be viewed as instructionally mutually supportive and interdependent. Phonics and meaning must each be carefully designed and sequenced, and close attention must be given to their effective integration.

The point I am trying to make can best be presented by chronicling the work of the Learning Research and Development Center (LRDC) with beginning reading instruction. LRDC's early attempts to individualize reading instruction used a commercially available program. During the course of its use, we sensed limitations in certain aspects of the commercial program which started us on a design-and-patch remedy. Attempts to fill some of the obvious gaps in the commercial program were successful, but as we began to formalize our knowledge about the requirements of effective reading instruction, we concluded that our experiences would work to best advantage through designing our own reading program. In this paper, I hope to convey what we have learned about the design of effective reading instruction through analyses of some specific weaknesses found through our experience with the commercial program and through a description of our own program which incorporates both phonics and meaning. Finally, some evaluative data will be presented to confirm that we appear to have found some important methods for enhancing reading achievement.

Initial development activities

Individualizing reading instruction

Ten years ago, when LRDC embarked upon its original mission to individualize elementary school instruction, the architects of Individually Prescribed Instruction (IPI) focused on the design of individualized curricula in reading, mathematics, and science. These curricula were built so that they could be implemented and so that the demands and requirements of individualization could thereby be studied and become better understood.

The model to be used for individualization was spelled out by Glaser (1965) and, in general, it included the following components: a) sequentially ordered curricular objectives stated in behavioral terms, b) instruments for monitoring and assessing each student's progress through the curricular sequence, c) instructional materials for attainment of mastery of the curricular objectives, d) a system for individually prescribing the learning tasks for each student, and e) self-improvement of the system through continuous feedback of information and evaluation.

Initially, two decisions were made regarding LRDC's work with individualizing primary grades reading: a) that the approach to beginning reading would emphasize code-breaking, and b) that LRDC would not develop its own reading program but would select from among existing commercial materials and adjust them as the Glaser model required.

The *Sullivan Associates Programmed Reading Series* (Buchanan, 1963)[1] was selected because it emphasized code-

---

[1]Throughout this paper, all statements about the *Sullivan Associates Programmed Reading Series* apply to the 1963 or 1967 editions.

breaking, it met some of the requirements of the Glaser model, and it was amenable to modification. It was implemented in the primary grades of the Oakleaf School, an elementary school near Pittsburgh, Pennsylvania, which served as LRDC's original developmental school. The core components of the series were student workbooks and teacher manuals. The teacher was responsible for presenting new content to the children (e.g., a grapheme/phoneme correspondence, an irregular function word) using a highly structured dialogue from the teacher's manual. At certain other places, the manual suggested additional stimuli presentations for the teacher to write on the board; at other places, the stimuli for the dialogue were specified pages in the student workbooks, The workbooks also contained pages which the children would complete individually *after* the new content was presented by the teacher.

It is, of course, very difficult for a group of 25 first-grade children to progress at their own rates if the teacher is the sole source for presenting new content. The teacher can attempt to get around to each child and teach him or her the new content when he or she is ready for it, but this is hardly feasible. Or, the teacher can wait for the accumulation of a group of children who need the same new content and then present the necessary instruction. But this method will not really permit each child to progress at his or her own rate.

In order to individualize the Sullivan materials, we developed audio lessons to teach some of the new content. The instructional strategies used in these audio lessons were the ones specified in the Sullivan teacher manuals. Variability of student rate through the program increased greatly with the implementation of these audio lessons, and the teacher was able to spend a greater amount of time "traveling" among the children, monitoring their performance, eliciting oral reading, and reinforcing or enriching individuals rather than groups. Stated more directly, the teacher was freed to teach each child what the teacher perceived the child needed.

Broadening the reading experience

Since individualization of instruction does not mean that children always need to work by themselves with self-instructional materials, management schemes were designed to gather children, who were progressing through the curriculum at various rates, together for group reading experiences. These small-group, teacher-led reading experiences featured opportunities for oral reading and discussion of the story line. Regarding story line, Chall notes that the Sullivan program contained "discrete words and sentences with humorous illustrations but no definite 'storyline'" (1967: 44). However, the Sullivan series did provide a short storybook to accompany each of its first 14 workbooks. The vocabulary in each storybook was compatible with the graphemic sequence of its companion workbook. The storybooks were used in the small-group, teacher-led setting in a typical basal reader fashion; that is, the teacher directed the story reading, questioned children, and stimulated discussion about the story.

It is important to emphasize that up to this time in this chronology of our early endeavors, LRDC's objective in beginning reading was to determine and provide the resources and classroom management schemes required for individualization. However, once the mechanics of individualization were under control and the "system" was up and running, the Reading Project staff began to observe, in a direct and detailed manner, the process of learning to read.

Attending to the text or reading for meaning

In this paper, I will use the terms *meaning* and *comprehension* synonomously. They both simply mean that the reader can demonstrate that he or she knows what is being communicated in the text. It was in this area that we first detected serious problems with the Sullivan program. Classroom teachers involved with the use of the Sullivan materials directed our attention to the problem by stating that "children aren't comprehending." In turn, we asked them to describe what they meant by this. A teacher who was working with children who were approximately half-way through the program (typically end of first grade, beginning of second grade) characterized her experience with directing the small-group story reading in this way: "When I ask the children to read two pages [i.e., approximately six to ten running sentences] to themselves and then ask easy questions [i.e., questions that are mappable back to the text], a lot of children can't answer the questions until I tell them to reread the pages." During the conversation, the teacher indicated that, for the most part, the children could answer the questions after she had required them to reread. Then she added, "You know, I have a group lesson [with each group] about every two weeks. Each time we start off, I have to make the children reread the first few pages to be able to answer questions. But, by the end of the story, they are able to answer my questions after the first reading."

The same day I heard this teacher's report, I visited a second-grade classroom and watched some children who were working independently in their workbooks. I immediately noticed the speed with which they were turning the pages. I could see that they were responding correctly even though they were proceeding rapidly. Inspection of the workbooks revealed why this was possible.

Figure 1 is a stereotypic representation of the kind of lesson page found in the Sullivan series. The page is arranged so that there are four responses required. At most, only one of them requires that the child read the five-sentence paragraph under the picture. Supplying the missing *a* in *cabin* and the missing *d* in *dog* are "copying responses" in that both words appear on the page correctly and all that the child needs to do is to locate a complete model of each word and then copy the missing letter. This "missing letter" format appears very frequently throughout the Sullivan program, and its use is problematic: a) It is insufficient to build skill in decoding, since practice in decoding should incorporate an auditory model or auditory feedback (confirmation). b) It often distracts the child from apprehending the meaning of the text since it requires him or her to stop and write (frequently in the middle of a sentence). c) When it is the only response required in the context of connected text (a common occurrence), it is clearly insufficient to ensure that children read the text. Children can ignore much of the connected text that surrounds the target word and respond either by supplying the missing letter from memory or by searching for a complete model of the word to find the letter(s) they need.

Other responses required by the formats in Figure 1 do not have their intended outcomes either. The first question, "Is Miss Ring in her cabin?" can be answered from the picture. If

This is Miss Ring. Miss Ring is a woman.
Miss Ring lives in a cabin. Her cabin
has a bed and sink in it. Miss Ring's
dog lives with her in the c __ bin.

Is Miss Ring in her cabin?   yes
                              no

Is Miss Ring a dog?   yes
                       no

Miss Ring's pet is a __og.

Figure 1. Representation of the type of workbook page found in the *Sullivan Associates Programmed Reading Series.*

the second question, "Is Miss Ring a dog?" should happen to be answered incorrectly (which I propose would not often happen, given the likelihood that the title Miss would be associated more frequently with a woman than with a dog), it could be corrected from the information found in the last sentence (i.e., Miss Ring's ownership of pet). In all, this analysis indicates that the sample frame in Figure 1 has a very high blackout ratio. Blackout ratio, as defined by Holland (1967), is the proportion of the text in a frame that does not have to be read in order to answer the questions correctly. A high blackout ratio indicates that very little of the material must be read. In other words, obtaining a correct answer is not contingent upon reading a lot of the textual material.

The sample frame in Figure 1 does not require that the child read the five sentence paragraph. However, the sample frame does require some reading. The child must read the question, "Is Miss Ring in her cabin?" and must demonstrate that he or she understands what "*in* the cabin" means; and the child must read the question, "Is Miss Ring a dog?" and must demonstrate his or her understanding that the name *Miss Ring* is associated with the woman. Requiring children to demonstrate that they comprehend the meaning of printed questions is a good example of a contingency that requires reading in some contexts, even when information needed to respond to the question can be found in the picture. However, why add five sentences of text, most of which is unnecessary for responding correctly? This tends to reinforce ignoring the text, rather than attending to it. Further analysis of the Sullivan text indicated that, in general, it had an extremely high blackout ratio.[2]

Since few contingencies were set up to require reading of the text, it is conceivable that the following speculation has merit: Perhaps the children who had to be directed to reread sections of a story in the group situation before they could answer a question were really reading for the *first* time, not *rereading*. They may have learned from the workbook

_____

[2]Before the decision was made at LRDC to develop our own program, we examined a variety of commercial reading programs. There was variability in the blackout ratio among programs. We found a number of programs whose workbook exercises had a high blackout ratio, and a few that had a generally low blackout ratio. It is suggested that this may be a salient variable for those evaluating reading programs to analyze.

exercises that "you don't need to read the story in order to answer the question." This bit of speculation is supported by the teacher's comment that each time she started the group reading activity she had to make the children reread the first few pages to be able to answer questions, but that by the end of the story, they were able to answer her questions after the first reading. Perhaps this is an example of the teacher establishing the contingencies and the children responding appropriately once they had learned what the contingencies were. The fact that the teacher had to require that the children reread at the beginning of each group lesson may have been due to the fact that group lessons occurred only about once every two weeks, and that during the interim, the children were relearning (through their interaction with the workbooks) that they didn't need to read the story in order to answer the questions.

Developing contingencies that required the children to attend to the connected text in the Sullivan workbooks was the most difficult problem the LRDC reading staff encountered, since the problem was so pervasive. Without actually rewriting most of the textual material, there was little we could do. We did request that the teachers, as they interacted with individual children who were working in their workbooks, question portions of the pages the children were working on that were not questioned by the program. For example, in the frame in Figure 1, there is a sentence in the text, "Her cabin has a bed and sink in it." A question such as "What is in the cabin?" is easily formulated and requires that the child read the text since the answer is not apparent from the picture.

It is virtually impossible to evaluate the effect of the questioning strategies. They were not implemented in any systematic way; nor was their use quantified. We did observe that teachers varied greatly in their ability to ask useful questions and that there was also great variation among teachers in the number and types of questions asked.

Let me present some achievement data which were collected before, and then during, the implementation of the questioning strategies. These data are from the first grades of LRDC's second developmental school, an innercity school, and cover a three-year span. They show a strong trend in increasing achievement on the Reading Subtest of the Metropolitan Achievement Test (Durost et al., 1970). The end-of-first grade scores move from a mean grade achievement of 1.7 at the end of the year, to 1.8 at the end of the second year, to 2.1 at the end of the third year. It was during the middle of the second year that we suggested the questioning strategies to the teachers. During the third year, we stressed their importance and kept reminding teachers why the questioning strategies were important. In addition, some LRDC reading staff members spent some time in classrooms demonstrating how the teacher could formulate questions while "traveling" among the children. The achievement trends above are, of course, quite favorable, but there is no way of attributing a direct link between the implementation of the strategies and the increase in achievement.

Designing instructional strategies for word attack

In addition to understandings gained about the limitations of the Sullivan program and about some general requirements of effective reading instruction, we also learned, in those early years, some important things about instructional strategies for word attack.

It will facilitate my discussion to clarify the sense in which I use terms associated with word attack. The terms *decoding, word attack, word recognition,* and *phonics,* are in some contexts used synonymously. In this paper each term has a specific meaning. *Decoding* is simply the translation of print to speech. In decoding there is a continuum of performance from laboriously "sounding out" a word, to recognizing words instantly. I will use the phrase *word attack* to represent the end of the decoding continuum where the reader brings into action (either overtly or covertly) implicit or explicit "rules" of pronunciation to unlock the pronunciation of a word. The term *word recognition* will be used to describe the end of the decoding continuum where the reader recognizes words instantly. The important point is that both word attack *and* word recognition are decoding. *Phonics* are various instructional methods that teach procedures for unlocking word pronunciation.

In the scholarly community at least, the "great debate" has subsided, little of the passion is left, and many people concerned with reading agree that "earlier and more systematic instruction in phonics is essential" (Diederich, 1973: 7). But, what kind of phonics? Analytic phonics, which attempts to teach grapheme/phoneme correspondences to the student by having him or her examine displays of words that share and contrast major spelling patterns? Or, synthetic phonics, which teaches grapheme/phoneme correspondences directly and has the student assemble words from phonemes?

The Sullivan program employed a synthetic approach because the instructional strategies recommended in the teacher manuals included having the student practice grapheme/phoneme relationships in isolation. However, there were no instructional strategies in the teacher manuals that suggested a process for teaching the child *how* to put the sounds together. Realizing that some children were having difficulty doing something that the Sullivan program made no provision to teach, we searched the teacher manuals of a variety of synthetic phonics programs looking for the instructional strategies employed to teach children to put sounds together. The results of our search indicated that there was a virtual absence of any such instructional strategies.

The teacher manuals did contain suggestions to the teacher to present a model of a blending process and have the child imitate the model. Acting on this suggestion, however, merely skims the top of the iceberg; it merely demonstrates what competence *is* rather than building it up through necessary instructional steps. Indeed, the known difficulty of learning the process of blending is considered a primary objection to synthetic phonics. As it turns out, inability to blend may be a natural consequence of the lack of any provision for instruction in blending.

While we were working with children who were having initial learning difficulties, we developed a successive blending routine that breaks blending into important functional units and enables most children to master blending. Instructional techniques for teaching this routine were developed. These techniques employ models, establishment of a series of prompts, and fading of those prompts. In addition, a blending booklet which a child manipulates while blending was devised to help externalize the process for the child. A detailed discussion and analysis of the blending routine are contained in a paper completed recently by Resnick and Beck (1976). For now,

I would like to point out that we attempted to link the successive blending routine to psychological theory, specifically information processing, in such a way that it could be analyzed in terms of theoretical constructs. We were able to demonstrate that since a substantial amount of processing must occur simultaneously during initial decoding, our successive blending routine reduces memory load.

We introduced the successive blending routine at the Oakleaf School in a systematic manner which made it easier for us to assess its effects. Comparisons of end-of-first grade achievements results obtained when the Sullivan strategies for teaching word attack were used with end-of-first grade scores when the new successive blending strategies were used show strong gains in mean student performance after the introduction of the LRDC strategies. These data are quite extensive and reflect five years of development and evaluation research. These data are reported in several documents (Beck and Mitroff, 1972; Beck, 1973; Eichelberger, Lee, and Leinhardt, 1974), so I will not dwell on them except to say that the results of the studies provided evidence to assure us that our strategies for sounding and blending were working to support increased reading achievement.

Deciding to design a new program

However, even with positive trends from the implementation of questioning strategies and improved sounding and blending routines, there were still children who were not reading as well as expected, both in terms of their achievement test results *and* our "clinical" assessment of them. We suspected that we could trace some of the remaining difficulties to a number of not yet mentioned deficiencies in the structure and sequence of the Sullivan program. Some of these deficiencies were that: a) Portions of the graphemic sequence introduced visually similar graphemes at the same time rather than distributing them in several sections of the text (e.g., early and close introduction of the *b* and *d*). b) At times, not enough examples of words containing the target phonemic element were provided (e.g., only three words with the /f/ phoneme as in *ph*one were provided). c) Phonemic elements were not varied across positions in a word (e.g., in the three words used as exemplars of the /f/ phoneme, the *ph* appeared only in the medial position). d) Response formats lacked variety and were overly repetitious.

The most pervasive remaining problem was the high blackout ratio. It severely hampered the development of rapid word recognition and failed to increase attention to the meaning of the text. Faced with these problems in the Sullivan program, we decided to design our own beginning reading program.

Analysis of the reading process. Before starting the actual design, we attempted to deepen our understanding of the nature of reading competence by performing some task analyses. Figure 2 contains a task analysis of the reading comprehension process. It shows the hypothesized flow of behavior for

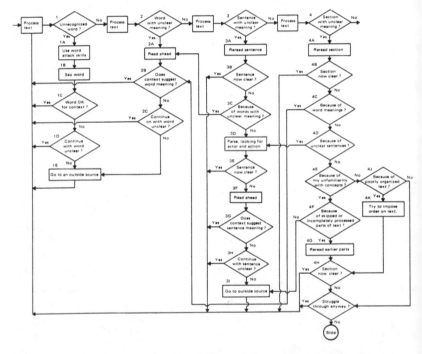

Figure 2. A schematic model of the reading comprehension process. Reproduced by permission from "Designing Instruction in Reading: Interaction of Theory and Practice" by L. B. Resnick and I. L. Beck, in J. T. Guthrie (Ed.), *Aspects of Reading Acquisition.* Baltimore: Johns Hopkins University Press, 1976, 198.

Beck

an effective reader reading a moderately difficult text. The reader might be a third-grader reading a social studies text about prehistoric animals, or a college student reading this paper.

The figure contains two kinds of statements: direction statements (rectangular boxes) and queries (diamonds). The four rectangles in the top line assume ongoing text-processing for a reader who encounters no difficulties. The four diamonds in the top row represent the broad categories of "difficulties" readers may encounter which can cause interruption in processing. The first such potential interruption is for an unrecognized word (Query 1). Skilled readers probably do not stop at every unrecognized word; when they do skip a word, they are likely to realize soon afterwards whether or not it interfered with getting the general meaning of the text. If they determine that the meaning has been restricted, they return to the unrecognized word and resort to word attack skills to attempt to unlock the pronunciation.

Boxes 1A and 1B, as shown under Query 1, are very condensed statements of some detailed decoding analyses which were performed during the early design stages of the New Primary Grade Reading System (NRS). They are discussed in detail in another paper (Resnick and Beck, 1976). Notice, however, Query 1C, where the reader judges whether the sounds he has produced form a recognizable word *and* whether the word "fits" the immediately surrounding text. Even in the process of attacking an unrecognized word, a search for meaning is presumed by the analysis. Word attack and meaning operate for practical purposes more or less in parallel; and the need for word attack arises when a word has not been recognized. If an acceptable word has been found, the reader returns to the main text-processing flow; otherwise, the reader must decide whether to continue reading with the word still unclear (1D) or to seek information from an outside source (1E). The "outside source" for a pronunciation problem is likely to be another person, although finding the same word in another context sometimes solves the problem.

The second interruption indicated occurs when a word is sounded that has an unclear meaning and that appears important enough to warrant further information search. We assume that the most frequent first response under these conditions is to read ahead a little, searching for context that will suggest a meaning (Query 2A). The success of this context search is tested at 2B. Success sends the reader back into the main processing strand, while failure gives him or her the same choices as before: to continue reading with the word unclear, or to utilize an outside source. Now, dictionaries, glossaries, and so on are available as outside sources, as well as are other people, although other people may remain the preferred "least effort" source. We will see in a moment that the decision to continue with words unclarified may effect subsequent processing. Nevertheless, depending upon the depth of comprehension required for a particular task, and upon the degree of informationa! redundancy, it is often a good choice in reading.

At Query 3, processing is interrupted by awareness of a sentence whose meaning is not completely clear. The reader's first action is probably to reread the sentence and to test for success in gaining meaning (3A and 3B). If simple rereading fails, a next reasonable test would be to determine whether individual words, perhaps those deliberately left unclear in early decisions, are the source of difficulty (3C); if this is so, then the word meaning strand is entered. If individual words are not the problem, attention must next be focused upon the syntactic and semantic structure of the sentences. The sentence must be parsed to reveal its basic structure (3D). If parsing is successful in revealing meaning (3E), then the reader reenters the main processing strand; if parsing fails then a set of decisions similar to those for individual words probably occurs. The reader may decide to proceed with the sentence (temporarily) unclear (3H), or he or she may turn to an outside source (3I).

We come finally, at Query 4, to a situation in which an entire section (paragraph, chapter, or whatever) is seen as unclear. As with sentences, the first likely act is rereading (4A). Next, unclear words (4C) or unclear sentences (4D) may be the source of difficulty. If so, the reader returns to the word meaning or sentence meaning strands. If neither of these seems to be the cause of difficulty, an interesting set of further tests may occur. The reader may try to decide whether the present difficulty is due to his or her own unfamiliarity with the concepts discussed in the text (4E). If this seems a likely cause, perhaps it is due to incomplete processing of earlier parts of the text

(4F); in this case rereading the earlier parts (4G) may help. If the difficulties do not appear to reside in the reader's unfamiliarity with the concepts (a "no" answer at 4E), then the skilled reader may begin to wonder whether the text itself is so poorly written that it is the cause of the problem (4J). He or she may then try to impose order on the text (4K). If all of these tests and actions fail to produce clarification (a "no" answer at 4J and 4H), a fundamental decision must finally be made—whether to struggle ahead anyway. We suspect that many children in school do struggle through, with very little comprehension, simply because they have been told to read something. People reading independently will rarely do this, nor would we reasonably expect them to.

The model, as presented in Figure 2, represents only a general mapping of the reading process. It suggests in broad terms the probable major components of the reading process and how these components might interact; it does not attempt to describe the process in detail. Nevertheless, we believe that even in this simplified outline state, the model helps to make evident certain important features of reading; and , as a general map of the terrain, it was very useful during the development of our new reading program as it alerted us to the necessity of providing certain reading experiences. Notice, for instance, how complicated the strands are under Query 3 (which is related to difficulty in apprehending the meaning of a sentence) and Query 4 (which is related to difficulty in apprehending the meaning of a section). Suppose that while reading a passage, a reader encounters more than a few words that are not instantly recognized. In this case , his or her attention will necessarily be directed to unlocking the pronunciation of those words, and he or she cannot focus on what is being communicated. Indeed, if word attack is being initiated too frequently and proceeds too laboriously, the reader will probably forget the ideas he or she has recently gathered; he or she will be unable to relate idea units; and, of course, he or she will be unable to perform the self-monitoring strategies implied by the model.

Skilled reading requires that the reader have a large reservoir of words that he or she instantly recognizes. If rapid word recognition is as important as we believe it is, then instruction must be designed to insure its development. Interestingly, some basic researchers have turned their attention to the importance of automaticity of word recognition, and some useful instructional strategies may eventually be extrapolated as that body of research grows (LaBerge and Samuels, 1974; Perfetti and Hogaboam, 1975; Samuels 1973). Building familiarity through repeated encounters may not be the only way to develop automaticity, but it is certainly an important way. Opportunities must be provided for children to encounter newly learned words in meaningful connected materials; that is, recently introduced words should be practiced in connected text. Previously learned words should be maintained in interesting and seductive ways. Both of these must be done with strict adherence to principles of instructional design; that is, attention to the textual materials must be insured by adequate contingencies.

LRDC's current development efforts in reading

We turn now to the new program itself. The New Primary Grades Reading System (NRS) covers what is traditionally considered the domain of the first three years of reading instruction. NRS is composed of a variety of instructional resources, each with its own function. However, it is termed a *system* because of the interrelationships among the instructional resources and the integration of these into a management scheme.

The scope of NRS requires a definition of reading in its broadest sense, "the perception and comprehension of written messages in a manner paralleling that of the corresponding spoken messages" (Carroll, 1964: 336). NRS has a terminal goal that upon finishing the program a child be able to read and demonstrate understanding of representative third grade reading selections. From its inception, NRS has been designed for use in an individualized environment, and the components and techniques for individualization, described in the first section of this paper, have been incorporated. In an individualized system, while some children may achieve the terminal goal in the middle of the second year, others may not achieve it until the end of three and one-half years. In NRS we attempt to provide situations that make the child and the teacher aware that learning is taking place. Our aim has been to build a system that allows for individual variation, but not for individual failure.

The system is composed of fourteen levels, each containing approximately ten instructional sequences. The term *level* was selected over such terms as *step, module,* or *unit* to connote a horizontal as well as a vertical progression. In other words, not every task the child performs is designed to add new content or skills; some activities maintain content or build fluency, some allow the student to read less demanding material, and some afford the pupil the opportunity for "discovery learning" of upcoming content.

No attempt will be made here to describe the system fully; rather, I will present examples from the program that will help to illustrate how its meaning component is integrated with the phonics component.

The integration of phonics and meaning

NRS is a code-emphasis program in the sense that it is organized and sequenced around grapheme/phoneme relationships and spelling patterns, thus producing initial vocabulary that emphasizes the regularities of the coding system. Instructional strategies employ both synthetic and analytic phonics techniques to teach children to respond to letters and to strings of letters. The instructional strategies teach children the actual grapheme-phoneme correspondences themselves rather than rules about them. For example, verbalized rules of pronunciation and special terms such as *short vowel, long vowel,* and *schwa* are not used.

NRS is a meaning-emphasis program since the text is constructed with contingencies that require the child to respond to its meaning. The total design of NRS is conceived as being a spiral rather than a hierarchical structure. A hierarchical structure implies that many of the important grapheme/phoneme correspondences would be taught to the child before attention would focus on his or her interaction with connected textual materials. In a hierarchical structure, the ability to decode (perhaps slowly and laboriously) a good portion of the language is prerequistie to extended reading experiences.

By contrast, in a spiraling structure the emphasis is on concurrent development of decoding and meaning. In a spiraling structure, the child initially learns to decode only a limited number of important correspondences; then many sentences and "story paragraphs" containing words with those decodable elements are made available to him or her in connected text. As the child reads with meaning through the known elements, the next loop in the spiral enlarges as he or she is introduced to new elements. The child continues to read extended meaningful texts that incorporate the new element with previously taught content.

Structure and content of levels 1 and 2

Levels 1 and 2 of NRS are structured quite differently from Levels 3 through 14. Levels 1 and 2 are teacher-centered. At this initial stage of learning to read, the teacher instructs children in small groups. Later, in levels 3 through 14, the bulk of learning occurs through children's interaction with the individualized materials. It is important that the teacher be a central part of instruction in the beginning stages, since the relationship between printed and oral language must be firmly established. In order for this to occur, the teacher must be present to evaluate and confirm many oral productions. The successive blending routine, mentioned earlier in this paper, also requires the teacher's presence since it is taught adaptively: The teacher presents a model, sets up a series of prompts, and through continuous evaluations of a child's performance, deliberately and systematically fades the prompts.

Level 1 consists of twelve 20 to 30 minute lessons that introduce 11 grapheme/phoneme correspondences, including some digraphs in order to prevent the children from becoming locked into "a single letter, single sound misunderstanding." The blending routine is established in level 1; when the children use their knowledge of correspondences with the blending routine, they learn 38 words. Then children match those words to pictures.

It is important that all the words introduced in the early lessons are in the child's oral/aural vocabulary before they are encountered in print. As the analysis in Figure 2 suggests, a reader searches for meaning even in the process of attacking an unrecognized word. If the sounds uttered do not match a previously known word (i.e., are not in the speaking or hearing vocabulary), the reader does not know whether he or she is right or whether his or her approximation needs to be modified.

It is essential that words with unfamiliar meanings be eliminated in the beginning stages of learning to read. Correspondences and blending are tools for the learner to use for getting to the meaning of the word. While he or she is still learning this procedure, a high success rate must be maintained in order to strengthen it and to build the child's confidence in his or her ability to get meaning from print. If the child cannot get meaning from proper application of this procedure, then he or she may revert to guessing. As an example, consider the word *tam*, a word used in NRS which in isolation appears to be a nonsense syllable to many children. In the case of *tam*, we observed a number of children who proceeded through correct phoneme production and correct blending, but who hesitated and tried *ten*, *tin*, *mat*, or some other word that they knew at the time when the word was to be pronounced. This did not occur with strongly known words such as *man* and *cat*. It appears that when decoding tools don't work, they are replaced by guessing strategies. To guard against guessing and to help insure that decoding strategies are used, we carefully monitored the vocabulary used in the early lessons and explicitly provided prefamiliarization activities with any words that we did not expect children to know. Of course, when sentences begin to be used, as happens in Level 2, context assists the child in deriving meaning. However, throughout the program word meanings are sometimes taught directly.

Only four new grapheme/phoneme correspondences are introduced in level 2 because the major emphasis in the level is placed upon moving the words learned in level 1 (and words which are new combinations of the correspondences learned in level 1) into the child's recognition vocabulary. Through repeated encounters with the same set of words, children begin to recognize the sound equivalents of larger units (e.g., spelling patterns) and begin to perform word analysis and synthesis covertly. This is, of course, a necessary step in the direction of developing automaticity of word recognition. The blending routine established in level 1 is faded, but not eliminated, during level 2. When children encounter difficulties in word recognition, the teacher still asks that they perform some overt blending in order to locate the difficulty, and thus, to be in a position to offer the assistance needed. Even more importantly, we have seen many children who are far along in the program resort to the blending routine on their own initiative when other clues (e.g., context) do not help them. In addition, level 2 introduces eight sight words,[3] sentences, and some of the first comprehension formats. Comprehension formats are so named because the required responses can be made only if the child has read and understood at least some of the textual material.

Comprehension, of course is a very complex behavior. Many theorists have stated that it is a function of the integration of perceptual, linguistic, cognitive, and knowledge components. While, through NRS, we are adding to the child's general perceptual, linguistic, and knowledge background, it is not clear to me that we *teach* comprehension; that is, it is not clear that we teach a child to understand things in print that he would not understand from oral language. Rather, we teach the child to attend to textual materials and we provide activities that are likely to enhance automaticity of word recognition.

Figure 3 shows a workbook page with three of the early comprehension formats used in NRS. The particular example in Figure 3 is a page that a child does independently towards the end of level 2. Throughout level 2, the teacher introduces each new type of comprehension format prior to its appearance on an independent page. For example, consider the middle frame in Figure 3. This format was first introduced earlier in level 2. At that time, the highly-structured teacher manual alerted the teacher to tell the children that when they encounter a picture and two sentences, they are to look at the picture, read both sentences, and then make a ring around the sentence that tells about the picture.

A variety of comprehension formats is introduced by the teacher in level 2. More sophisticated versions of some of these same comprehension formats continue throughout the program, and new types of comprehension formats are introduced by the audio lessons in succeeding levels. Notice the

---

[3] Sight words in NRS are either irregular words or regular words containing graphemic elements not yet introduced. For instance, *and* which is regular, is introduced as a whole word before the grapheme/phoneme correspondence for *d* is introduced. The early introduction of *and* is considered useful for developing variation in sentences.

A   fish   is   in   a   net.

The   fish   is   Sam's.

Sam's   fish   is   fat.

1.

Is   Sam   in   a   net?

yes   no

2.

Is   the   fish   fat?

yes   no

Nan   is   napping.

Nan   sees   Ben's   feet.

Color   the   cat   that   is   fat.

Figure 3.   Examples of three comprehension formats from Level 2 of the New
Primary Grades Reading System (NRS).

bottom frame in Figure 3, the one with the direction "Color the cat that is fat." This is an early example from a "direction following" strand that has proven to be very successful because the blackout ratio can be kept low in this type of frame.

In this section thus far, I have concentrated upon the instructional design for effective reading instruction in the early levels. As any designer of an instructional program knows, the effectiveness also depends upon the care with which the management scheme has been developed. In order for individualization to occur, children must acquire a variety of self-management skills. Just as the skills of reading are taught in a gradual cumulative sequence, NRS also teaches self-management skills in a gradual cumulative sequence. I will not dwell on this important aspect of the program, but I want to indicate that these self-management skills are introduced gradually throughout levels 1 and 2, so that by the time the child reaches level 3, he or she has been taught each type of self-management skill needed to progress through subsequent levels.

Instructional resources in levels 3 through 14

Figure 4 attempts to suggest how the instructional resources of NRS "fit" into an effective management scheme for individualization. The workbook is seen as the central component of NRS because it either contains the resources needed by both teacher and child or it triggers the use of the other resources. I will describe each of the resources very briefly and then focus on the components that are starred by providing examples that relate to the major topic of this paper, the role of comprehension during the acquisition of decoding skills.

Let's begin with the box at 12 o'clock, in Figure 4, the box entitled "Lesson Overview." In an individualized program in which children in one classroom are working in various places, perhaps over a range of six or eight levels, the teacher needs information about a particular lesson to be readily accessible. Therefore, preceding each lesson in the child's workbook is a green page addressed to the teacher which provides an outline of the new content and stresses any aspects of the content to which the teacher should be alert. While functioning in the

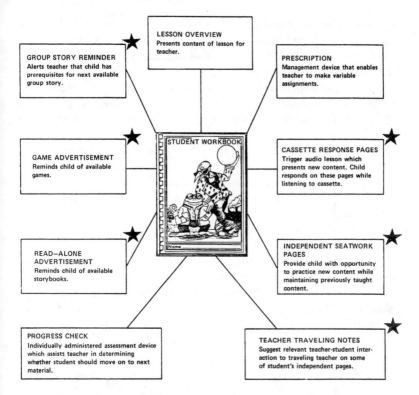

Figure 4. Instructional resources in Level 3 through 14 of NRS.

"traveling" role, the teacher can glance at the outline to familiarize himself or herself quickly with the content a particular child is learning.

"Prescriptions" are listings of the instructional resources that are available for each lesson. They are management devices that enable the teacher to make variable assignments.

"Cassette Response Pages" direct the child to listen to the appropriate cassette as he or she completes these pages by responding to directions given on the cassette. These audio lessons are a key device for individualization with beginning readers because they present new content.

"Independent Seatwork Pages" follow the audio lessons and provide the child with opportunities to read material which contains the new content and which maintains previously-taught content.

"Teacher Traveling Notes" are an important aid in an individualized system since part of the teacher's role in such a system is to "travel" among the children, tutoring and reinforcing them as they interact with the materials. The traveling notes appear in reduced type at the bottom of some of the child's independent seatwork pages and suggest relevant teacher/child interactions concerning the text on a particular page.

"Progress Checks" are individually-administered assessment devices. Again, they are located in the workbooks exactly where the teacher needs them. In addition, if the child hasn't learned the content taught in a lesson well enough to proceed to a new element, additional instructional material is provided following the progress check.

"Read-Alone Advertisements." NRS includes, as an integral part of its design, a variety of storybooks which a child can choose to read. The vocabulary in these stories is correlated with the content the children have learned in instructional settings. Advertisements for these books are placed throughout each workbook.

"Game Advertisements." We also include, as an integral part of NRS, a variety of games which a child can choose to play. The vocabulary in these games is also correlated with the content that the children have learned in instructional settings. Advertisements for the games are placed throughout each workbook.

"Group Story Reminders." Group stories are situations in which the teacher and a group of children read a story together and discuss and share interpretations of that story. Group stories occur at designated places throughout all levels of NRS. The group story reminder is printed in the workbook and is simply a part of a management scheme we have developed to enable the teacher to assemble a group of children.

Now we will take a look at some examples of the content in some of the components and examine them to see how phonics and comprehension have been designed in harmony.

Cassette introduction for a new grapheme/phoneme correspondence. In order to present a flavor of how a new grapheme/phoneme correspondence is introduced by cassette, we will use the example in Figure 5, which is part of an actual cassette response page from level 8. This lesson introduces the phoneme /ō/ for the graphemes *oa* and *ow*.

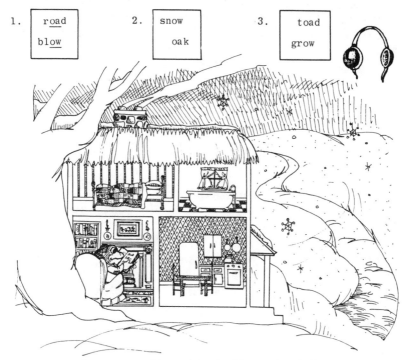

1. r<u>oa</u>d
   bl<u>ow</u>

2. snow
   oak

3. t oad
   gr ow

Once upon a time, deep in the woods at the end of a <u>road</u>, there lived a <u>Toad</u>. He lived under an old <u>oak</u> tree. It was winter time and sometimes the wind would blow the <u>snow</u> against the door so the <u>Toad</u> couldn't get out of his house. He just sat by the fire and rested. It was quiet and cozy in the <u>Toad's</u> house under the old <u>oak</u> tree.

4. Where does the Toad live?

   ☐ at the end of a road under an oak tree

   ☐ at the end of a road under an apple tree

Figure 5. Example of a cassette response page which introduces the phoneme /ō/ as in <u>road</u> and g<u>row</u>.

The narrator on the cassette directs the child to the words next to numeral 1 in Figure 5, reads each word, and asks the child to repeat the words. Then the child is told to point to the underlined letters in *road* while the narrator makes the sound of the underlined letters. The child then is asked to repeat the sound. The same procedure is followed for the bottom word in box 1.

Moving to numeral 2, the child is prompted that each word in box 2 contains the $/\overline{o}/$ sound and he or she is asked to read the words. After a sufficient pause, the narrator says the words. Then the child is directed to underline the letters in each word that make the $/\overline{o}/$ sound.

In number 3, the child is directed to read the words and to underline the letters in each word that make the $/\overline{o}/$ sound.

Next, the narrator directs the child to the picture and makes some relevant comments about it. The child is told to read the paragraph under the picture aloud with the narrator, but that each time they arrive at an underlined word, the child will be reading that word aloud himself or herself. The narrator pauses for three seconds at each underlined word and continues the text after each pause.

After the paragraph has been read, the child is directed to answer question 4. The purpose of question 4 is to establish the character of the Toad, since this particular cassette lesson continues for three more pages with a story line developed around the Toad. A variety of word analysis frames, such as those at the top of the figure, are interspersed with episodes in the story. After interruptions for word analysis, the narrator provides transition back to the story.

The most relevant aspect of the example in Figure 5 is the fact that the introduction of a new grapheme/phoneme correspondence takes place in meaningful connected text.

Independent Seatwork Pages. We now move to examples of workbook pages that the child completes independently. Figures 6 and 7 are from a sequence of workbook pages that follows the cassette instruction for the $/\overline{o}/$ phoneme as in r*oa*d and gr*ow*. In Figure 6, each sentence contains the word *Toad* and at least one other word that contains the new element. Close examination of the sentences will indicate that the child must read at least some of the target words in order to match the sentences with the correct pictures. Notice the reduced print at the bottom of Figure 6; this is a "teacher traveling note." As defined earlier in this paper, teacher traveling notes suggest relevant teacher/student interactions.

1. The Toad is sleeping
    on a big pillow.

2. The Toad is putting
    on his coat.

3. The Toad is hopping
    down the road.

4. The Toad is rowing
    his boat across the
    lake.

5. The Toad is soaking
    in his bathtub.

6. The Toad is watching
    the snow falling.

Point to a word containing <u>oa</u> and a word containing <u>ow</u>. Have the child read the words and underline the letters that make the /ō/ sound in each word.

Figure 6. First independent seatwork page following cassette introduction of the /ō/ phoneme as in <u>road</u> and <u>grow</u>.

Since the page in Figure 6 is the first independent seatwork page to follow the cassette introduction of the new correspondence, the traveling note directs the teacher to check the child's oral reading of the words that contain the target element.

1. One of the toads just closed the window.
   He has on a yellow coat. Make an X on
   the animal that just closed the window.
2. One of the crows loves to ride on railroad
   trains. He is eating a bowl of oatmeal.
   Make a ring around the animal that loves
   to ride on railroad trains.
3. One of the toads likes to play in the snow
   in the winter. He is eating some toast.
   Make a line over the animal that likes to
   play in the snow.
4. One of the crows always takes a bath with
   yellow soap. He is drinking tea now. Make
   a star on the animal that takes a bath with
   yellow soap.

[If there are errors, help the child extract the relevant information.]

Figure 7. Example of a later independent seatwork page following cassette instruction of /ō/ phoneme as in r*o*ad and gr*o*w.

Figure 7 is an example drawn from the "direction following" strand that began in level 2. This strand has gradually evolved to the kind of complex activity shown in Figure 7. The traveling note which suggests helping the child who has made an error to "extract the relevant information" is a cue to the teacher to have the child read each sentence and to ask the child leading questions about the sentence. For example, using the text next to numeral 4, after the child had read the first sentence, the teacher would ask, "Who always takes a bath with yellow soap?" After the second sentence had been read, the teacher would ask, "Who is drinking tea now?" and would explicitly establish that the *He* in the second sentence is the crow that always takes a bath with yellow soap.

Figures 6 and 7 are examples of independent seatwork pages that contain short textual material. It is very important to point out that longer texts with story lines are contained in every sequence of independent pages. For instance, the sequence that follows the introduction of the /ō/ phoneme (as in r*o*ad and gr*o*w) includes a two page story about a toad and a squirrel who are planning a party. There is also a factual story about real toads which explains some of the differences between toads and frogs. While I have not presented examples of these longer selections, I want to emphasize that a great number of extended stories are included in the child's workbooks in order to try to motivate the child to read through interesting text.

Figures 8 through 13 are other samples of comprehension formats from various sequences. Figure 8 is another example of the "direction following" strand. In this particular example, the target element is the /ôl/ pattern as in b*all*. Notice the low blackout ratio; the child has to read the target words in order to make the correct responses.

In Figure 9, the target element is the word *would*. Notice that each even-numbered direction requires the child to confirm his or her response to the preceding odd-numbered question.

Figure 10 presents a page that focuses on the words *above* and *below* as concepts. Even though these concepts were introduced in the cassette instruction, the independent frames are sequenced to help "shape" the concept.

In Figure 11, questions 1 and 3 are the key features. Unlike traditional who, what, where, when, and why questions about textual material, questions 1 and 3 require the child to determine whether or not certain information is contained in the text. One reason for including this type of question is to attempt to establish the important understanding that a particular text doesn't necessarily tell everything about a given topic. How often in the intermediate grades do we see children "researching" a topic by going to the encyclopedia and assuming that all relevant information has been included in the encyclopedia? Indeed, we introduce this type of question in a cassette lesson that specifically tells the child that "a story tells you some things about a subject, but one story can't usually tell you everything about a subject."

1.   Color all the plānǿs red.

2.   Mākǿ a ring around the big ball.

3.   Mākǿ an X on each of the small balls.

4.   Color the tall elf.

Figure 8.   Example of independent seatwork page containing comprehension format from the "direction following" strand.

1. Would you like to be the pitcher?

        yes   no

2. If you would like to be the pitcher,
   make an X on the pitcher.

3. Would you like to be the catcher?

        yes   no

4. If you would like to be the catcher,
   make an X on the catcher.

5. Would you like to be the batter?

        yes   no

6. If you would like to be the batter,
   make a ring around the batter.

7. Would you like to see the children playing
   this game?

        yes   no

Question 1: Ask the child to draw a ring around the word <u>Would</u>. Then have him read the question outloud. Discuss with child reasons why he would or would not like to be some of the things suggested on the page.

Figure 9. Another example of independent seatwork page containing comprehension format from the "direction following" strand.

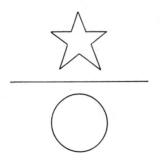

The star is above the line.
The circle is below the line.

1. Is the star below the line?

    yes   no

2. The circle is | above / below |

    the line.

1. The picture is hanging

    | above / below | the clock.

2. The box is | above / below | the

    clock.

1. Make an X on the books that
    are above the window.

2. Make a ring around the books
    that are below the window.

Top Frame: Have the child find and read a sentence containing the word <u>above</u> and a sentence containing the word <u>below</u>. If necessary, clarify the meaning of the words.

Figure 10. Example of independent seatwork page establishing the words *above* and *below* as concepts.

Ben and Pete were camping in Ben's tent. The tent
was next to Pete's house. Just as the boys were about to
go to sleep, something went "bump, bump" outside the
tent. Then it went "bump, bump" again. The boys
got frightened. They wanted to run into the house.

Then Ben took the flashlight and shined it on the
grass outside the tent. The light flashed on a turtle
trying to climb over the bag of snacks the boys had
left on the grass.

"Pete," said Ben, "look at the turtle. I think he
wants to sleep in the tent, too."

1. Does the story tell you who was in the tent?

            yes   no

2. When did the boys hear the "bump, bump?"

    ☐ just as they were about to eat their snacks

    ☐ just as they were about to go to sleep

3. Does the story tell you what kind of snacks the
    boys had in their snack bag?

            yes   no

Figure 11. Example of independent seatwork page containing comprehension format requiring child to decide whether certain information
is contained in text.

In Figure 12, directions 1 and 4 require the child to underline specific sentences in the text. The purpose of this format is to give the child experience in searching a text for specific information, a behavior performed by many adult readers. Directions 2 and 3 extend the notion that a single text contains limited information. In addition, in order to follow the directions, it is likely that children will have to reread sections to respond correctly to directions 2 and 3. The notion of occasionally providing activities that require a child to reread is based on the analysis of the reading process in Figure 2 which suggests that effective readers do sometimes reread sections of text.

It would be, of course, a huge leap (based on faith alone) to assume that the particular responses required in directions 2 and 3 of Figure 12 would transfer to the child monitoring his or her own comprehension and rereading when he or she determines that a section is unclear. What we can say with assurance is that the directions in Figure 12 do set up contingencies that require the child to attend to the text.

Figure 13 presents an example of some syntactical analysis. This format was suggested by the part of the analysis of the reading process in Figure 2 which hypothesizes that a reader who is having difficulty with a sentence may reread the sentence to simplify it by isolating the actor and the action. Therefore, it seemed useful to provide opportunities for the child to isolate the actor, action, and the object of the action in a sentence. Notice that grammatical terms are avoided in the use of this format. When we intoduce this format in the cassette, we establish the notion of "important words" in a sentence, rather than using grammatical terms such as *subject*, *verb*, and *object*.

While the examples in Figure 6 through 13 contain limited textual material, it was noted earlier that workbooks also include longer selections with more developed story lines. These longer selections have a far higher blackout ratio. Indeed, if all the reading material had a low blackout ratio, children might be shaped to attend too thoroughly to all texts. Whereas the high blackout ratio throughout the Sullivan series may have taught children that "you don't have to read the story to answer the questions," a low blackout ratio in all textual material could teach them that "you have to read everything all the time." Neither is true for effective reading. Effective reading requires a diversity in levels of attention. In addition to the extended stories in the workbooks, NRS contains two other resources featuring extended stories; these are the Read-Alone Storybooks and the Group Story Books.

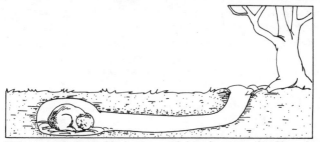

This animal is called a ground hog because it digs deep, long holes in the ground. In the spring and summer, the ground hog finds plants to eat in meadows and farmlands. The ground hog eats a lot and gets very, very fat.

By the beginning of fall, the ground hog is ready to go underground. It goes underground long before the cold weather arrives. The ground hog sleeps underground for part of the fall and almost all of the winter. Then the ground hog comes out again when winter is almost over.

1. Make a line under the sentence in the story that tells you what a ground hog finds to eat.

2. If there is a sentence in the story that tells you what color a ground hog is, make a line under that sentence.

3. If there is a sentence in the story that tells you when the ground hog is ready to go underground, make a line under that sentence.

4. Make a line under the sentence in the story that tells you when the ground hog comes out from underground.

> Numerals 2 and 3 are new formats which were introduced in the preceding cassette. Make sure all directions were followed, and in particular, make sure the child understands the contingent "If" statement. There should be no underlined sentence for numeral 2.

Figure 12. Example of independent seatwork page containing comprehension formats requiring child to underline sentence in text and demonstrate understanding of contingent "If" statement.

Once a week, the woman gives lectures about different
jungle animals.

1. Who does something in this sentence?

    ☐ woman

    ☐ week

    ☐ jungle

2. What does the woman do in the sentence?

    ☐ runs

    ☐ gives

    ☐ different

3. What does the woman give in the sentence?

    ☐ animals

    ☐ lectures

    ☐ jungle

4. What are the three important words in the sentence?

    _____

___

The brown and white cows eat green grass in the pasture.

1. What are the three important words in this sentence?

    ☐ pasture eats cows

    ☐ cows eat grass

    ☐ grass grows green

> Bottom Frame: This is the first frame where the child directly identifies the three important words
> in a sentence. If necessary, go through the logic involved in identifying the important words
> with him (i.e., the first important word tells who eats in the sentence, the second important word
> tells what the cows do, and the third important word tells what the cows eat).

Figure 13. Example of independent seatwork page containing syntactical
analysis format.

Read-Alone Storybooks. Beginning with level 2, each NRS level includes eight to twelve separate story booklets which children may elect to read. As instructional designers, we have attempted to provide varied and lively reading materials whose vocabulary is compatible with the correspondences children know at any given level of the program. The Read-Alone stories exhibit variety in terms of topic, style, length, degree of difficulty, and treatment of subject matter. They also provide children with reading "books" composed of decodable content during the interim period between their earliest attempts to read and their development of the decoding skills necessary to read commercial storybooks with less restricted vocabulary.

Group Story Books. As noted in the discussion of the NRS components in Figure 4, each child's workbooks contain "Group Story Reminders" which are part of the management scheme that enables the teacher to assemble a group of children who have the appropriate requisites for reading and discussing a particular story under the teacher's direction. Since the teacher is available to provide assistance in a group story situation, the stories tend to contain more complicated syntax, more sophisticated vocabulary, and more thoroughly developed plots than appear in the workbook stories or Read-Alone stories. Some group stories integrate the situation of "children reading" with the situation of "children being read to." In the teacher's editions of the group stories, suggestions are made to the teacher to read a few of the more complicated passages of a given story to the children. Through a discussion of those passages, the notions that are important for understanding subsequent passages are established. Then the children read portions themselves and discuss those passages. In general, the instructional purposes for group stories are for the teacher to assist children with: increasingly complex syntax, polysyllabic words, word meanings, and story line development. The group story situations are also important for social reasons, in that they provide an opportunity for sustained peer contact and teacher-student contact. In an individualized environment, children are in frequent short-term contact with the teacher when they receive their prescriptions, when they take tests, and when the teacher briefly stops during the "traveling" to reinforce and tutor. Children are, of course, in touch with each other in many informal ways such as when they get materials and when they compare what they are doing. They interact especially in the "choice" area (to be described later) where they select among games that are designed for more than one child to play. The group story situation adds yet another environment for more sustained peer contact and teacher-student contact. This situation would be beneficial if it were based on social reasons alone. However, the strong instructional benefits mentioned above also exist in the small-group, teacher-led environments.

Games. Each level of NRS contains a variety of games with vocabulary emphasizing the correspondences taught in that level while also utilizing previously-taught content. In order to provide a sense of how the games contribute to reading fluency, I will briefly describe three of them. The first picture in Figure 14 is a representation of the "War" game. War is introduced in level 2 and is an adaptation of a game played with regular playing cards. A category (in this case, either alive" or "not alive," established by flipping the disc) determines the rank of printed word cards in the deck (e.g., if "alive" were the category chosen, the word card *man* would outrank the card *cape*). Two children read cards that are turned over one at a time. If the pair *man* and *cape* were turned up, the child who had the word card *man* would take both the *man* card and the *cape* card. War is declared when both players turn up

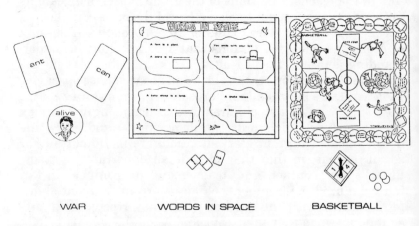

WAR   WORDS IN SPACE   BASKETBALL

Figure 14. Pictorial representation of three NRS games.

cards from the same category (e.g., if *cab* and *can* appeared). When war is declared each player puts one card face down. Then the next of each child's cards is turned over. As soon as one of the players turns up an example of something "alive" and the other player turns up a "not alive" example (e.g., *Sam* and *can*), the player who has the "alive" card takes the whole pile. The winner is the child who collects the most cards during a round.

I propose that this kind of game enhances automaticity. We have observed children who were reading slowly in their workbooks begin to call out the words on the cards not only rapidly, but loudly! The "War" game described above is introduced in level 2; that is, the teacher teaches a group of children the rules of the game, using a deck containing level 2 words. As children proceed through the levels, War games using words from subsequent levels become available. Categories in the games change (e.g., names of animals and names of vegetables; things usually found inside a house and things usually found outside a house, etc.).

The second game pictured in Figure 14, "Words in Space," is introduced in level 7. It consists of four game boards with fill-in-the-blank sentences printed on them (e.g., "Mittens go on your hands; socks go on your _____ .") and 16 printed cards containing the words that complete the sentences. Players simultaneously attempt to complete their boards by selecting cards from the 16 word cards that have been placed face down, and rejecting the cards that have inappropriate words. The player who first completes his or her board correctly is the winner. Words in Space is a fast-paced game that encourages rapid sentence processing through the use of a kind of "contrast/parallel structure" context clue. In subsequent levels, the Words in Space games feature use of other context clues (e.g., synonyms, common expressions, etc.).

The third game pictured in Figure 14 is "Basketball," which is introduced in level 9. Players read aloud directions printed on various spaces on the board (e.g., "You walked with the ball instead of dribbling. Miss one turn."). On some spaces, they must select a card with a multiple choice question on it (e.g., "Which one of these things would a king put on his head? a crown/a gown"). Players receive chips for correctly answering questions, and the winner of the game is the player who collects the most chips by the time any player has completed a circuit of the board. The game is a very popular one and its purpose is to provide children with an occasion to read in a way that is fun for them. As with other games, Basketball becomes available in subsequent levels employing words from the correspondences taught in those levels.

Through this brief description of the components of NRS and through specific examples of some of the content, I have attempted to illustrate some of the concepts that I think are important in the design of effective reading instruction. Therefore, the remaining question is: Is NRS effective?

Preliminary evaluation data

There are two sets of data that bear on the effectiveness of NRS. One set comes from the two LRDC developmental schools, the other from a school that had no previous relationship with LRDC programs prior to the implementation of NRS. The latter school has many characteristics of an urban school.

In 1973-1974, NRS was implemented in the first grades of the LRDC developmental schools. Comparisons of end-of-year achievement of NRS students with students from the previous year under the "patched" Sullivan program showed slight gains in favor of NRS. These data were encouraging; but, as might be expected, the amount of gain due to NRS was small, primarily because the comparison group was already achieving fairly well since it had had the advantage of LRDC's individualized Sullivan program. In addition, the reading achievement data from LRDC's developmental schools are confounded by the fact that during the years we worked with the Sullivan program, LRDC Reading Project personnel spent time in the classrooms working with individual children. This was done in order to better understand the instructional processes; however, it also provided "clinical" assistance to a number of children. It should be noted that, during the 1973-1974 implementation of NRS in the developmental schools, this clinical support was removed. Therefore, we feel the small gains with NRS are quite encouraging.

A better measure of the success of NRS comes from the school that had no previous relationship with LRDC. The data were gathered from first-grade classrooms where implementation of our program was initiated during the 1974-1975 school year. Prior to implementation of NRS, first-graders in this school were taught to read through a basal program that contained a rather heavy phonics component.

Table 1.   Mean Grade Equivalent Comparisons on Five SAT Subtests of End-of-First Grade Achievement between 1973-1974 Classes Using a Basal Program and 1974-1975 Classes Using NRS

SAT Subtest	N	$\overline{X}$ (Grade Equivalent)	S.D.	t	df	P
Word Reading						
Basal	43	1.66	.42	3.44	81	<.001
NRS	40	2.05	.61			
Paragraph Meaning						
Basal	43	1.66	.41	2.62	81	<.02
NRS	40	1.96	.63			
Word Study Skills						
Basal	43	1.80	.48	1.06	81	N.S.
NRS	40	1.93	.58			
Spelling						
Basal	43	1.64	.51	-1.07	81	N.S.
NRS	40	1.50	.67			
Vocabulary						
Basal	43	2.03	.71	1.39	81	N.S.
NRS	40	2.23	.60			

The data in Table 1 are reported on five subtests of the SAT, Stanford Achievement Test (Kelley et al., 1964). The table shows comparisons between first-grade achievement in the spring of the 1973-1974 school year when children were using the Basal program, and first-grade achievement in the spring of the 1974-1975 school year when children were using NRS. In both groups, only those students who were enrolled in the school from the beginning to the end of their first-grade year (40 in the NRS group and 43 in the Basal group) are compared. The NRS group and the Basal group had mean IQs as derived from the Pintner-Cunningham Primary Test (Pintner, Cunningham, and Durost, 1966) of 108.24 and 108.98, respectively.

Table 1 shows student achievement on the five language arts subtests, expressed in mean grade equivalents, for the students in the Basal program and NRS, and the values of the corresponding t statistics. The first three subtests in the table, Word Reading, Paragraph Meaning and Word Study Skills are classified by the authors of the SAT as measures of reading skills. All comparisons on these reading-related subtests favored NRS students over those in the Basal program, with significant differences between the two groups in the Word Reading and Paragraph Meaning subtests. The authors of the SAT do not classify their Vocabulary subtest as one that directly measures reading skills since the items on this subtest are read to the child; hence this particular subtest measures pupils' vocabulary knowledge independent of their reading skills. Spelling was taught in neither the Basal program nor in NRS. The Vocabulary and Spelling subtests are included in this analysis of the effects of NRS to illustrate that the comparison and NRS groups appear similar in other skills that may be related to the acquisition of reading skills. From that we strengthen our belief that differences in achievement in the reading subtests are due to differences in instructional treatment rather than to differences in group characteristics. Further analysis of the above data and additional descriptive data are available in McCaslin (1975).

Conclusions

I have undertaken to describe some of the factors that need to be considered for the design of effective instruction in beginning reading. One important factor is adherence to principles of instructional design. Application of principles of instructional design must be complemented with some understanding of the nature of the reading process itself. This understanding can be fostered through the use of analytic devices such as the task analysis of the reading process shown in Figure 2. The resultant "map" of the reading process enabled us to view the integration of separate kinds of reading competencies and led to the conclusion that instruction must be provided for the effective integration, rather than sequential mastery, of several separate components. Indeed, it was this that led us to the position that phonics and meaning are most sensibly viewed as mutually supportive and interdependent.

However, curriculum design is not only a matter of the application of instructional principles and the use of available knowledge about the reading process itself. Curriculum development also requires the integration of science and intuition with structure and playfulness. The curriculum designer must have a strong sense of children, of the variety of social systems operating in various classrooms, and of the busy primary grades teacher attending to so many needs unrelated to reading. Each time a design decision is made, multiple considerations are necessary.

In the design and development of NRS we used notions from both theory and practice. As we study NRS in operation in various classrooms and analyze data from those classrooms, we should learn more about principles of instruction and the learning to read process itself. In turn, what we learn may contribute to both theory and practice.

REFERENCES

Beck, I. L. *The New Primary Grades Reading System: Preview of an adaptive reading system.* Paper presented at the meeting of the American Educational Research Association, New Orleans, March 1973.

Beck, I. L., and Mitroff, D. D. *The rationale and design of a primary grades reading system for an individualized classroom.* Pittsburgh: University of Pittsburgh, Learning Research and Development Center, 1972. (Publication No. 1972/4; ERIC Document Reproduction Service No. ED 063 100)

Buchanan, C. D. *Sullivan associates programmed reading.* St. Louis: McGraw-Hill, 1963.

Carroll, J. B. The analysis of reading instruction: Perspectives from psychology and linguistics. In E. R. Hilgard (Ed.), *Theories of Learning and Instruction — The Sixty-Third Yearbook of the National Society for the Study of Education, Part 1.* Chicago: University of Chicago Press, 1964, 336-353.

Chall, J. C. *Learning to Read: The great debate.* New York: McGraw-Hill, 1967.

Diederich, P. B. II. *Research 1960-70 on methods and materials in reading.* TM Report 22, ERIC Clearinghouse on Tests, Measurement, and Evaluation. Princeton: Educational Testing Service, January 1973.

Durost, W. N.; Bixler, H. H.; Wrightstone, J. W.; Prescott, G. A.; and Balow, I. H. Metropolitan achievement tests. New York: Harcourt, Brace, Jovanovich, 1970.

Eichelberger, R. T.; Lee, J. B.; and Leinhardt, G. *LRDC adaptive educational programs and academic achievement results obtained at two developmental schools.* Unpublished manuscript, Learning Research and Development Center, University of Pittsburgh, 1974.

Glaser, R. Toward a behavioral science base for instructional design. In R. Glaser (Ed.), *Teaching Machines and Programmed Learning, II: Data and Directions.* Washington, D.C.: National Education Association, 1965.

Holland, J. G. A quantitative measure for programmed instruction. *American Educational Research Journal,* 1967, *4,* 87-101.

Kelley, T. L.; Madden, R.; Gardner, E. F.; and Rudman, H. C. Stanford achievement test. New York: Harcourt, Brace and World, 1964.

LaBerge, D., and Samuels, S. J. Toward a theory of automatic information processing in reading. *Cognitive Psychology,* 1974, *6,* 293-323.

McCaslin, E. S. *A first year implementation of the New Primary Grades Reading System.* Unpublished manuscript, Learning Research and Development Center, University of Pittsburgh, 1975.

Perfetti, C. A., and Hogaboam, T. The relationship between single word decoding and reading comprehension skill. *Journal of Educational Psychology,* 1975, *67,* 461-469.

Pintner, R.; Cunningham, B. V.; and Durost W. Pintner-Cunningham primary test. New York: Harcourt, Brace and World, 1966.

Resnick, L. B., and Beck, I. L. Designing instruction in reading: Interaction of theory and practice. In J. T. Guthrie (Ed.), *Aspects of Reading Acquisition.* Baltimore: Johns Hopkins University Press, 1976.

Samuels, S. J. *Automatic decoding and its role in reading comprehension.* Paper presented at the meeting of the American Education Research Association, New Orleans, March 1973.

Comments on
Comprehension during
the Acquisition of Decoding Skills

John B. Carroll

Isabel Beck's paper is a fine statement and a report of a promising new reading program. I hope nobody will be disappointed if I say that I find no points of difference or disagreement with it. Indeed I would want to applaud many of her statements very heartily—for example, the point that in teaching beginning reading, an emphasis on phonics does *not* mean that attention to meaning must inevitably decrease. *Of course* you can teach meaning while teaching phonics, and doing otherwise is counterproductive and absurd. Yet, as Isabel Beck points out, one can find reading programs that fail to give enough attention to meaning, either by stressing phonics too much or simply by not realizing that the child will not read for meaning, necessarily, unless the proper contingencies are set up for him to do so. So, a very valuable feature of the New Reading Series is that it arranges matters so that the child will learn to read for meaning while attending to other aspects of the reading process.

The work of Beck and her associates is also to be praised from the standpoint of its attention to problems of instructional design. Under the leadership of Robert Glaser, the Pittsburgh Learning Research and Development Center has pioneered in research on sound instructional design and I presume that Beck's reading program has profited greatly from this. Already she presents evidence that the new reading program *can* make a difference, and this is encouraging in view of the long history of failures of reading programs. It is also gratifying that the New Reading Series is being developed with ample funding for program validation, particularly formative evaluation. Most reading programs, after all, have been developed mainly by a kind of "seat of the pants" intuition about what works and what doesn't—intuition that is not always a good guide.

The New Reading Series is designed only for teaching beginning reading but some of the principles underlying it can be applied in more advanced programs. One of these principles is that exercises must be constructed in such a way that the learner is *required* to attend to meaning in order to complete them. As Beck puts it, the exercises must have a low blackout ratio, such that if you try deleting a lot of the textual material, you would find that you are deleting the material that the learner must read in order to find answers. Note that determining a blackout ratio, or trying to estimate what the blackout ratio would be, is something that would be done by an instructional designer or preparer of instructional materials; it's not something a teacher would ordinarily do except possibly in designing his own exercise materials. It's an operational way of specifying the extent to which the material of instruction is relevant to what it is trying to accomplish. I suggest, however, that the technique has an intimate relation to the notion of comprehension because the more material the learner is required to read, the more the material is going to require the activation of comprehension processes, whatever they may be.

There are many other fine things about the Pittsburgh reading program, although they may not be immediately related to comprehension. For example, I've been impressed with the excellent way in which the analytic decoding processes have been programed—carefully teaching children to recognize words in phrases, then to recognize syllables in words, and then particular phonemes in words. This is only one example of the way in which a careful analysis of the hierarchy of tasks in learning to read has produced striking improvements in methods of instruction. Such an analysis is implicit in the schematic model of the reading comprehension process that is included in Beck's paper. Though such models may appear frighteningly complex, the instructional designer has need of such models and must patiently explore their

158   *Carroll*

implications if materials are to be properly and efficiently designed.

Reading has been taught for centuries—perhaps not on the scale that it now is attempted, and perhaps not always to all children; but one cannot deny that at every era of history since the time of the ancient Greeks and Romans, at least some children have learned to read—without benefit of basal readers, standardized reading tests, or psycholinguistic theories of reading. Some of us have learned to read with only the most primitive methods of teaching, and yet we have developed into mature and skilled readers, even claiming sufficient expertness to be able to teach others to read, or at least coach others in their teaching. Why, then, do we need reading conferences? Why do we need new reading series?

Around 1950, when I had just joined the faculty at the Harvard Graduate School of Education, I remember attending a lecture on education by Margaret Mead. One thing she said has always stuck with me—that education needs a new theory every three or four years. It doesn't have to be really novel, or even correct, but it must have at least some elements of correctness and novelty. To catch on among teachers, it helps if the new theory has a bit of new terminology and a few pet slogans. What Margaret Mead was saying, I think, was that a new theory of education is needed every few years in order to get teachers to reconsider what they are doing. Perhaps that is one of the purposes of reading conferences—to get participants to rethink their objectives and methods; to get them to learn new terminology and concepts; review the latest research findings (even if the findings seem only to provide the obvious); and go away refreshed with the thought that, on arrival back home, they can lick all the problems that previously seemed insoluble.

Likewise, new reading series may be needed every few years in order to catch up with new developments; provide up-to-date, fresh materials; and revive interest in both teachers and students. But perhaps the Pittsburgh reading series is not "just another" reading series. With the attention it pays to the components of the reading process and the principles of instructional design, it has the promise of establishing a totally new standard of excellence.

An Applied Behavior Analysis Approach to Reading Comprehension

Cheryl Hansen and Thomas Lovitt

There is, among teachers, researchers, and parents, total agreement in respect to the importance of developing pupil abilities in reading comprehension. Although there has been continued debate about the contributions of this or that approach to beginning reading, the merits of programed texts, ability grouping, individualized instruction, and many other matters, few persons question that the ultimate objective of teaching a child to read is to enable him to read with enough proficiency to comprehend what the writer intended to be understood.

Most teachers also agree that it is one thing to instruct pupils to say words or decode, but quite another to assist them to comprehend or encode. They are in agreement that it is much more difficult to teach the latter skill. Teachers report that a great percentage of their pupils, many of whom are capable decoders, have poorly developed comprehension skills.

The general area of comprehension has stimulated research for some time. For example, Washburne published a report in 1929. Since that time, there has been a continued concern over the matter of comprehension.

In spite of the long history of investigations concerned with reading comprehension, many of the basic problems of this process remain unsolved. Some of them were stated in a report by Davis in 1971 when he proposed several research themes which would respond to the fundamental issues. He indicated, for instance, that research should seek to demonstrate the relationship between several basic variables and comprehension: cultural level of the home, level of oral word knowledge, and level of oral reading fluency. He also believed that investigations should be established to determine the proportion of our youngsters which perform below average in comprehension as a result of inadequate decoding skills, below average knowledge of word meaning, and other factors.

Others have pointed out the fact that research has not resolved the fundamental issues of reading comprehension. The editors of *Reading Research Quarterly* (1974-75) hypothesized that the reason research has not responded to practical needs in the general area of reading was because educational researchers used only traditional psychological research methodologies; they were restricted by traditional concepts of how a study should be designed. The editors referred to this condition as *methodological incarceration*. They went on to say that although many of the studies of these investigators were sound and sophisticated in respect to design and implementation, they generally avoided "...some of the most important questions in the reading arena." The editors were referring to a research methodology which was developed originally by agronomists and used later by psychologists and other behavioral scientists. Basically, this methodology requires that experimental and control groups should be formed, a test administered, a treatment provided the experimental group, the test readministered, and the data analyzed statistically. The editors proclaimed a need for "...research designs and new approaches that allow variables to emerge from the situation being studied, that admit to a lack of answers and even to a lack of questions, that allow for study in a natural setting...."

It is our belief that the Applied Behavior Analysis method is such a new approach, and furthermore, should be considered seriously as an alternate methodology. Initially, we will explain the components of this system and attempt to justify its suitability for investigating educational matters, including reading comprehension. Next, we will review some of the studies conducted by applied behavior analysts in the general area of reading.

Components of Applied Behavior Analysis

In regard to Applied Behavior Analysis, four ingredients comprise this system: direct measurement, daily measurement, individual analysis, and experimental control. While experimental control is a necessary component of all research methodologies, the other three ingredients are unique to this system.

Direct measurement

This simply means that the behavior of interest is measured directly. If the teacher or researcher is concerned with a pupil's ability to answer questions of the who, what, or where variety, he is asked questions of that type. If he wants to assess his ability to answer the prepared questions which follow selections in *Reading for Concepts* (Liddle, 1971), his performance in respect to those questions would be measured. This form of measurement is contrasted to other methods such as achievement tests which might not measure the exact behaviors the pupil was being taught.

Daily measurement

This implies that the topic behavior is measured daily, or at least quite often. If, for instance, the pinpointed behavior is the pupil's ability to answer who, what, and where type questions, he would respond to questions of that form for several days before an instructional technique was scheduled. Those data would continue to be obtained under the same conditions for several days during the period when the intervention was in effect. The experimenter with such data would be able to evaluate confidently the effects of the intervention. He would be able to discern the extent which the measured behavior was modified and the point at which performance was altered. Daily measurement is in contrast to many current research methodologies which recommend that standardized tests be administered at the beginning and end of a school year or before and after an intervention is scheduled.

Individual analysis

The very heart of the Applied Behavior Analysis methodology is that the data from individuals are studied in detail. In fact, some have referred to this methodology as the Single-Subject Method. In an Applied Behavior Analysis investigation, if data are obtained from five students each pupil's performance is analyzed and graphed separately. In so doing, all of the idiosyncratic behavioral patterns become obvious. An inspection of these graphs might reveal that an intervention affected all five in generally the same way, e.g., their performances improved from baseline to intervention, but that each pattern was unique. This emphasis on individual performance makes this approach different from other research systems which analyze and report the data of groups: experimental and control.

Experimental control

In every research study, regardless of the methodology, the researcher attempts, in one way or another, to convince others that the effects on the dependent variable can be attributed only to the manipulated independent variable. This is referred to as establishing a functional relationship between variables. The reason for such effort is extremely important; for if researchers recommend to teachers of reading that they should use method C because it improves certain types of reading, they must be certain that this variable and none other caused the improvement.

The applied behavior analyst would use a form of experimental control to establish functional relationships between independent and dependent variables. He would, as indicated earlier, at least obtain several days of data before an intervention was scheduled and several days of data during the period the intervention was in effect. At other times the researcher would attempt to replicate the condition in effect before the treatment was scheduled and thus arrange what is known as an ABA design. During the first A phase, no treatment is arranged. Then a treatment is scheduled throughout the B condition. In the replication phase, the instructional technique is removed. If the frequency of the behavior changed in the B phase and reverted to its original level in the third phase, a convincing argument can be made that a functional relationship was discovered. Several other replication techniques are available to applied behavior analysts.

Researchers who use other methodologies often use a form of statistical control in contrast to experimental control.

Typically, they subject their research data to a statistical test, then calculate a probability level and hope it will significantly defeat demon chance.

Review of Applied Behavior Analysis studies on reading

Applied behavior analysts have published about 100 studies pertaining to reading since 1962. Although we do not intend to review all that literature, certain of those investigations will be noted. We will also comment on the trends of Applied Behavior Analysis reading investigations.

A majority of the Applied Behavior Analysis studies investigated the effects of various reinforcement contingencies on children's ability to perform specified reading tasks (Staats, et al., 1962; Pikulski, 1971; Raygor, Wark, and Warren, 1966; Whitlock and Bushell, 1967). In those studies the students earned tokens or points for reading accurately and fluently. The tokens were later exchanged for edibles, trinkets, or free time.

In 1970, Lovitt, Schaaf, and Sayre published a report made up of three case studies which broadened the perspective of applied behavior analysts. They reported on the effects of circumstances other than reinforcement contingencies on the reading performances of children. In the first study, they analyzed the reading performance of an eight-year-old boy as he read from three different books. Daily, correct and incorrect rate data were obtained as the pupil read orally. Although the stated grade levels of those books were between 3.5 and 4.5, he read them with equal proficiency. In the second study, they investigated the effects of different prereading tactics. It was concluded that the most effective technique was when the pupil listened to and looked at a story before he read it orally. In the third study, they compared students' reading performances when they read individually and in groups. Their data indicated that the students read more fluently and accurately in individual settings than in group situations.

Since 1970, several applied behavior analysts studied the effects of a variety of instructional variables on aspects of reading. These include studies on shaping (Sidman, 1971), fading (Corey and Shamov, 1972), cueing systems (Massard and Etzel, 1972; Lahey, Weller, and Brown, 1972-73; Knapczyk and Livingston, 1974), feedback (Willis, 1974), and fixed page vs. fixed time assignments (Semb and Semb, 1975).

For the most part these investigations focused on (*aspects of*) decoding; one of the most rudimentary of which was the ability to match. A few studies dealt with matching pictures or whole words with pictures or other graphic representations (e.g., Sidman). Other investigations focused on saying part words and whole words. In the former, the pupils were required to say various word elements such as blends or short vowels (e.g., Massard and Etzel). In the latter studies, pupils were required to say words taken from basal series or from standardized lists (e.g., Staats, et al.). Other studies dealt with reading stories orally (e.g., Corey and Shamov).

Relatively few Applied Behavior Analysis studies have been concerned with comprehension or the meaning of words. As was true of the early efforts of these people when they studied decoding, when they *did* investigate comprehension, they relied heavily on their favorite intervention—reinforcement contingencies. For example, Lahey, McNess, and Brown (1973) reported improved comprehension scores when social praise and pennies were awarded for correct answers to comprehension questions. Similarly, Sidman (1971) and Speller (1974) used a combination of tokens and shaping procedures to facilitate the comprehension of words.

Reading investigations at the Experimental Education Unit

At the Experimental Education Unit (EEU), University of Washington, several studies have been conducted in the area of oral reading. In one of these investigations two measurement systems were compared: the pre-post test method with the direct and daily approach (Eaton and Lovitt, 1972). In another study the effects of various reinforcement contingencies on oral reading performance were assessed (Lovitt, et al., 1971). In yet another investigation, the relationship between phonics instruction and oral reading was studied (Lovitt and Hurlbut, 1974).

At the EEU we have also conducted some studies which focused on various aspects of comprehension. Some of these were descriptive studies in which we assessed comprehension performance as influenced by such factors as readability or grade level, and method of reading, either silent or oral. Other studies were experimental in that some variable was altered in an effort to effect change. In all our investigations, whether descriptive or experimental, we used the Applied Behavior Analysis methodology.

In an effort to explain more clearly the features of this system we will describe five of our studies. Following the presentation of these investigations, we will make some concluding remarks, discuss the limitations of our research, and offer some considerations for future research.

Relationship between readability and describing passages

The ability of seven boys between the ages of 8 and 11 to read and describe stories of five different levels of difficulty was investigated in this study. The pupils read from three levels of the *Lippincott Basic Reading Series* (McCracken and Walcutt, 1970): the level at which they were placed for instruction, a level one year below, and a level one year above their instructional levels. They also read from *Red Badge of Courage* by Stephen Crane (1968) and an article by Ulrich, Wolfe, and Dulaney (1969) in the *Journal of the Experimental Analysis of Behavior* (JEAB). According to the Fry formula, *Red Badge of Courage* was at the seventh grade level and the *JEAB* article was twelfth grade level.

The study was conducted for eight weeks. Each day the students read orally from every book for one minute and then told as much as they could about the passages. The students' oral reading and retelling performances were tape recorded and a portion of these tapes was later transcribed for purposes of analysis.

When these data were analyzed, we learned that the students' oral reading performances varied in accordance with the difficulty level of the materials. Generally, their oral reading rates were satisfactory when they read from the *Lippincott* readers, but they were very low when they read from the *Red Badge of Courage* and the *JEAB*. In reference to their descriptions of the passages, the students were relatively fluent and used approximately the same number of words when they described the *Lippincott* stories. They were markedly less fluent, however, when they told about the selections from the *Red Badge of Courage* and the *JEAB*.

David's performance exemplified the others. One day after he read from the *Lippincott D* reader (his instructional text), he said, "Robbie Rabbit, he fell into a potato patch. He went to this farm and jumped into this potato patch or something and then he got all yukky. So his mom came and she washed his whole body, his ears. She said, 'you have to put on your new Sunday suit.' So he put on his new Sunday suit." On that same day after he read from the *Red Badge of Courage,* his comments were, "They were out of liquid...not much more." When he talked about the *JEAB* article, he said, "Well [it's about] rats and cats and monkeys...ah well, I'm not sure some of the words are right."

Clearly, David was less able to comprehend the latter two books than he was the instructional text. Figure 1 is provided to show the number of words David used to describe passages from the five texts. (These data are the number of words he said prior to being prompted by his teacher to say more.) The data indicate that David generally said twice as many words about the *Lippincott* stories as he did when required to describe the other two texts.

The reading errors of the students were also analyzed by using the Reading Miscue Inventory (Goodman and Burke, 1972). Table 1 summarizes the amount of comprehension loss predicted by this technique. Less than one-fourth of David's reading errors in the *Lippincott* books resulted in a comprehension loss, whereas more than two-thirds of his errors in *Red Badge of Courage* and the *JAEB* resulted in a comprehension loss.

Throughout this study the pupils read from books whose levels ranged from first through twelfth grade. When our data were summarized, they indicated that, generally, the ability to comprehend was related to grade level. Although pupil ability

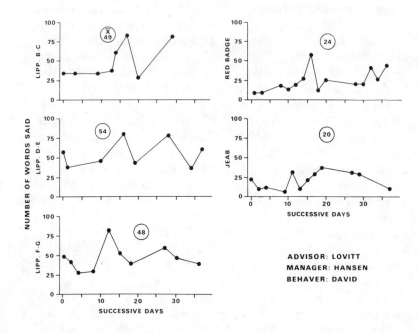

Figure 1. Number of words David used to describe passages from three *Lippincott* texts, *Red Badge of Courage,* and the *JEAB.* Data from every text were not analyzed each day, therefore, the plots occur on various days. For example, data were analyzed on the first day of this experiment for the three *Lippincott* books and the *JEAB.* They were analyzed the next day for only *Lippincott* D-E.

Table 1. Analysis of David's Loss in Comprehension Due to Reading Errors, According to Miscue Inventory.

Book	Number of Samples	Average No. of Errors	Amount Comprehension None	Partial	Loss Total
Lippincott C	9	3.0	77.8	11.1	11.1
Lippincott E	8	3.4	77.8	14.8	7.4
Lippincott G	10	3.0	76.7	3.3	20.0
Red Badge of Courage	14	5.6	32.1	5.1	62.8
JEAB	12	6.0	26.4	8.3	65.3

to comprehend fluctuated from one day to the next within any book, the performances gradually deteriorated as the difficulty of the text increased. The students did not suddenly reach a point at which they could not comprehend. This relationship between grade level and ability to comprehend is pointed out more clearly in the next study.

Relationship between readability and answering comprehension questions

This study was conducted a few years ago with seven learning disabled youngsters at the EEU (Lovitt and Hansen, 1976a). The pupils were between the ages of 8 and 11. The purpose of the project was to place them at their instructional reading levels.

From our previous data, we had observed that when children were placed in readers in which their correct rates were between 45 and 65 words per minute, and their comprehension scores were no less than 50 percent, they were able to progress when only minimal instruction was provided. It was, therefore, the aim of this project to place the pupils in the highest reader in a series in which those conditions were met.

In order to do this, the teacher required them to read orally from eight different books representing grade levels of 1.5 to 6.0 in the *Lippincott* reading series. They were required to read 100-word selections from each book for five consecutive days. They were also required to answer comprehension questions. After each selection was read, the teacher asked six questions: two recall, two sequential, and two inferential. Recall questions pertained to facts in the story. In order to answer the sequential questions, the pupil had to tell what happened before or after a specific event. Inferential questions included the skills of translation, interpretation, and synthesis. The correct and incorrect oral reading rates, and the correct percentage score for answering the comprehension questions were graphed and the teacher studied these data to determine the appropriate reading level for each pupil.

The results for one boy are presented in Figure 2. The top graph indicates Marty's correct and incorrect rates for oral reading in each of the texts; the lower graph shows his correct

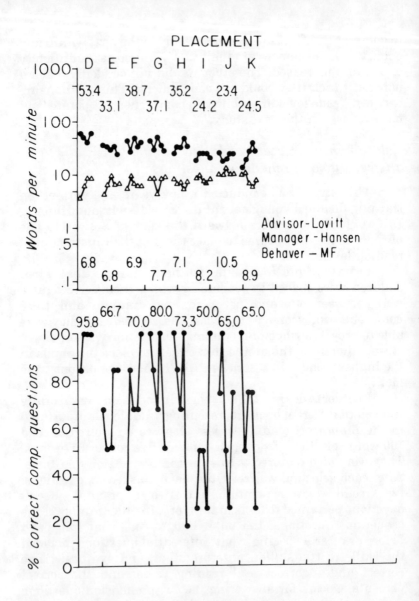

Figure 2. The top graph shows the correct and incorrect rates from *Lippincott* books D through K. The numerals above the data are the correct rate means for each book, the numerals below the data refer to the incorrect rate means. The bottom graph shows the correct percentage of comprehension answers.

percentage for answering comprehension questions. His average comprehension scores ranged from 95.8 percent in the *Lippincott D* book (grade 1.5) to 50.0 percent in the *Lippincott I* text (grade 4). Although the first grade material was generally easier for Marty to comprehend, his percentage scores fluctuated widely in each book: he achieved a 100 percent score in seven of eight books, and a score below 50 percent in seven of eight books. When these data were analyzed he was placed in the *Lippincott D* reader for instruction.

This placement technique was used with 14 boys at the EEU over a two-year period. During the first year, five reading samples were obtained from each text. When these data were analyzed we learned that three samples per text were sufficient to predict an instructional reading level; therefore, the students during the second year were required to read only three samples. The data of the other students were very similar to Marty's: their correct rates and comprehension scores gradually declined and their incorrect reading rates rose as the grade level of the texts increased.

These data strengthen a conclusion pointed out in the first study; when the difficulty of the material increases, the pupil's ability to read and comprehend gradually worsens. This decline, however, is more clearly noted for oral reading than for comprehension, at least for the types of comprehension monitored in this study.

Comparison of oral and silent reading and comprehension

This study with seven learning disabled boys ran for nine months: three academic quarters (Hansen and Lovitt, 1976). Four measures were obtained daily: oral reading rate, answering comprehension questions from orally read material, silent reading rate, and answering questions from material read silently. During the first two quarters, the pupils read orally from a *Lippincott* reader and silently from a *Ginn* text (Clymer and Gates, 1973). The books were matched for difficulty.

Each day the pupils read 500 words orally from the *Lippincott* reader. As they read, the teacher corrected missing and mispronounced words. Next they read silently and wrote answers to 30 comprehension questions. The pupils then read 500 words silently from a *Ginn* reader; then they read silently and wrote answers to 30 comprehension questions. No feedback was provided for silent reading or its accompanying comprehension questions. Three types of comprehension questions were assigned: 10 recall, 10 sequential, and 10 inferential. The types of comprehension questions corresponded to those used in the previous study.

Following a baseline period, during which time neither instruction nor reinforcement contingencies were in effect, the students were divided into two groups. For one group a contingency was scheduled for oral reading rate; for the other group, a contingency was arranged for the comprehension of orally read material.

The contingency for both groups focused on errors. When applied to oral reading, a projected trend was drawn on the student's oral reading graph. If on any day his correct reading rate was lower than that slope, he had to practice the words he mis-read. Each error was embedded in a phrase and he practiced reading those phrases for several minutes. Later, he recited the phrases to the teacher.

When applied to comprehension, a similar projected trend was drawn on the students' comprehension graph. Any day a pupil's comprehension score was below this line, he had to re-do the questions he had answered incorrectly. The students were allowed to refer to their texts to correct recall and sequential questions. In order to demonstrate their proficiency with inferential questions, the students discussed them with the teacher.

A crossover design was used for this research. During the first quarter, the contingency was in effect for one group of pupils on correct reading rate, and for other pupils on comprehension. Throughout the second quarter the contingencies were alternated. For those pupils for whom the contingency was on correct rate, the contingency was now on comprehension. The reverse was true for the other pupils.

The project was continued throughout the spring quarter. During that time, the reading texts were alternated; the students read silently from the *Lippincott* and orally from the *Ginn* text. During that quarter, both contingencies were alternately arranged for all pupils. If, during the first part of the quarter, the contingency was on correct rate for a pupil, the contingency was arranged for comprehension in the second half of the quarter.

Three important findings from this study should be noted. 1) The ability to comprehend was highest on recall and lowest on inferential questions. 2) The ability to comprehend all types of questions improved throughout the year; however, the relative performance on the types remained unchanged. Furthermore, improvement varied according to the question type. In general, recall questions were less amenable to change than either sequential or inferential questions. 3) One instructional technique (requiring pupils to correct their answers to comprehension questions) generally resulted in improved performance on all types of comprehension questions.

Stanley's comprehension data from his oral reading are presented in Figure 3 to illustrate the results of this study. *Base* refers to those conditions during which no error contingencies were in effect. *Oral* means that Stanley was required to correct his oral reading errors. During the two *Comp* conditions Stanley corrected his answers to comprehension questions if his performance failed to meet a specified minimum criteria.

These data indicated that the pupil's ability to answer factual questions was consistently superior to that of answering sequential or inferential questions. With the exception of one Comp condition, Stanley was less able to answer inferential questions than other types of questions. These data also revealed a general improvement in his ability to answer all three types of questions from the beginning to the end of the year.

The direct effects of the interventions on Stanley's comprehension performance are unclear. When drill was first arranged for oral reading errors, his performance improved on all types of questions. In contrast, his comprehension scores decreased on all three measures the second time drill was arranged for oral reading errors. When Stanley was initially required to correct his answers to comprehension questions, direct effects were noted on only his accuracy for answering inferential questions. During the final phase of the study, when comprehension drill was again instituted, his performance improved on all three comprehension measures.

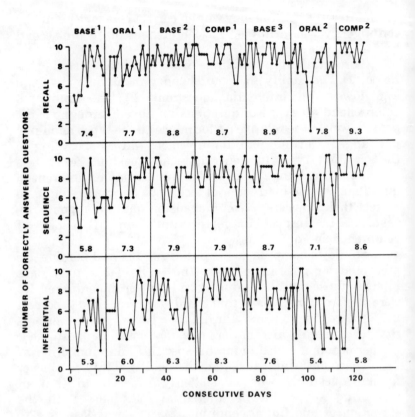

Figure 3. The number of correctly answered comprehension questions throughout the seven phases of the study. The numbers below the data in each phase indicate the means.

Arranging contingent skipping and drilling

This study was based on the second investigation reported here and was conducted with seven intermediate aged boys at the EEU. At the beginning of the study each student was assigned to the highest book in which his correct rate was between 45 and 65 words per minute; his incorrect rate, between 4 and 8 words per minute; and his comprehension score, above 50 percent.

Daily, each student orally read a selection of 500 words and answered several comprehension questions (Lovitt and Hansen, 1976b). Once again, we used the *Lippincott* reading series. The students who read from the first to third grade readers were given 30 questions: 10 recall, 10 sequential, and 10 inferential. The students who read from the fourth to sixth grade books were given 20 questions: 5 recall, 5 sequential, 5 inferential, and 5 vocabulary. The pupils read the questions silently and wrote their answers. Short answers were required for the recall, sequential, and inferential questions. A multiple choice format was used for the vocabulary questions.

An ABA design was used in this investigation. During the baseline condition, the students received minimal feedback in respect to their efforts. This condition lasted for seven days.

In the second condition, skipping and drilling were introduced. Each student was informed that he would be allowed to skip (not read) one-fourth of his text, if on any day his oral reading and comprehension performances exceeded his average baseline scores by 25 percent.

If a pupil did not skip for four days, drill procedures were instituted. Three types of drill were arranged. If a student's correct rate did not exceed his average baseline rate by 25 percent, he was required to read orally several 100-word passages from his daily assignment until his performance met this criterion. The second type of drill was scheduled if a student's incorrect rate wasn't 25 percent lower than the average baseline rate. When this form of drill was arranged, the pupil practiced phrases in which his error words were embedded. The third type of drill was employed if a student didn't answer 25 percent more comprehension questions than he had during the baseline phase. When this drill was used, the student was required to re-do his incorrect answers. These procedures continued each day until the student skipped.

During the last two weeks of the quarter, the baseline procedures were reestablished. The students read orally and answered questions as they had before, but the skipping and drilling provisions were not in effect.

Throughout the baseline condition the average oral correct and incorrect rates for the group were 50.7 and 3.1 words per minute. During the skip and drill condition, the average correct and incorrect rates were 60.0 and 2.9 words per

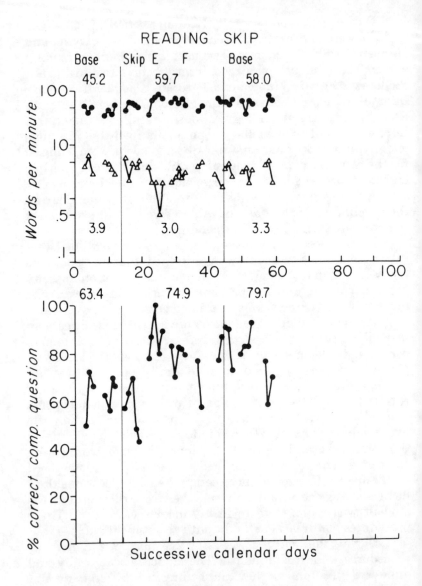

Figure 4. The data in the top graph are the daily correct and incorrect rates throughout the three phases of the project. The numbers above and below the data are the means for those conditions. The bottom graph shows the correct percentages for answering the comprehension questions.

minute. When these data were compared with the baseline scores it was noted that the correct rates for all students improved and the incorrect rates for four students improved.

Meanwhile, the average comprehension score during the first phrase was 65.9, and 77.8 percent during the second condition. The comprehension scores of all pupils improved when the skipping and drilling procedures were scheduled. Throughout the second condition, the pupils skipped 33 times, an average of .24 skips per day.

When the skip and drill intervention was removed in the third phase, the performances of the students were generally maintained. In fact, the average oral reading and comprehension scores of some students improved during this condition.

Following this study, we conducted two investigations in order to determine the relative effects of skipping and drilling. We arranged only the skipping provision with some students and only the drilling procedures with others. These data did not clearly indicate the relative effects of either component.

Figure 4 is included to show Marty's daily oral reading and comprehension scores. All three aspects of his performance were influenced by the skipping and drilling interventions.

Interventions for two types of comprehension

This study was conducted for about nine weeks and is still in progress. Four learning disabled youngsters were initially involved; they ranged in age from 8 to 11.

Each day the pupils read silently a different story in the *Reading for Concepts* series. These stories are about 125 to 150 words in length. As the pupils read they could request assistance for unknown words. The teacher timed each reading and graphed their words per minute rates.

After they read the story, the students were asked to tell about what they read. While they described the events, the teacher tallied the number of facts they related. (Each new piece of information was counted as a fact.) If the fact pertained to the story it was counted as correct; if not, it was counted as incorrect. (Most of these situations were tape recorded, thus the teacher later verified her tallies with the tape.) The pupils were allowed to tell about the story as long as they wanted. When they first hesitated, the teacher asked them to tell more. A second request to provide more information was given before the session ended. The teacher timed these descriptions. Later, she calculated and graphed the rates of saying facts correctly and incorrectly.

When the students finished describing the story, they were asked to answer the seven comprehension questions which followed every story. They were required to read the questions silently and write their answers. The teacher timed the students from the time they began reading the questions until they responded to the final question. When they finished, the teacher checked each answer as either correct or incorrect. She then calculated and graphed the number of correct answers and the rates for correctly and incorrectly answering the questions.

During the baseline phase, the pupils received little feedback and no instruction. If they asked about their scores, they were given that information, but there were few inquiries of this type.

Throughout the second phase, three interventions were simultaneously arranged. For one, the story was previewed before the pupils read it. They were asked to read the title and, from that, infer what the story was about. If their response was accurate, the session proceeded, if not, they were told the subject matter of the story. For the second intervention, the seven comprehension questions were previewed. After the students read the story silently, they were required to read each question orally. After a question was read, the teacher asked the pupils to indicate the strategy they would use to answer it. They would explain, for example, that a letter should be circled, a blank filled, or whatever. This approach was followed for each of the seven questions, since several response strategies were required. Following this, they silently read the questions and wrote their answers just as they had in the first phase. After they answered the questions, the third intervention was scheduled. Now, they received feedback on each of the questions; they were told whether their answers were correct or incorrect. If an answer was incorrect they were told the correct response and the strategy for arriving at the answer.

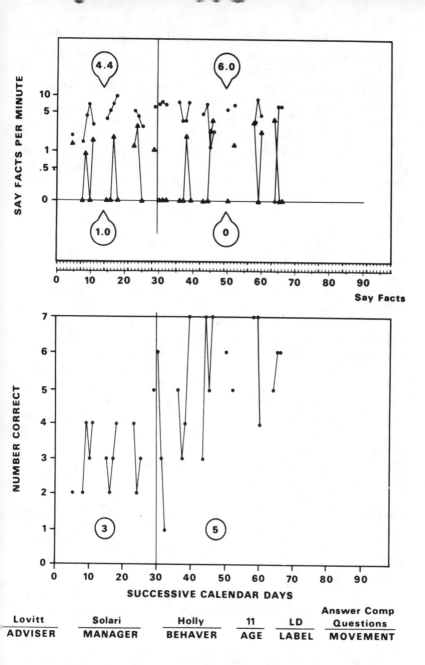

Figure 5. The data in the top graph pertain to correct and incorrectly said facts about each story. The numbers above and below the data are the median correct and incorrect rates. The data in the bottom graph show the number of correctly answered comprehension questions.

In general, we were encouraged by the effects of these interventions. We were particularly pleased with Holly's performance. During the baseline phase she answered about three questions correctly each day. Her scores ranged from two to four. Throughout the second phase her median score was five correct, the scores ranged from one to seven. On five days she answered all the questions correctly.

Holly also improved somewhat in her ability to say facts. Her median correct rate throughout the baseline phase was 4.4 facts per minute and in the second phase that rate was 6.0 per minute. On some days she told about as many facts as was possible about a story. Her performances are shown in Figure 5.

Throughout this study, the performances of three other pupils also improved. One boy's median number of correct answers in the baseline phase was two. During the second phase, when the same intervention as described earlier was in effect, his median number of correct answers was four.

It was necessary to schedule another intervention for two boys in our study, since the first technique did not alter their performances. We extended the manner in which the seven questions were previewed for one boy. Since he consistently erred on the three fill-in-the-blanks questions, he was required to locate the answer to those questions in the story. He did not, however, write the answers at that time. After he located the answers to the three fill-in-the-blanks questions he read all seven of them silently and then wrote his answers. During the first two phases of the project his median number of correct answers was one; it was three during the third phase.

Self-charting was used as an intervention in the third phase for the other boy. During this period, he plotted his own scores for the seven comprehension questions immediately following his performance. His median score for the first two phases was three. It rose to five in the third phase.

Discussion

In this chapter, the Applied Behavior Analysis methodology was presented as an alternative strategy for studying aspects of reading, particularly reading comprehension. In the first part of the paper the characteristics of this method were listed, then five studies which featured those components were described.

In those studies, we measured several aspects of comprehension. In the first, we measured the number of words said by students after they read stories of differing levels of difficulty. In the fifth study, we also required the pupils to describe stories they had read; correct and incorrectly said facts were counted in that investigation.

In Study 2 we asked the pupils six questions per passage. These questions were of three types: recall, sequential, and inferential. All the questions required oral responses. In the third study the students were required to answer 30 questions from their silent reading and 30 from their oral reading. These questions were the same types as those used in Study 2. The students were required to read these questions, however, and respond in writing.

In the fourth study, the questions were the same types as those in Studies 2 and 3. Furthermore, the pupils read the questions and wrote their answers in Study 4 just as they had in Study 3. One difference between the third and fourth studies was that the pupils in the latter study who read from the fourth to sixth grade texts answered 20 questions each day of four types: recall, sequential, inferential, and vocabulary. In the fifth study, the pupils were required to read seven questions which accompanied each story and write their responses, in addition to telling about each story.

In summary, we presented the material to the pupils visually and orally and we required them to respond orally or in writing. Several types of questions were asked: recall, sequential, inferential, vocabulary, and the many types used in the *Reading for Concepts* book.

The easiest questions seemed to be of the recall type. The hardest questions appeared to be the sequential and inferential types. Our children also experienced great difficulties with some of the questions in the *Reading for Concepts* text, particularly those which required the children to fill in a blank.

We used a variety of methods to modify various aspects of comprehension. In the fourth study we used contingent skipping and drilling, whereas in the third study we used contingent drilling. In the fifth study we combined several interventions: previewing the story, previewing the questions, and providing feedback for answering the written questions. Most of these techniques were moderately effective.

There are some decided limitations with our research that others should consider. For one thing, most of our studies were conducted with few students: in many instances there were seven boys. We must hasten to add, however, that although there were few pupils in our studies we obtained a great deal of data in respect to their performances. In some of the studies, we monitored the pupils' performances daily for nearly a year.

Other limitations have to do with the type of population we used. Our youngsters were all handicapped, particularly in the area of reading. They were between the ages of 8 and 11, and all except one were boys.

There were other methodological problems with some of the studies. For example, in the fifth study, three interventions were used simultaneously. Although effects were noted in that project, it is impossible to attribute them to any one variable. Our initial intent was to produce effects. Later, we intend to analyze discrete components. In the fourth study we used two interventions simultaneously: skipping and drilling. Although we attempted to analyze those components in subsequent research, our efforts were not successful.

In the introduction of this paper we referred to an editorial in the *Reading Research Quarterly* which called for new research methodologies to focus on the problems of reading. We contend that the Applied Behavior Analysis system is such a methodology. In the following issue of the *Reading Research Quarterly,* the editors continued to criticize the current state of reading research, and in an editorial they recommended that the people "...involved with the teaching of reading need to become involved in the development of new research methodologies." They warned that unless current teaching practices are evaluated in the classrooms "...we will continue to select programs on the basis of the newest fad or those that make the greatest promises" (1975-76).We maintain that the Applied Behavior Analysis system certainly responds to this plea.

When this system is used practitioners and researchers can investigate current reading problems in classrooms or other places where reading ordinarily occurs. Indeed, some of the features of the studies reported here have been replicated in public school classrooms, even though the research took place in an experimental setting. For example, our research with placement (Study 2) and our Skip program (Study 4) are used by dozens of special and regular education teachers in the Northwest and in many other parts of the country.

In our research we have used common materials and techniques. In our current research (Study 5) we used questions from a commercially developed program. We have used commercial textbooks in all our research, although we generally wrote our own questions. We have used not only the *Reading for Concepts* series but the *Lippincott* and *Ginn* series. Certainly these are not esoteric materials. Likewise, the techniques we have investigated are those commonly used in many classrooms throughout the nation. Our intent in these studies has been to analyze these well known procedures in order to ascertain whether or not they affect student performance.

One of the reasons the Applied Behavior Analysis system can be used by researchers and practitioners trained in this methodology is that they use common procedures; they speak the same language. Since the basic ingredients of the system can be used equally satisfactorily by knowledgeable teachers and researchers, it should intensify the rapport between the two groups. The manner in which behaviors are defined and pinpointed is the same. The method for gathering and charting data is essentially the same. Research designs or teaching patterns are alike for the two groups. The techniques for analyzing the data from the two sectors are identical.

This uniform system for both laborers should do much to unify and coordinate their efforts, but there are still other shared benefits. Because the language and the methodological components are common to both groups, an individual from one group can easily move over to the other. If a teacher, for example, has been gathering data from her pupils using these procedures, she will have little trouble transferring those techniques to a research setting. The reverse movement would be just as expeditious.

It would be presumptuous of us if we said, in response to the editorials in *Reading Research Quarterly,* that we have found the illusive methodology and, therefore, the search for alternatives can be abandoned. We intend to seek useful components from other methodologies and to improve our method so that more issues can be investigated. We do, however, recommend that others—researchers and teachers— try to use the Applied Behavior Analysis method in their laboratories and classrooms to investigate the problems in reading that have for so long baffled us.

A great deal of work remains to be done, irrespective of the chosen methodology. Considerable effort should be expended in efforts to identify the elements which may comprise comprehension. To date, a number of behaviors have been listed which might make up the process of comprehension, but these elements and taxonomies are based largely on rhetoric. In this regard we have been pleased with the expressive measures of comprehension we have used: say words and facts.

Some interesting studies could be arranged to assess the relative differences of input and output channels. Research might be arranged to study pupil performance when they listen to or read the questions. Likewise, studies might evaluate effects of writing the answers or verbalizing the answers.

Several investigations must also be arranged to locate more effective ways to modify students' abilities to comprehend what they read. There has been a great deal more talk about how to effect change than research to demonstrate those effects. In this regard we have been moderately pleased with some of the interventions we have used. For example, we have been satisfied when we used a reinforcement contingency in combination with another technique in our clinical and research situations. Paradoxically, we have not studied systematically reinforcement contingencies, those techniques which are often believed to be synonymous with our methodology. We intend to rectify that shortcoming in the future.

REFERENCES

Clymer, T., and Gates, D. *Ginn 360 reading series.* Lexington, Massachusetts: Ginn and Company, 1973.

Corey, J.R., and Shamov, J. Effects of fading on the acquisition and retention of oral reading. *Journal of Applied Behavior Analysis,* 1972, *5*, 311-315.

Crane, S. *Red Badge of Courage.* New York: Golden Press, 1968.

Davis, F.B. (Ed.) *The literature of research in reading with emphasis on models.* Graduate School of Education, Rutgers—The State University, New Brunswick, New Jersey, 1971.

Eaton, M., and Lovitt, T.C. Achievement tests vs. direct and daily measurement. In G. Semb (Ed.), *Behavior analysis and education*—1972. Lawrence, Kansas: University of Kansas Press, 1972, 78-87.

Goodman, Y.M., and Burke, C.L. *Reading miscue inventory kit: Procedure for diagnosis and evaluation.* New York: The Macmillan Co., 1972.

Hansen, C.L., and Lovitt, T.C. The relationship between question type and mode of reading on the ability to comprehend. *Journal of Special Education*, 1976, *10*, 53-60.

Knapczyk, D.R., and Livingston, G. The effect of prompting question-asking upon on-task behavior and reading comprehension. *Journal of Applied Behavior Analysis*, 1974, *7*, 115-121.

Lahey, B.B.; McNess, M.P.; and Brown, C.C. Modification of deficits in reading for comprehension. *Journal of Applied Behavior Analysis*, 1973, *6*, 475-480.

Lahey, B.B.; Weller, D.R.; and Brown, W.R. The behavior analysis approach to reading: Phonic discriminations. *Journal of Reading Behavior*, 1972-73, *5*, 200-206.

Liddle, W. *Reading for concepts reading series: Book A.* New York: McGraw Hill, 1971.

Lovitt, T.C.; Eaton, M.; Kirkwood, M.E.; and Pelander, J. Effects of Various reinforcement contingencies on oral reading rate. In E.A. Ramp and B. L. Hopkins (Eds.), *A new direction for education: Behavior analysis.* Lawrence, Kansas: University of Kansas Press, 1971, 54-71.

Lovitt, T.C., and Hansen, C.L. Round one—placing the child in the right reader. *Journal of Learning Disabilities*, 1976a, *9*, 347-353.

Lovitt, T.C., and Hansen, C.L. The use of contingent skipping and drilling to improve oral reading and comprehension. *Journal of Learning Disabilities*, 1976b, *9*, 481-487.

Lovitt, T.C., and Hurlbut, M. Using behavior-analysis techniques to assess the relationship between phonics instruction and oral reading. *Journal of Special Education*, 1974, *8*, 57-72.

Lovitt, T.C.; Schaaf, M.; and Sayre, E. The use of direct and continuous measurement to evaluate reading materials and pupil performance. *Focus on Exceptional Children*, 1970, *2*, 1-11.

Massard, V.I., and Etzel, B.C. Acquisition of phonetic sounds by pre-school children. I. Effects of response and reinforcement frequency. II. Effects of tactile differences in discriminative stimuli. In G. Semb (Ed.), *Behavior analysis and education*—1972. Lawrence, Kansas: University of Kansas Press, 1972, pp. 88-111.

McCracken, G., and Walcutt, G.C., *Lippincott basic reading.* New York: J.B. Lippincott, 1970.

Methodological incarcertation. *Reading Research Quarterly,* 1974-75, *10*, 549-552.

Pikulski, J.J. Candy, word recognition, and the "disadvantaged." *Reading Teacher*, 1971, *25*, 243-246.

Practitioners should play a role in developing new methodologies. *Reading Research Quarterly,* 1975-76, *11,* 123-125.

Raygor, A.L.; Wark, D.M.; and Warren, A.D. Operant conditioning of reading rate: The effect of a secondary reinforcer. *Journal of Reading,* 1966, *9,* 147-156.

Semb, G., and Semb, S. A comparison of fixed-page and fixed-time reading assignments in elementary school children. In E. Ramp and G. Semb (Eds.), *Behavior analysis: Areas of research and application.* Englewood Cliffs, New Jersey: Prentice-Hall, 1975, 233-243.

Sidman, M. Reading and auditory-visual equivalences. *Journal of Speech and Hearing Research,* 1971, *14,* 5-13.

Speller, P. Reading comprehension: An experimental analysis. Paper presented at *Fifth Annual Conference on Behavior Analysis in Education,* Kansas City, Missouri, October, 1974.

Staats, A.W.; Staats, C.K.; Schutz, R.E.; and Wolf, M.M. The conditioning of textual responses using "extrinsic" reinforcers. *Journal of the Experimental Analysis of Behavior,* 1962, *5,* 33-40.

Ulrich, R.; Wolfe, M.; and Dulaney, S. Punishment of shock induced aggression. *Journal of the Experimental Analysis of Behavior,* 1969, *12,* 1009-1015.

Washburne, J.N. The use of questions in social science material. *Journal of Educational Psychology,* 1929, *20,* 321-359.

Whitlock, C.; and Bushell, D. Some effects of "back-up" reinforcers on reading behavior. *Journal of Experimental Child Psychology,* 1967, *5,* 50-57.

Willis, J. Effects of systematic feedback and self-charting on a remedial tutorial program in reading. *Journal of Experimental Education,* 1974, *42,* 83-85.

Comments on
An Applied Behavior Analysis Approach
to Reading Comprehension

Lawrence T. Frase

Applied focus

Applied Behavior Analysis, as characterized by Hansen and Lovitt, deals with real life tasks. This contrasts with many research studies, in which the focus of experimentation, the instructional task, often seems constructed to make a theoretical point rather than to reflect upon the processes involved in day to day reading activities. Research can be criticized for neglecting to rationalize more carefully the selection of the problems that it tries to solve. It is ironic when reading research solves problems for which there is no counterpart in the real world.

But there are problems, in this regard, for behavior analysis, too. Perhaps the applied focus is even more important an issue for behavior analysis since it attempts to deal with socially important changes in behavior. Consider attempts to modify reading comprehension. Should behavior modification focus on student performance on test items that someone else has called "comprehension," or should it ask deeper questions about the repertoire of behaviors that a person needs in order to read documents that have functional significance? For instance, should application concern itself with shaping performance on interpretation or inference test items, or should it more explicitly rationalize the contents and operations that will be required to read a sign, to fill out a simple form, to read charts of chemical properties to be used in next semester's work?

Perhaps this is a curriculum question, better left to those who do curriculum planning. But it has its narrower focus, too. I am not sure that comprehension test items, as now conceived, provide a proper focus for the application of behavioral analysis. Behavior analyzers should be wary of preformed conceptions of comprehension. Although they give focus to the behaviors to be shaped, they provide little information about the importance of these behaviors in real life, nor do they clarify the conceptual analysis of comprehension. Clarifying this analysis is important. If we were to gather more systematic data on the kinds of reading activities in which people must engage at various points in life, we might evolve a somewhat different conception of what is and is not important reading behavior.

Behavior analysis

The question of the kinds of behaviors that should be reinforced is related to the problem of applied focus. But there is a narrower issue that concerns the level at which performance should be discussed. An obvious difference between Hansen and Lovitt's approach and mine lies in our propensities for talking about processes like encoding, rehearsal, retrieval, and so on. The authors avoid this terminology, although there are things like recall, sequence, and interpretation questions in their paper. Differences in the processes elicited by those questions are implied. I talk about the reinforcement of classroom behaviors about as much as Hansen and Lovitt talk about cognitive operations. And so, although we discuss the effects of similar things, like questions, our styles differ.

But suppose we look at the research literature relating to behavior analyses. In this literature, one is hard put to find studies on the reinforcement of higher mental processes, such as comprehension. As Hansen and Lovitt point out, this research is just beginning. One reason for this lack of research may be the tendency to emphasize behavior more than the analysis that goes into what applied behavior analysts do. Don't get me wrong. I have considerable respect for the potential of behavior analysis for the modification of human behavior. But I think that the tendency to steer clear of conjectures about covert processing operations is not in the best interest of the field. In point of fact, good behavior analysts are often good hypothesizers about process, if not heavy theorizers.

The approach of behavior analysis, if I understand it correctly, suggests that performance in a task can be analyzed into small easily attainable repertoires of behavior. This is the heart of the matter. Do performances on interpretation and sequence test items represent easily attainable repertoires of behavior? I think not, and I am moved to the conclusion that behavioral analysts should not avoid talking about process when it comes to comprehension. Interesting behaviors, like sequencing and translation, involve complex chains of covert activities that should be made explicit. This does not mean that process language should supersede behavioral data. On the contrary, overt acts by readers should provide the grist for monitoring interventions. But I am arguing for a more explicit discussion of the covert behaviors that overt performance reflects.

Why is it important to talk about what a reader does covertly? Because we might then be able to discern reasonable behavioral indicants that can become the focus for intervening in complex thought processes. This seems to me a central problem for behavior analysis, since verbal behavior entails many covert processes. What is being reinforced is not the behaviors observed, but the behaviors of which overt responses are a weak shadow.

An example

Let's consider, briefly, what could be involved in answering a comprehension test item like the ones employed by Hansen and Lovitt. Assume that a text includes, among others, the following two sentences. "Jim belongs to the Boy Scouts. The scouts in Jim's troop come from poor families." Question: Jim comes from a poor family. True or false?

Assume, further, that this question is asked after a child has read the text. Several component stages are involved in answering this question. Starting with the processes during reading, one stage required for correct solution (aside from random correct answers due to guessing) is that the reader *encode* the information from the two sentences. The information must be represented in some way in memory. This might also entail maintenance operation, like *rehearsal* (a second stage).

A third stage, at the time of testing, involves *retrieval* of the appropriate information about each sentence. People remember many things that they are sometimes unable to retrieve upon demand. Some encoding activities may result in more effective retrieval, so my stages of comprehension are not entirely independent.

A fourth stage involves *relating* the two sentences to each other. Here, processing activities involve difficult class inclusion relations, and they may require extensive additional analysis by the instructional developer. For instance, humans are likely to overgeneralize verbal relations that are stated in a text. If the second sentence in the previous example were, "Some of the scouts in Jim's troop come from poor families.", we know that many subjects would conclude that Jim came from a poor family, although the relations asserted in the text do not logically allow that conclusion.

If our procedure is an instructional one, in which we expose readers to test items after reading and then go on to new passages, we make the assumption that all four processes (encoding, rehearsal, retrieval, and relation) will occur with greater frequency on later passages as a consequence of the questions seen about earlier passages. Yet this chain of operation, if it is real, is left pretty much to the reader.

Furthermore, we have added another complexity by expecting performance to be altered on new passages. The content of consecutive passages changes, hence the subject must engage in the activities of encoding, rehearsal, retrieval, and relation in the presence of changed cues. Performance seems rather loosely controlled with this much variability in the instructional environment. Consider the rat, trained to press a bar for food at the end of a runway. When transferred to a T-maze it may be some time before the rat learns to correctly turn right or left, although the chain of bar-pressing behaviors, previously shaped, is left intact. New cues are confusing, although previously learned skills may still be available.

There are ways in which intervention might be made more precise. For instance, we might remove the retrieval and relation demands, concentrating first on encoding. This could be done by having subjects engage in overt behaviors *with the text present*. These behaviors might include oral reading, translating sentences into their own words, and so on. Oral reading would be an indicant of what I have called encoding. It is interesting to note that oral reading was especially effective in Hansen's project. Perhaps the constraint to speak the text out loud ensures minimal encoding of all the text.

A second stage would entail relating the sentences to each other with the text present, for instance, answering questions of the form "Was Jim poor?" and so on.

A third stage would consist of introducing rehearsal demands, like turning the page over and reciting the last sentence that was read out loud. Immediate review might be permitted at this stage to provide feedback to the reader.

A fourth stage consists of increasing these memory demands so that retrieval from long term memory becomes relevant for successful performance. Performance on recall questions, after reading the entire passage, might be useful here as a datum.

A fifth stage would begin to involve retrieval and the relation of information in the head. Test items like "Did Jim come from a poor family?" would be appropriate. Note that we have elaborated five previous stages of training and have only now arrived at our original comprehension test item.

Sixth, we might now begin to introduce minimal changes in text content, and in later stages quite different content could be introduced.

The kind of instructional program that I have in mind involves several cycles, each focusing on behaviors that reflect encoding, rehearsal, retrieval, and relation activities. These cycles would progress from simple tasks (two or three sentences) to more complex tasks (several sentences containing different relations).

The first cycle might go as follows:

1. Encoding—read sentences aloud
2. Rehearsal—close eyes and repeat sentence
3. Retrieval—repeat sentence aloud at later time (text absent)
4. Relation—judge implication from two sentences
5. Retrieval and relation—judge implication from two sentences at later time (text absent)

The first cycle would employ a short two sentence passage. The second cycle would entail the same activities but more sentences. Subsequent cycles might begin to vanish the overt response requirements for encoding, and later cycles would increase the number and type of relations in the sentences.

Some aspects of my example are overdrawn. For instance, we would not expect a reader to repeat, verbatim, many sentences from a text, and paraphrases and so on might be acceptable performance. But the example serves to make the point that explicit lists of processing activities, hypothetical though they may be, can suggest a rationale for interventions.

I have suggested several component stages to shaping reading behaviors, but there remain many unexplored issues. For instance, it would be desirable to clarify classes of discriminative stimuli, the stimuli that are to provide the occasion for encoding, retrieval, rehearsal, and relation activities. Can our conception of stimuli, nominal stimuli, be transferred directly to our conception of them as internalized verbal behavior? We need to consider how the form of encoding alters internal representation. If so, the analysis of reinforcement in later stages of learning may have little apparent relation to the text material.

How should we use reinforcement principles? What is the effective reinforcer in reading? Should we minimize incorrect responses, or should we elicit them, allowing the reader to make errors so that common incorrect responses can be discriminated from correct ones? How difficult should the problems be? If performance demands are too difficult, learning may become a punishing experience.

Summary

My point, in all of this, is to suggest that we need to consider more explicitly the molecular characteristics of comprehension tasks in order to make intelligent decisions about intervention techniques. On the view that I've presented, categories of test items like knowledge, application, synthesis, and so on provide an insufficient focus for instruction in comprehension. Instructional programs, written from the standpoint of behavioral analysis, try to shape specific components of comprehension, such as the comprehension of if-then relations. Talking about the analysis of the small steps and sequences that compose these larger comprehension performances, although it may have a cognitive ring, can provide a more effective base for behavioral interventions and for research. Hearing people with an applied interest talk more about these molecular processes might help researchers to focus their own work on relevant problems.

Design for Developing
Comprehension Skills

Wayne Otto

The title of this volume, *Cognition, Curriculum, and Comprehension*, reveals no inclinations, preferences, or biases. And so it should be, for books of this sort are meant to examine and explore and, perhaps, to discover. On the other hand, the title of this chapter, "Design for Developing Comprehension Skills," reveals inclinations, preferences, and biases. And so it should be, for the separate chapters ought to get the issues out where they can be examined. Be assured that if one of the issues is whether we should take a holistic or a subskill development approach to the development of reading comprehension, then this paper is addressed to that issue. Be assured, too, that there will be no attempt in this paper to present both sides of the issue. This paper deals with the skill development side.

I am convinced that the most straightforward way to get at the development of reading comprehension is through the development of subskills. Now let me qualify that a bit: The most straightforward way to get on with the *teaching* of reading comprehension is by teaching the important subskills. I don't mean to hide behind semantics, but I do believe that we need some special stipulations when we talk about *teaching* comprehension that we might not need when we talk about developing comprehension. On the first hand, the process would be directed, systematic, and explicit; whereas, on the second hand, the process would be more free-flowing and opportunistic. Nevertheless, if you will permit me to reach for a metaphor, I think that each hand should know what the other is doing and, if we use a bit of common sense, that both hands can be joined in common endeavor. But I'll return to this point a bit later. The point I want to stress now is that this paper is about the *teaching* of the subskills of comprehension.

As principal investigator for one of the projects at the Wisconsin Research and Development Center for Cognitive Learning, a good share of my effort has been devoted to developing the Wisconsin Design for Reading Skill Development. And a good share of the project effort, particularly in the last three or four years, has been devoted to the Comprehension component of the Design. I'd like to do two things in this paper: I'd like to tell you where we are with the Comprehension component, and I'd like to tell you how we got there. And that, I'm sure you will see, has very much to do with the *teaching* of comprehension *skills*.

First, I shall examine very briefly the rationale for a skill development approach; and then, I'll describe a conception of research and development that we've evolved in our work. And, finally, I'll tell you where we are with the Comprehension element of the Design. So . . . first I'll tell you how we got there, and then I'll tell you where we are.

Rationale for skills orientation

I will not develop an elaborate rationale for taking a skill-centered approach to the development of reading comprehension. The battle between the supporters of the holistic and the subskills approaches will probably continue to be fought in seminars and symposia for as long as human beings continue to have difficulty comprehending the printed messages of other human beings. There are intelligent, sincere, reasonable people on both sides. And, so long as good people are concerned about the development of reading comprehension, I'm confident not only that kids will learn but also that their learning will become more efficient as a result of the controversy. Controversy keeps us on our toes.

To be totally frank—and to risk persecution for heresy to my cause—I must say that sometimes I find myself on either side of the issue. Certainly kids "comprehend" long before they've been taught a single skill. And certainly they can be helped to comprehend a given passage without being taught any specific "skills." I like to think that when we teach skills we *sharpen* critical aspects of the comprehension process. But we can attempt to strike a balance later. The question here is: Why Skills?

To me, the answer is clear and it is inescapable: Because we need them in order to focus instruction. Or individualize instruction...or differentiate instruction...whatever terminology we use to describe a process whereby we (a) decide what we want learners to know, (b) find out what individuals do and do not know, and (c) teach individuals—probably with other individuals who have the same need—what they don't already know. Anyone who rejects the notion of focused instruction rejects skills.

One would, I suppose, expect the converse: Anyone who rejects skills rejects the notion of focused instruction. Nevertheless, to my amazement, I find that many people who write reading methods texts say little or nothing specific about skills; yet they feel free to rhapsodize about individualization and to admonish their readers to take a diagnostic approach in their teaching. Seems like telling people to shoot at the target without having the foggiest notion what or where the target is. The price we pay for focused instruction is skills. Without them, diagnosis is meaningless and individualization is an empty slogan.

The question then is whether the *price* is right. I truly believe that this question is closer to the hearts of teachers than the holistic versus subskills issue we identified earlier. Lots of teachers who believe in skills and recognize the benefits of teaching them hold back because they claim to be wary of "teaching skills in isolation." If the price of efficient focused teaching were indeed skills in isolation, then the price would be too high. It is utter nonsense to teach skills for their own sake. Other teachers who believe in skills cheerfully do the extra planning and record keeping—which is the true price of a skill-centered approach to teaching comprehension—because they feel the price *is* right. And they don't worry about skills in isolation because they don't teach them that way.

Why skills? Because we *need* them. We need them to sharpen the focus of our teaching. But we must choose them sensibly and we must keep them in perspective.

Even a cursory search of the literature will yield dozens of lists of comprehension skills. Every basal reading and every curriculum guide will yield still another. But examine most of them closely and you have reason to hold skill lists in low esteem. The skills listed tend to be so general or so specific that they can serve no function in teaching or learning, more often than not the essential *literal* aspects of comprehension are neglected in favor of the more esoteric interpretive and creative aspects, and there seems to be no concern whatever for whether the skills are in fact teachable. If I thought that was the best we could do, I would want to cast the first stone to put skill lists and skill listers out of their misery.

I believe we can do better. We can extrapolate from the literature and from the experiences of successful teachers to identify skills that can and should be taught; then we can follow up with research to examine the outcomes of such efforts.

Once we concern ourselves with sensibly chosen skills—skills that are both important and teachable—I think there will be less tendency to view them or to teach them in isolation. I see skills and the teaching of skills as the *substance* and the *means* for sharpening the process of developing reading comprehension. Skills must be identified, taught, and applied in context. In perspective skills can be the vehicle for moving children to independence in their reading comprehension. Without the explicit focus of skills, I'm afraid we abandon too many learners while they are still dependent on the crutches of "classroom questions," "directed reading activities," and other alternatives to explicit skill development. The alternatives, too, need perspective.

My rationale for skills is mainly pragmatic. In my view, if we are going to *teach* comprehension, then we must teach the skills of comprehending. My position embodies my bias, and I present it primarily as an hypothesis, as yet largely untested.

Substantial theoretical support for the skills position—or, perhaps more properly, a skills in perspective position—has been offered by Samuels (1976) in a carefully conceived paper titled "Hierarchical Subskills in the Reading Acquisition Process." In that paper he examined the controversy between holistic and part methods of instruction, compared speech and reading acquisition, analyzed what is presently known about skill hierarchies in reading, and offered some implications for reading instruction. The implications are succinctly stated and they are completely relevant in the present context, so the rather lengthy quote from Samuels is offered in further defense of skills in perspective.

A major point made by critics of the subskill approach is that fractionating the reading process interferes with the essential characteristic of reading, which is comprehension. This point is well taken. Many teachers who use the subskill approach have lost sight of the fact that the subskill approach is simply a means to an end. What has happened in many classrooms is that goal displacement has occurred and the means have become ends in themselves. In using the subskill approach care must be taken to prevent the subskills from becoming the focal point of instruction. Once again, perhaps, this point should be made that it is important for the child to get ample practice reading meaningful and interesting material in context.

While agreeing with the critics of the subskill approach that too much emphasis can be placed on these subordinate skills, the critics probably are in error in failing to recognize the importance of subskills in the developmental sequence of skill attainment. Just because fluent readers are able to derive meaning from the printed page is no reason to believe that beginning readers can do the same or that we can transfer the sophisticated strategies of the fluent reader to the beginning reader. While it is true that sophisticated strategies can be taught to the less sophisticated, these transfers of skills have been accomplished by doing a task analysis of the sophisticated strategies and teaching these subskills to the beginner.

As the advocates of the holistic approach point out, the essential element of reading—deriving meaning—is destroyed by taking a whole and breaking it down. However, current research suggests that before one deals with wholes, smaller aspects have to be mastered first. For example, before one can visually process letter clusters as a unit, individual letters have to be unitized. The controversy between letter-by-letter and whole word processing in word recognition seems somewhat resolved now that we have evidence to indicate that familiar words can be processed by fluent readers as a unit while unfamiliar words tend to get processed letter-by-letter.

Many critics of the subskill approach suggest that meaningful reading material should be given to a child and subskills should be taught when the student asks for help or shows evidence of needing particular skills. This approach has shortcomings when one realizes the logistical and managerial problems facing the teacher with a large group.

With regard to this last point, it is important to consider that many students do not know what kind of help to request and many teachers are not sufficiently trained to diagnose and pinpoint the cause of the student's difficulty. Even when the teacher is able to diagnose the cause of the problem with accuracy, the managerial problems of giving individual help as needed loom so large as to make the system difficult to operate, if not unworkable. It would seem more manageable to assume on a prior grounds that there are certain subskills beginning readers require. These skills would be taught routinely to students. For those students who fail to master these skills, additional time could be allocated and different methods could be tried.

Earlier in this paper the point was made that the adverse relationship between holistic and subskill approaches may not exist. Both approaches recognize there are subskills. Subskill approaches start with smaller units and move to larger and more complex units. On the other hand, the holistic approach begins with the larger unit and moves to smaller units. One of the important factors differentiating the two approaches is that of sequencing. In considering this factor, we must think about which tasks and which unit size one would use to start instruction and how one would program the sequence of skills to be taught as the student progresses in skill.

Another similarity between the two approaches is that both recognize the importance of diagnosis of difficulty in reading and the need to remedy the problem. The subskill approach, however, attempts to reduce the number of students who will experience difficulty with reading by teaching the prerequisite skills before a problem appears. (p. 176-77)

Components of the Wisconsin Design

So much—at least for now—for the skills aspect of this chapter. The title of the chapter is "Design for Developing Comprehension Skills," so let's look briefly at the *design for developing* aspect.

Sensibly selected skills viewed in perspective are, I'm convinced, the bits and pieces from which a program for teaching reading comprehension can be built. But they will remain, bits and pieces until they are put together in some coherent manner that permits teachers to teach them and learners to learn them in some systematic, manageable way. For some time now I have been involved in a project where we have been attempting to do the putting together. One outcome has been the Wisconsin Design for Reading Skill Development, which I will describe in some detail a bit later. It represents our attempt to develop the support system that will permit teachers to teach skills and to individualize instruction with confidence and efficiency.

Other outcomes have been two companion books, *Focused Reading Instruction* (Otto, et al., 1974) and *Objective-Based Reading* (Otto and Chester, 1975). The content covered is similar, but the books are written for different contexts. Either book can be used as a primary or a supplementary text for a reading methods course. I cite them here because they, along with the Wisconsin Design, spell out in detail the effort that I feel is needed in a total design for developing comprehension skills (and, of course, other essential reading skills).

All of this developmental effort has been guided by what I have begun to call a pragmatic-empirical approach. An excerpt from the last chapter of *Objective-Based Reading* (Otto and Chester, 1975) gives a brief explanation of what I mean.

> ...we have described what amounts to a pragmatic-empirical approach to the teaching of reading. By pragmatic we mean *practical*; and by empirical we mean *guided by experience or experiment*. The approach recognizes that in order to deal effectively with individual differences, teachers must adapt instruction to the individual student. The differentiation of instruction through the use of (skills and) objectives is presented as a practical way to deal with differences among individuals. Our suggestions for implementing the (skill-and) objective-based approach are derived from personal observations in developing and working with the *Wisconsin Design for Reading Skill Development*, from the experiences of many teachers and principals, and from data gathered in more formal, field test situations. But what we have described represents only a beginning. Change is implicit in a pragmatic-empirical approach because experiment and experience will be a constant source for modification and improvement in the practices and procedures employed in teaching reading. (p. 211)

I have described the approach in greater detail in another paper (Otto, 1975).

Here I wish to stress three main points. First, if the identification and listing of skills is to have any practical impact on what goes on in the classroom, the skills must be backed up by a delivery system that is credible and palatable to teachers, and workable in the schools. Second, our efforts to provide such a delivery system have been pragmatically based and they continue to be guided by experience and experiment. We apply the pragmatic-empirical approach in our attempt to bridge the traditional gap between the needs and realities of the classroom and the inputs and demands of the researcher. Third, our efforts to identify the essential skills have also been guided by the pragmatic-empirical approach. I will discuss the third point more fully in another section of this paper.

Our work in comprehension has all been done within the context of the Wisconsin Design for Reading Skill Development. Comprehension is one major area of the WDRSD, which is the objective-based system we are developing to provide the total support we feel is needed to teach skills successfully. A brief overview of the WDRSD will provide a context for looking more specifically at the Comprehension element. It will also show the outcome of our application of the pragmatic-empirical approach to developing a backup system for teaching skills.

The WDRSD is an objective-based system that provides both structure and substance for an elementary school reading program, kindergarten through grade six. The structure and substance of the Design itself are probably best demonstrated by an examination of the components: skills and objectives, assessment materials, instructional resources, and management techniques and materials. The skills are grouped into six main areas: I. Word Attack Skills; II. Study Skills; III. Comprehension Skills; IV. Self-Directed Reading Skills; V. Interpretive Reading Skills; and VI. Creative Reading Skills. Each area is subdivided into levels that correspond roughly to grade levels as shown below.

ORGANIZATION OF THE OUTLINE OF READING SKILLS

AREA	GRADE/SKILL LEVEL						
	K	1	2	3	4	5	6
Word Attack Skills	A	B	C	D	—	—	—
Study Skills	A	B	C	D	E	F	G
Comprehension Skills	A	B	C	D	E	F	G
Self-Directed Reading Skills	(A ------------- C)			(DE)		(FG)	
Interpretive Reading Skills	(A ------------- C)			(DE)		(FG)	
Creative Reading Skills	(A ------------- C)			(DE)		(FG)	

A terminal objective has been stated for each skill area and an instructional objective has been developed for each skill in the Outline. (See Otto and Askov, 1974, for the instructional objectives. See also the *Teacher's Planning Guide* for each area

for the terminal objectives and for the instructional objectives.)
The terminal objective for an area sets expectations as to the
outcome once all of the instructional objectives have been
covered. Thus, the terminal objective for the word attack area
calls for independence in attacking phonically and
structurally regular and selected sight words as covered by the
word attack objectives. The instructional objective for each
skill *prescribes* or *describes*—depending on the type of
objective—the expectations with regard to each specific skill.

Two types of instructional objectives have been developed
for the skill areas of the WDRSD. There are behavioral, or
prescriptive, objectives for the Word Attack, Study Skills, and
Comprehension areas; and there are expressive, or *descriptive,*
objectives for the Self-Directed, Interpretive, and Creative
areas. Consider a behavioral objective from Level G of the
Comprehension Skills.

> *Uses context clues: obscure meanings of familiar words.* The
> child determines the obscure meaning of a familiar word in
> context by using the contextual devices of cause and effect,
> direct description, and contrast.

Note that the behavioral objective specifies what a child
is to do when he has attained mastery of the skill. All of the
behavioral objectives are written at a *mid-level* of specificity,
somewhere between the level of broad, terminal objectives and
of extremely narrow objectives that specify each step in a
learning sequence. Written at this mid-level, objectives can
provide teachers with guidance in assessment and instruction
without imposing so many prescriptive constraints that they
become unwieldy. The expressive objectives are quite different
in that they amount mainly to descriptions of activities that
are judged to be relevant to the development of skills in the Self-
Directed, Interpretive, and Creative areas.

Criterion-referenced assessment devices have been
developed for all of the behavioral objectives of the WDRSD.
That is, using the behavioral objectives as the description of
criterion, or mastery, performance for each skill, both formal
and informal assessment procedures have been worked out
and made available.

Formal assessment is done with paper-and-pencil tests, called The Wisconsin Tests of Reading Skill Development. There is a test for each objective in the Word Attack, Study Skills, and Comprehension areas. The tests are available in two parallel forms and in one of two formats—single sheet for a single objective or booklet for all the objectives at a given level. They can be group administered and scored either by hand or by computer. Typically, the booklets are used for pretesting in order to find individuals' instructional levels; the single-sheet tests are used after skill instruction to assess individuals' attainment of criterion performance. Each test includes about fifteen items. The goal of the developers was to make them as brief as possible and yet attain a reliability coefficient of about .8 or better and be assured of covering the behavior described in the objective.

Informal assessment exercises, called *Guides to Informal Individual Skill Observation,* are also available for certain skills. The *Guides,* which are supplied as a part of the *Teacher's Resource Files,* provide directions for observing pupil behavior or for directing a brief performance test. The *Guides* are, of course, criterion referenced in the same sense as the paper-and-pencil tests: They are designed to sample criterion behaviors that are prescribed by objectives. In practice, they serve as alternatives and/or supplements to formal tests. Where the formal tests bring objectivity and reliability to the assessment process, the informal guides offer flexibility and, in some instances, credibility.

In the Self-Directed, Interpretive, and Creative Reading areas there are, of course, no criterion-referenced assessment exercises. Teachers are urged to observe pupils' performance in the activities related to each skill and to keep systematic records of exposure to and participation in the activities.

The WDRSD does not include instructional materials per se. The developers decided that sufficient materials for teaching most of the essential skills are already available. Consequently, the Design includes a component called the *Teacher's Resource Files,* which amounts to a means for organizing existing materials and activities.

There is a *Teacher's Resource File* for each skill area with behavioral objectives: Word Attack, Study Skills, and Comprehension. Within each file, materials and activities are identified and organized by objective. Thus, in each of the *Files* there is a collection of materials and activities appropriate for teaching/learning and criterion behavior(s) prescribed by each objective. Of course the *Files* available from the publisher include only a limited sample or "starter set" of appropriate resources related to each objective. Teachers are invited to add whatever local resources they judge to be relevant to the objectiyes and to the needs of their pupils.

The *Files* offer a number of positive points. In the first place, they permit a school staff to make use of existing materials and ideas by keying them to the objectives. Second, they provide niuch flexibility, for once the local additions are made they should represent local resources and needs in a way that could never be imposed from outside. And, finally, they permit teachers to be true eclectics insofar as the instruction related to any given objective is concerned.

There is a single *Teacher's Resource File* for the Self-Directed, Interpretive, and Creative Reading areas. Its organization is generally similar to that of the *Files* for the other areas, with a specific file for each skill. The main difference is that the material related to each skill is organized to provide breadth of exposure rather than mastery of prescribed criterion behavior.

Three components of the Design are directed specifically to providing assistance with its management and implementation. The *Rationale and Guidelines* (Otto and Askov, 1974) covers all six skill areas of the Design and amounts to what its title implies. It provides a rationale for the development of the Design and guidelines for its implementation. There is a *Teacher's Planning Guide* for each skill area, with a separate book for Word Attack, for Study Skills, and for Comprehension and a single combined book for Self-Directed, Interpretive, and Creative Reading. The *Planning Guides* include the specific information teachers need to get on with the implementation of an objective-based approach to each skill area. Taken together, the *Rationale and Guidelines* and the *Teacher's Planning Guides* provide the practical assistance that will enable a school staff to plan and carry out the assessment, grouping, scheduling, and record keeping that is required for successful implementation. Note that the WDRSD is still under development. Consequently, there are frequent changes in all of the components as a result of experience and formal field test results. Most changes are reflected in annual revisions of the *Rationale and Guidelines*. The latest edition should be consulted to resolve apparent inconsistencies that are attributable to revision of the components. Current lists of available materials can be obtained from National Computer Systems.

A final component is the *Pupil Profile Card. Cards* are provided for keeping a current record of each individual pupil's skill development in each skill area. Thus, when an individual's *Profile Card* is current for any given area—say, Word Attack—it provides information as to which objectives he has and has not attained at the moment in time. (See the *Teacher's Planning Guides* for a more comprehensive discussion of the *Profile Cards* and how they are used.)

The WDRSD is not meant to be a "complete reading program." It offers the skills and objectives that can serve as a framework for such a program but it does not prescribe the program format, content, or procedures. Nor is it meant to be a comprehensive program in the classic tradition of the basal readers. Again, the WDRSD offers the skills and objectives for organizing such a program, but it does not prescribe content. The WDRSD focuses on the skills that are judged—at this point in time—to be essential to success in reading and it provides the backup found to be essential to teach the skills. But responsibility for developing a total reading program and for seeing to it that skills are applied to content rests squarely with school administrators and teachers who use the program.

The critical question to ask about a skill-centered, objective-based approach to the teaching of reading is not the traditional, is it better? The main problem with that question is that it is usually answered in terms of comparative scores on standardized achievement tests. If the test scores get better, the treatment is judged to be better than whatever it is being compared to. There are real difficulties in evaluating a specific approach with non-specific measures. That is, it doesn't really make sense to examine the impact of teaching specific objectives by looking at the results of achievement tests that sample superficially from areas that may or may not be related in any reasonably direct way to areas covered by the objectives.

A much more relevant question to ask is: Can the approach be implemented? Or, to put it another way: Can the skills (objectives) be taught? I do not mean to suggest that *skills* and *objectives* are the same thing. But, in the present context, objectives are statements that translate skills into observable behaviors. Consequently, when I say "Teach skills," I mean "Teach the objectives that pin down the skill-related behaviors that are expected." We look for outcomes that could reasonably be expected to result from what we set out to do in the first place. Such a question suggests that we need to be sold on the objectives we set. But once we set them, attaining the objectives—not some nebulous number on a general test—ought to be the goal.

Developmental edition of the comprehension element

Now let us examine the comprehension element of the WDRSD. Most educators seem to agree that reading comprehension amounts to "understanding" what is read, but beyond that the consensus drops off sharply. There are many unresolved issues and the practices suggested for teaching/developing comprehension are often in conflict and seldom in concert. While we have attempted to keep out of the infighting, we did find it necessary to make some rather basic decisions in developing the comprehension element of the WDRSD. Perhaps I can best represent some of those decisions by quoting from the *Teacher's Planning Guide-Comprehension,* Developmental Edition (Chester et al., 1974).

> ... the Comprehension component of the WDRSD deals only with "reading comprehension" as distinguished from "comprehension" in the more general sense. We feel that it is inaccurate to label a student as having a problem in reading comprehension if that same student, because of intellectual, physical, or psychological problems, is incapable of comprehending information presented in a form other than written material. We assume that this type of student has a (general) comprehension problem.
>
> In further defining Comprehension ... we found it necessary to distinguish between skills requiring convergent thinking and those requiring divergent thinking. Unfortunately many testing and instructional materials have failed to make this distinction, thus contributing to ... the confusion in the area today. Convergent thinking is involved in such skills as

identifying topic sentences, determining sequence, recall of detail, etc., which require the reader and writer to gain some common meaning from written material. If they do not find some common area of convergence, communication breaks down. When a writer offers a series of events which are sequentially related in some fashion, it is important for the reader to comprehend, or understand, what that relationship is. To this extent there are right and wrong answers which are not open to interpretation.

Divergent thinking, on the other hand, offers no right and wrong answers. If the child is asked for his interpretation of a poem, his opinion of a character, or his evaluation of a situation, his answer will always be correct. It may be an interpretation, opinion, or evaluation different from that of his teacher or classmates, but it is nevertheless correct. There may be ten or a hundred correct answers based on differences in background experience, intelligence, emotional attitude, or even something as mundane as decoding ability. The fact remains, questions which have answers that are open to interpretation have no one correct answer.

The point here is that both types of thinking, convergent and divergent, are important and necessary in a total reading program. Problems arise only when we get the two confused and expect convergent answers for problems which should allow for divergent responses (pp. 7-8).

We limited our focus in the comprehension element of the WDRSD to skills which require convergent thinking. This enables us to deal with the skills in terms of prescriptive or behavioral objectives. The objectives are manageable because there are right and wrong answers and because mastery of an objective can be prescribed in terms of criterion behaviors. We have dealt with skills that either allow or call for divergent thinking in other elements of the WDRSD, particularly the interpretive reading and creative reading elements. There the objectives are descriptive, or expressive, and they accommodate latitude in responding.

What we attempted to do, in effect, was to limit the comprehension element to literal comprehension. Operationally, we decided that we would concern ourselves mainly with getting learners to deal with material actually presented by calling only for responses derived explicitly from the material presented. This we have done to the best of our ability. Yet we were haunted by the specter of inferential thinking. This is how we dealt with it in the *Teacher's Planning Guide-Comprehension*:

Another difference you will find between our model of comprehension and that offered in traditional materials lies in our treatment of inferential thinking. Many programs offer a skill commonly referred to as "Inferential Thinking." Again, after analyzing the processes involved, we found not one but many different skills. We found that inferential thinking cuts across all strands and levels. To us, the difference between inferring a main idea and inferring an outcome appears to be as great as the difference between determining the answer to a question when it involves factual recall and determining the answer to a question when it must be inferred. The difference between one inferential skill and another may at times be greater than the difference between factual skills and inferential skills. Therefore, rather than having an inference skill in the Comprehension (element), we chose to develop skills which necessitate inferring the main idea, inferring an outcome, inferring an effect given a cause, inferring the meaning of a word given context clues, etc. (p. 8).

To put it another way, we chose to deal with inferences in multiple contexts of related skills (e.g. main idea, context clues) rather than to abandon them to some Never Never Land terminology like "Draws inferences." In line with our commitment to literal comprehension, we are limited to *literal* inferences in the comprehension element. That is, the substance required for drawing an inference must be *actually presented* in each instance. Thus, when an objective calls for inferring the main idea of a selection, the condition is that *all* of the support for the main idea be presented in the selection. We deal with interpretive inferences in the interpretive reading element; and we do it with *descriptive,* not *prescriptive,* objectives.

Finally, in attempting to arrange the skills in some manageable manner, we came up with what we call *strands,* which are in turn arranged in what we call hierarchies. A strand amounts to a cluster of related skills, like the main idea skill strand or the sequence skill strand. Within each strand the skills are presented at sequential levels, as described earlier in the discussion of the entire WDRSD. We are becoming increasingly aware that a sequence doesn't necessarily make a hierarchy, and I'll return to that point later. Meanwhile, this is what we said in the *Teachers Planning Guide-Comprehension:*

...the skills in (the Comprehension element) are arranged by strands and each strand has a hierarchy. Each step within a strand represents a different and discrete skill built on, or subsuming, previous skills within that strand. To illustrate, we will use the main idea strand. Many traditional programs offer at every level a skill called "Determining the Main Idea." However, when we analyzed the process involved, we found not one but several skills, each of which contributed to the summary skill but each of which was different in some way. We were also able to determine that these skills were sequentially related in that they progressed from determining topics, to identifying main ideas, to inferring main ideas. Global terms, such as determining the main idea, are ineffective in providing focus for specific skill instruction and, unless they can be broken down in more descriptive terms, they are essentially meaningless. Consequently, in the Comprehension (element) you will not find "Determining the Main Idea" at every level. What you will find is a sequence of six separate skills in the main idea strand arranged in a hierarchy according to level of difficulty... (p.8).

Six strands of Comprehension skills were identified for the developmental edition. The strands and the levels at which skills/objectives are identified are given in the schema that follows.

Strand	A	B	C	D	E	F	G
Main Idea	X	X	X	X	X	X	-
Sequence	X	X	X	X	X	X	X
Reasoning	X	X	X	X	X	X	X
Detail	-	X	X	X	X	X	-
Context Clues	-	-	-	X	X	-	X
Affixes	-	-	-	-	X	X	-

The actual skills and objectives are presented *by level*. Within each level, the strand is identified in caps; the skill follows; and the related objective(s) is given on the next line.

LEVEL A

MAIN IDEA—Identifies a topic: pictures
Objective: The child identifies the topic of a picture.

SEQUENCE—Determines sequence: first or last event
Objective: The child identifies the first or last event in an oral selection.

REASONING—Uses logical reasoning
a. Synthesizes information
Objective: The child identifies an activity that represents a synthesis of two events given in an oral sentence.
b. Predicts outcomes
Objective: The child identifies the outcome of an activity described in an oral sentence.

LEVEL B

MAIN IDEA—Identifies a topic: paragraphs
Objective: The child identifies the topic of a written-oral selection.

SEQUENCE—Determines sequence: event before or after
Objective: The child identifies pictured events that occur before or after specific events in an oral selection.

REASONING—Uses logical reasoning: predicts outcomes
Objective: The child synthesizes the information given orally in a three-event activity and identifies a logical outcome.

DETAIL—Reads for detail
Objective: The child attends to and derives meaning from the important details in a simple written-oral selection in the active voice.

LEVEL C

MAIN IDEA—Identifies a topic: paragraphs
Objective: The child identifies the topic of a written selection.

SEQUENCE—Determines sequence: event before or after
Objective: The child identifies events that occur before or after specific events in an oral selection.

REASONING—Uses logical reasoning: determines cause-
effect relationships
Objective: The child identifies cause-effect relationships.

DETAIL—Reads for detail
a. Notes detail in sentences in active voice
Objective: The child attends to and derives meaning from
the important details in a simple selection
written in the active voice.
b. Interprets negative sentences
Objective: The child attends to and derives meaning from
negatives in simple selections written in the
active voice.

LEVEL D

MAIN IDEA—Identifies a topic sentence
Objective: The child identifies the topic sentence of a
paragraph.

SEQUENCE—Determines sequence: explicit relationships
Objective: The child determines the order of events in
paragraphs with explicit sequential relationships.
Note: Explicit sequential relationships are identified by
specific cue words (e.g., next, finally, before, after, first,
last).

REASONING—Reasons deductively
Objective: The child determines whether a conclusion to a
syllogism that has one major and one minor
premise is right or wrong.

DETAIL—Reads for detail
a. Interprets sentences with clauses at the beginning or
end
Objective: The child derives meaning from sentences
written in the active voice by synthesizing the
information from the main clause with that
from the introductory or terminal subordinate
clause.

b. Interprets sentences written in the passive voice
Objective: The child derives meaning from sentences written in the passive voice.

CONTEXT—Uses context clues: unknown words
Objective: The child determines the meaning of an unknown word in context by using the contextual devices of direct description and cause-effect.

LEVEL E

MAIN IDEA—Identifies a main idea: paragraph
Objective: The child identifies the main idea of a paragraph with no topic sentence.

SEQUENCE—Determines sequence: implicit relationships
Objective: The child determines the order of events in selections when the sequential relationships are implicit.

Note: Implicit sequential relationships are identified by means other than specific cue words or position in paragraph.

REASONING—Reasons deductively
Objective: The child determines whether a conclusion to a syllogism that has one or two major premises and one minor premise, either in or out of order, is right or wrong.

DETAIL—Reads for detail: sentences with one centrally embedded part
Objective: The child derives meaning from sentences by synthesizing the information from the main clause with that from the centrally-embedded part.

Note: A centrally-embedded part is an appositive, phrase, or clause between the main subject and the verb.

CONTEXT—Uses context clues: unknown words
Objective: The child determines the meaning of an unknown word in context by using the contextual

devices of direct description and contrast.

AFFIXES—Determines the meaning of prefixes
Objective: The child derives the meaning of a word with a prefix by synthesizing the meaning of the prefix with that of the known word.

LEVEL F

MAIN IDEA—Identifies a main idea: two paragraphs
Objective: The child identifies the main idea of a passage containing two paragraphs, either or both of which may have topic sentences.

SEQUENCE—Orders events along a timeline
Objective: The child uses explicit and/or implicit sequential cues to order events on a timeline.

REASONING—Reasons deductively: indeterminate conclusions
Objective: The child determines whether a conclusion to a syllogism that has one major and one minor premise is right, wrong, or indeterminate.

Note: An indeterminate conclusion is a conclusion that could be either right or wrong. It is a conclusion that can't be made with certainty from the statements as given.

DETAIL—Reads for detail: sentences with one centrally-embedded part and an introductory or terminal clause
Objective: The child derives meaning from complex sentences by synthesizing the information from the main clause with that from both the centrally-embedded part and the introductory or terminal subordinate clause.

AFFIXES—Determines the meaning of suffixes
Objective: The child derives the meaning of a word with a

suffix by synthesizing the meaning of the suffix with that of the known word.

LEVEL G

SEQUENCE—Determines sequence: multiple explicit relationships
> Objective: The child determines the order of events in paragraphs with multiple explicit sequential relationships.

REASONING—Uses logical reasoning
a. Reasons deductively
> Objective: The child identifies the correct conclusion to a syllogism with one major and one minor premise embedded in context.

b. Reasons deductively
> Objective: The child infers a general principle from a selection in which specific pieces of information supporting that general principle are given.

CONTEXT—Uses context clues: obscure meanings of familiar words
> Objective: The child determines the obscure meaning of a familiar word in context by using the contextual devices of cause and effect, direct description, and contrast.

The skills and objectives for the developmental edition are very much a product of the pragmatic-empirical approach. After a general review of research and practice related to the teaching of comprehension skills, we identified the six strands that are outlined in the schema above. As we saw it then, these strands reflected the major subareas or clusters of skills presented in the literature. In developing each strand, we attempted to identify a sequence of skills that would be compatible with the grade/skill level model we evolved for the WDRSD. For some strands we were able to identify and state seven discrete skills/objectives and to arrange them—at least to our satisfaction—in an ascending order of difficulty. For other strands, we did not feel we had seven discrete skills/objectives. Then we simply inserted what we found into the leveling sequence at the point most compatible with the development in the other strands. Then we tried out what we had and made changes as they seemed appropriate.

Throughout the development of skills and objectives for the development edition we were strongly influenced by measurement constraints. If, for example, we found that a tentatively stated objective presented major problems in developing a paper-and-pencil criterion referenced test, we were inclined to restate the objective. This may seem like a classic case of the tail wagging the dog, but we were—and we are—firmly committed to the development of reliable paper-and-pencil criterion referenced tests.

Persistent problems

We feel that we have progressed to a point where we can—if nothing else—identify and assign priorities to some of our most troublesome and persistent problems. Here I will discuss five problems and how we are dealing with them.

1. *Skills in perspective.* I would like to acknowledge an apparent problem that probably turns out to be a non-problem if we view it in perspective. Actually, it also turns out to be the same problem I acknowledged at the outset: How do we strike a balance between an *approach* that focuses on the subskills of comprehension and a *process* that clearly requires the simultaneous application of a vast array of skills? The question can be a difficult one, because it tends to push us toward taking either a holistic or a subskills position. The answer, in my opinion, is that we must acknowledge the need to concern ourselves not only with the teaching of subskills but also with the development of the process. We really do not need to make a choice between conflicting realities, because a conflict exists only if we make one.

I see no conflict in directing the development of children's comprehension through questions and activities while at the same time teaching comprehension by focusing on the mastery of specific subskills. To me, the approaches are a perfect complement. On the one hand we stimulate thinking and stress application; on the other hand, we stress the sharpening of the specifics in order to enhance overall performance. What we need most is to develop our procedures so as to be assured that the activities for sharpening skills and opportunities for applying them are always in concert.

2. *Overlap of skills/objectives*. The fact of overlap among skills and objectives in the different *comprehension* strands is real and it has been recognized from the start. One cannot say with much conviction that, for example, the *context clue* skills are wholly discrete from the skills in the *affixes* strand. Nor can we claim that the *main idea* objectives are unrelated to the *detail* objectives. And, when we examine the intercorrelations of scores on the criterion referenced tests for skills in different strands, we find the coefficients are both positive and substantial. All of this suggests that what we may be doing is simply tapping some global, underlying "skill" with different measures; so each time we sample we come up with something that is quite similar to what we got before in terms of performance. The cynics—or you might call them the purists if your views are similar—have said this means there are no subskills for comprehension. They suggest that we either a) discover skills that are discrete and unrelated, or b) abandon the skill-centered approach and simply teach "comprehension."

The problem that confronts us is not *whether* there is overlap among the skills we are identifying. There is, and we acknowledge the fact. The problem really amounts to a question of whether we should develop skills that are indeed interrelated or search for skills that are discrete. Actually, we have had little difficulty arriving at an answer to that question. We are convinced that the most straightforward way to help children become independent in tackling a diversity of comprehension tasks is to help them sharpen specific skills that are related to the process of comprehending. For purposes of efficient measurement, discrete subtests (subskills) may be desirable. But for purposes of coherent teaching, development of the overall process by sharpening related behaviors seems sensible.

3. *Assigning skills to levels*. As I've pointed out, skills in the WDRSD are clustered at seven levels which are roughly equivalent to the seven levels—kindergarten through grade

six—of the elementary school experience. The intent is not to lock levels to grades; but we have found that it is essential to have some well established referent to guide the placement and development of skills and objectives. The grade level referent is the best we have.

We have no serious difficulty in assigning skills/objectives to levels on the basis of logical and/or content analysis. The levels we assign get the consensual support of consultants, including classroom teachers. But when we get data from the criterion referenced tests designed to assess mastery of the objectives, sometimes we get inversions or, occasionally, breakdowns in mastery performance. The pragmatic does not always square with the empirical!

The dilemma is whether we should be guided most by the pragmatic or by the empirical *at this stage of development*. On the one hand, if the data are unequivocal we could simply make the changes suggested. But on the other hand, if the logical/content/consensual analysis is valid, we must wonder whether a) the criterion referenced test used to get the data is valid, b) the subjects tested are really typical, and/or c) things might not have turned out differently if we had *taught* the skills in the prescribed order *from the beginning*.

In general, my inclination—again, *at this stage of development*—is to put my eggs in the pragmatic basket. That means we look long and hard at our content/logical analyses before we do any changing. And we come up with simple sequences of comprehension skills.

4. *Teachability of the objectives.* All of our objectives ought to be teachable, no question about that. The main question, then, is: How soon? And a question that often comes up is: By whom? Let's look at both questions.

Aside from the sequence and hierarchy implications of the first question, there is a practical aspect that must be dealt with in the schools. As I have already said, the skill levels correspond roughly to grade levels. Everybody knows that individuals differ and that *grade level* is just a referent and that individuals ought to be permitted to progress at their own rate. However, lots of people want to know a) when we will publish grade-level norms for our criterion referenced tests, and b) whether it is okay to teach the upper level skills in the junior high school.

We could evade such questions by insisting that they are not ours to answer or that they are unanswerable in any sensible way. And yet we know that they reflect real and pragmatically legitimate concerns. What we would like to do— and this turns out to be expensive because it is time consuming—is to follow up our commercial edition with case studies in schools. We can do small scale pilots to satisfy ourselves that specific objectives are teachable, and we have done them. But the only way we will ever determine whether the skills can be taught in sequence and on some reasonable time line is by doing large scale, longitudinal followups after the program is fully operational. This is the only way we will ever *really* find out whether the skill-centered, objective-based approach is in fact accomplishing the goal of developing reading comprehension.

The teachable-by-whom question is another that has practical implications. Is it enough that we find a *superteacher* who can teach each skill for demonstration purposes? We think not, for we are committed to developing a backup system that enables teachers to teach all of the skills successfully. Again, the need for longitudinal case study and for rather extensive development of instructional "inputs" (exact nature to be determined) seems clear.

5. *Development within strands.* In view of concerns I have already expressed and information we have gained, we are inclined to look again at the specific skills/objectives and their arrangement within strands. Perhaps the best way for me to explain how we have proceeded is to give an example of what we are doing. The example that follows is adapted from a paper explaining the pragmatic-empirical appraoch to research in reading (Otto, 1975).

In the fall of 1974, the Main Idea strand amounted to six objectives to be taught and mastered in the elementary school. The most basic objective had to do with the identification of the topic of a picture and the most advanced had to do with the identification of the main idea of two paragraphs, which might or might not include explicity stated topic sentences. The objectives were based heavily on research done earlier by the Laboratory for Research in Basic Skills at the University of Wisconsin-Madison. Data from limited tryouts indicated that children could attain the objectives and that the objectives were acceptable to teachers. To be brief, the strand looked respectable and teachers could use it.

But we wondered about a number of things.

1. To what extent should the strand be reflecting the great mass of research findings that are accumulating with regard to advance organizers, cognitive organizers, paragraph organizations? Certainly there was no lack of existing research. If anything there was too much, with diverse approaches and orientations and sometimes conflicting results. Lots of promise, but perhaps as many question as answers.

2. Is it easier to identify the topic (one or two words) of a selection than a more explicit title? Practice suggests that it is, but no data were available. It is harder still to identify a main idea statement? What if a topic sentence is provided? Again, practice seemed to be unsupported by data and practitioners shared our concern.

3. Are children who can identify a main idea statement also able to *state* a main idea? Common sense could take us either way in answering that one. Again, no real data are available. And, again, practitioners wondered, too.

We have to make some decisions. A change in objectives would mean changes in criterion referenced test and in supporting materials for teaching and implementing the strand. All would have to be accomplished within the time/resource allocation. We decided that our reservations were serious enough to warrant changes, so this is what we have done or are now in the process of doing.

1. We reviewed the existing research relating to paragraph organization and the use of various types of organizers. On the basis of all that, we decided the objectives in the strand probably should prescribe—or at least describe—the organization of test passages as well as call for identification of a topic. We wrote seven objectives—one additional—for the strand to reflect organization of passage as well as expected outcomes. To the practitioner, this means that while the strand is being taught over the elementary school experience, explicit attention will be paid to what appear now to be important aspects of organization. To the researcher, this means that some rather tentative suggestions from research are being tried out and need, in turn, to be examined as they are presently operationalized. (Either that, of course, or that the suggestions be further developed—which *could* mean they would become contraindicative of present suggestions. This would be the traditional approach and would keep outcomes out of any wide scale application indefinitely.) To the developer this means putting the whole strand together again with a new thrust.

2. We have done a study to find out whether topic, title and main idea statement do indeed differ in difficulty. They do; and

this information has been looped directly back into the development of the strand in terms of how the objectives are stated and sequenced.

3. We have done a study to find out whether children who can identify a main idea statement when it is given can state a main idea on their own. We've gotten far enough with that one to conclude that they cannot—or at least *do* not come up with statements that are definitive enough to be considered adequate. So we are adding a top level objective to the strand. The child génerates a main idea for a passage that may or may not have an organizer and has both relevant and irrelevant details. (*Happy Note:* We have done this despite the fact that this virtually precludes a paper-and-pencil criterion referenced test.)

As we put the strand back together, we operationalize each objective by a) devising an appropriate criterion referenced test, and b) deciding what materials and procedures we can identify and suggest to help children reach the objective. In that process we work with teachers and children routinely. We send drafts of the objectives out for review by educators who are knowledge-able in the area. We try to use common sense and we check it out when we see a need. We try to keep it all palatable to practition-ers and we check that out constantly. And we go out to the schools to see whether it works. Next we'll try to find out whether it does any good. We *employ* the pragmatic-empirical approach.

Revisions of the comprehension element

We followed a procedure similar to that just described for the main idea strand in looking at each of the strands included in the developmental edition. As a result of that effort, we have decided to do a major revamping of the substrands of the comprehension element. The strands are now being developed as shown in the schema that follows.

COMPREHENSION STRANDS

Word Meaning	Sentence Meaning		Passage Meaning	*Sequence
*Affixes	*Detail	}Sentence	*Central	
*Context clues	Paraphrase	Structure	Thought (main idea)	
			*Relationships/ Conclusions	

*Major strands in the Developmental Edition.

The most apparent change is that we are now focusing explicitly on Word Meaning, Sentence Meaning and Passage Meaning as aspects of literal comprehension. This is clearly in line with what the psycholinguists are saying; but, more important, we have found it to be conducive to the coherent development of the skills within a strand. Consider, for example, the Sentence Meaning strand. With the focus now clearly on the meaning conveyed by sentences, we are developing the strand to deal not only with the *detail* aspect but also with sentence structure and paraphrase. This, we feel, moves us to where we are in fact providing teachers and learners not only with essential skills/objectives but also with a better vehicle for pursuing them.

A close look at the Word Meaning strand will illustrate how we have proceeded with the revision of all of the strands. The basic assumption underlying the Sentence Meaning strand of the Comprehension element is that getting meaning from a sentence, or a complete thought, is an integral step in the reading process. After a reader has begun to decode individual words and get meaning from them, he must learn to perceive "groups" of words and understand the ideas they represent. The primary intent of the strand is to provide the child with the opportunity to increase his abilities to note detail, see sentence organization, attend to word order, and realize there may be a variety of ways to convey a single meaning.

The Sentence Meaning strand is developed through two sets of skills, one dealing with *synthesis* and one with *analysis*. The organization of the strand is shown schematically in Figure 1. Objectives dealing with analysis (detail) are offered at Levels B, C, D and E; and objectives dealing with synthesis (paraphrase) are offered at Levels C, D, E, F and G. The organizing thread for the entire strand is sentence structure, with varied and generally more complex structures at each subsequent level. To put it another way, sentence complexity is the vehicle for moving through the levels of the strand. Sentence meaning is dealt with, on the one hand, through analysis, which focuses on specific details in the context of different, increasingly more complex structures. And, on the other hand, meaning is examined through synthesis, which calls for paraphrase (restatement) of different structures.

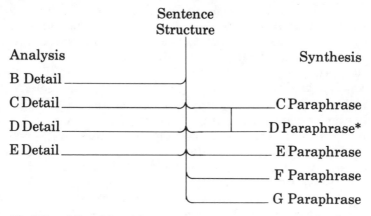

*Both Level C and Level D sentence structures are used to test level D paraphrase skills.

Figure 1. Sentence Meaning Strand.

The analysis aspect of the strand requires the learner to focus solely on a single detail within a sentence. The underlying assumption is very straightforward: Sentence comprehension is built from the understanding of specific details. Too often this basic first step is overlooked or given less attention than it demands. While most learners should have little difficulty with the detail objectives, there is reason to expect that any difficulty at this most basic level must be dealt with before progress can continue.

The synthesis aspect of the strand involves the learner in paraphrasing given structures. Here the assumption is that one of the most effective ways in which a learner can demonstrate his understanding of a sentence is by restating it in a different but meaningfully equivalent way. Paraphrase can follow either of two strategies: *rearranging* words or *substituting* words (synonyms).

Rearranging the words of a sentence or "transforming" it alters the syntactic structure. According to Chomsky (1969) the meaning of a sentence is very much affected by the syntactic structure. Likewise, Fries (1940) says that "the order of the words as they stand in a sentence has become for modern English an important device to show grammatical or structural relationships." And after an extensive review of the literature, Foust (1973) concluded that it is "a well-established conclusion that word order plays an important role in the conveyance of meaning through English sentences." Because of the evidence supporting the idea of a strong relationship between word order and the meaning conveyed, the skill of changing word order within a sentence without altering meaning was included as part of the paraphrase skill.

Substituting for one or more words requires the learner to express a given meaning in a different way. The process can, among other things, help him to recognize redundancies in the English language. Smith (1971) has suggested that one cause of the difficulty encountered by poor readers is their inability to make full use of syntactic and semantic redundancy. He argues that fluent readers of familiar materials go directly from the visual features of prose to the deep structure by making use of the syntactic and semantic redundancy that exists within sequences of words. Such fluency is attained only through practice and experience.

Sentence structure provides the context in which the skills in the analysis and synthesis aspects are developed and tested. The general specifications for writing sentences at each level in the strand are described in the paragraph that follows. Explicit structural specifications are described in detail in the next section of the paper.

The basic structures emphasized at each level are summarized in Figure 2. Note that the structure at each level relates to the synthesis and analysis aspects at each level by providing the context for developing the specific detail and paraphrase skills.

Simple sentences are designated at Levels B and C. The main difference is that at Level B the sentences are read aloud by the teacher, while at Level C the learners are expected to work independently. Compound sentences and complex sentences with one clause are introduced at Level D. At Level E the sentences may include two clauses, and at Level F the clauses, themselves, become more complex with the addition of prepositional phrases. At Level G the only restriction is that the sentences be of the types learners typically encounter by the end of

Structure

Analysis Aspect		Synthesis Aspect

B Detail ◄──────── Simple sentences (written-
                        oral)*

C Detail ◄──────── Simple sentences ──────────────► Paraphrase

D Detail ◄──────── Compound or complex
                   (1 clause) sentences ──────────► Paraphrase

E Detail ◄──────── Compound and/or complex
                   (2 clauses) sentences ──────────► Paraphrase

F   Two clauses with 2+
                   prepositional phrases ──────────► Paraphrase

G   One or more sentences of
                   any type ───────────────────────► Paraphrase

*Sentences read by teacher.

Figure 2. Basic Sentence Structures.

their elementary school experience. While sentence structure is systematically varied at subsequent levels in the strand to increase complexity, present knowledge would not support a claim that the levels are arranged in any hierarchy of absolute difficulty. The structures offered do provide the learner with a variety of contexts for dealing with sentence meaning.

In addition to general structure, sentence length and vocabulary complexity were considered when appropriate in developing materials for the strand. For example, the Spache and Dale-Chall readability formulas were applied to the materials prepared for the primary and intermediate levels, respectively. And, of course, all materials were subject to expert review and try-out with children in a conscientious effort to ensure appropriate conceptual load at each level.

To give substance to the general structures summarized in Figure 2, more explicit specifications were developed for the sentences written at each level. These specifications are given in Table 1. In practice, the specification at a given level provides an additional focus for instruction designed to help learners deal with sentences as they are actually written. The specifications concern function words, substantive words, and negatives at various levels in the strand.

Function words are included because they are the "connectors" of meaning in the English language. Fernald (1904) defined the role of connectives in language quite adequately.

> There are certain words that express the great essentials of human thought, as objects, qualities or actions; these are nouns, adjectives, and verbs. Such words must always make up the substance of language. Yet these are dependent for their full value and utility upon another class of words, the thought-connectives, that simply indicate relation; these are prepositions, conjunctions, relative pronouns and adverbs. If we compare words of the former class to the bricks that make up the substance of a wall, we may compare those of the latter class—the thought-connectives—to the mortar that binds the separate elements into the cohesion and unity of a single structure [p. vii].

Katz and Brent (1968) studied the developmental differences in understanding linguistic connectives and statements of relationships. Their results showed that between grades one and six there is a marked increase in children's ability to clearly verbalize both causal and temporal relationships and the manner in which they are related by connectives. Also, there appeared to be an increase in preference for the linguistic order of clauses to reflect the actual chronological order of events. Robertson (1968) found a significant relationship between fourth, fifth, and sixth graders' understanding of connectives in reading and of ability in listening, reading and written language. Her results also showed a significant variation in students' understanding of a connective at each grade level. As a result of his study, Rodgers (1974) stated that "An awareness of connectives as signals of relationships between ideas is vital to intelligent reading and intelligible speaking."

The function words or connectives have been grouped into several categories for purposes of instructional emphasis. The categories include coordinate conjunctions, subordinate conjunctions, prepositions, and common word orderings—passive construction. The specific structure descriptors in Table 1 show how the function words have been placed and emphasized at given levels. The meaning of each function word is always tested via the paraphrase skills.

The coordinate conjunctions are placed at Levels B, C and D. The subordinate conjunctions are introduced at Level D. The conjunctions were included because there is evidence to link them with comprehension. Clark (1970) studied the oral speech of young children and confirmed his prediction that coordination is the first construction to appear; and that subordination with the subordinate clause appearing in second place precedes subordination with the clause appearing in first place. Stoodt (1972) examined the relationship between a subject's understanding of conjunctions and his reading comprehension and found the two to be significantly correlated.

Positional, directional, and temporal/abstract usages of prepositions are emphasized at Levels B, C, and D, respectively. Foust (1973) determined that although learners use prepositons quite early, they are unable to define their meaning. He categorized a group of frequently occurring prepositions into the positional, directional, temporal, and abstract classes and found a respective hierarchy. The placements shown in Table 1 are based on Foust's work.

Function words which usually occur in a particular order, such as the "by" and "to" in the passive construction, are focused on at Level D. Gleason (1969) has pointed out that the English language places special reliance on the role of syntax in the comprehension process. He states,

> ...the burden of the message is carried by the way in which words are arranged into sentences, the syntax . . . . Word order is so important in English that when it becomes reversed, as it is in the passive, it becomes very hard to learn. If, for instance, you show first graders two pictures, one of a cat chasing a dog and the other of a dog chasing a cat, and tell them to point to the picture called "The cat is chased by the dog," only about half will respond correctly. They ignore the little words, including the prepositions that signal the passive and pay attention to the word order [p. 18-19].

Since the passive voice has been identified as a specific construction related to comprehension difficulties, it was selected for instructional emphasis.

Substantive Words. In addition to the types of function words already discussed, selected substantive words are given attention in determining the specific structures as summarized in Table 1. At Levels B and C, the substantive words are dealt

Table 1. Specifications for sentence structure

Level	Basic Structure	Function Words	Substantive Words	Negatives
			Specific Structure	
B	Simple sentence (written-oral)	Coordinate: and Prepositions: positional	Objects: direct, prepositional Modifiers: adjectives, adverbs	See discussion in text
C	Simple sentences	Coordinate: or Prepositions: directional	Objects: indirect, prepositional, infinitive Pronouns: all	
D	Compound or complex (1 clause) sentences	Coordinate: but Subordinates: causal, relative pronouns Prepositions: temporal/abstract Common word orderings: passive voice		
E	Compound and/or complex (2 clauses) sentences	Subordinates: temporal Prepositions: all usage		
F	Two clauses with 2+ prepositional phrases	Subordinates: adversative		
G	One or more sentences of any type	Conjunctions: sentence linkers		

with in the context of simple sentences and within the *detail* aspect of the Sentence Meaning strand. At subsequent levels the substantive words may be dealt with in either the detail or the paraphrase aspect. Objects, modifiers, and pronouns were selected for special emphasis on the basis of experiences gained in developing materials for pilot versions of what has turned out to be the Sentence Meaning strand. The observation was that pupils who were generally able to handle assessment items dealing with the detail aspect of sentences meaning had inordinate difficulty with items in which these substantive words contributed directly to the correct responses to test items.

Negatives. Negative constructions are included in the specification because some researchers (Kennedy, 1970) feel that their presence makes comprehension more difficult. Certain studies (Wason, 1959, 1961, 1965; Wason and Jones, 1963; and Gough, 1965, 1966) have indicated that reaction time to negative sentences is longer than to affirmative sentences. Just and Carpenter (1971) report,

> The fact that affirmatives are unmarked and negatives are linguistically marked is completely correlated with the finding in this study and previous studies that affirmatives are psychologically less complex than negatives.

They further suggested from Greenberg's (1966) linguistic data the generalization across languages that all syntactic negatives are psychologically more difficult to process than corresponding affirmatives. This evidence seems to warrant the inclusion of negatives as a specific focus for instruction designed to improve the comprehension of sentences.

Specific skills and objectives
for sentence meaning revision

As shown in the discussion of Figure 1, specific skills in the Sentence Meaning strand are developed through two sets of objectives: a) an analysis aspect, where the focus is on identification and understanding of details, and b) a synthesis aspect, where the learner paraphrases, or restates, the meanings conveyed by varied sentence structures. Sentence structure, as shown in Figure 2, is treated as a vehicle for developing the skills and stating the objectives in each aspect of the strand. Treatment of the entire strand is summarized in

Table 2, which shows the sentence structures and the focus of each set of objectives at subsequent levels.

Table 2.   Sentence meaning strand

Level	Analysis aspect	Basic Structure	Synthesis aspect
B	Detail	Simple sentences (written-oral)	
C	Detail	Simple sentences	Rearranges and substitutes for a phrase
D	Detail	Compound or complex (1 clause) sentences	Rearranges and substitutes for a phrase
E	Detail	Compound and/or complex (2 clauses) sentences	Rearranges and substitutes for more than a phrase (whole sentences)
F		Two clauses with 2+ prepositional phrases	Rearranges and substitutes (focuses on phrases)
G		One or more sentences of any type	Rearranges and substitutes in more than one sentence

The skills and objectives for the revised Sentence Meaning strand are given in Table 3.

Detail aspect. Objectives for the detail skills (Levels B, C, D, and E) require the learner to get meaning from a single substantive word or a short phrase presented in a sentence. At Level B the word may be a direct object, the object of a positional preposition, or a modifier. At Level C the word or phrase may be the object of a directional preposition, an indirect object, the object of an infinitive, or a pronoun is a simple sentence with or without a negative. At Level D the emphasis is on temporal and/or abstract prepositional phrases in sentences with clauses introduced by causal conjunctions or relative pronouns. At Level E detail is noted in sentences with prepositional phrases and clauses introduced by temporal conjunctions.

The detail skills should be taught concurrently with the paraphrase skills at each level. No sequence is suggested because in his daily life the learner must cope concurrently with tasks that require application of both types of skills.

Table 3.   Skills and objectives for the sentence meaning strand

	Detail	Paraphrase
Level B	Derives meaning from sentences: notes detail Objective: Given a short written-oral selection of simple sentences in the active voice, the child derives meaning from direct objects, objects of positional prepositions, and modifiers.	
Level C	Derives meaning from sentences: notes detail Objective: Given a short written selection of simple positive and negative sentences, the child derives meaning from indirect objects, objects of infinitives, objects of directional prepositions, and pronouns.	Derives meaning from sentences: paraphrases negative and positive sentences Objective: The child is able to a) restate negative sentences in the negative and in the positive and b) positive sentences in the negative and in the positive by rearranging the order of words in the sentence and/or substituting for a word or phrase.
Level D	Derives meaning from sentences: notes detail in sentences with subordinate clauses Objective: The child attends to detail in sentences which are written in the active voice and contain a) temporal and/or abstract prepositional phrases and b) either a terminal clause or an embedded part.	Derives meaning from sentences: paraphrases active and passive sentences Objective: The child is able to restate sentences in the active voice to the passive voice and in the passive voice to the active voice by rearranging the order of words in the sentence and/or substituting for a word or phrase.
Level E	Derives meaning from sentences: sentences with two subordinate clauses Objective: The child attends to detail in sentences containing a) any type of prepositional phrase and b) an introductory,	Derives meaning from sentences: paraphrases complex sentences Objective: The child restates sentences with an introductory and/or between subject and verb and/or terminal sub-

(Table 3 continued)

	and/or between subject and verb, and/or terminal subordinate clause.	ordinate clause by rearranging and/or substituting for more than a short phrase.
Level F		Derives meaning from sentences: paraphrases complex sentences with two or more prepositional phrases.
		Objective: The child paraphrases complex sentences containing two or more prepositional phrases by rearranging words and substituting for more than a short phrase.
Level G		Derives meaning from sentences: paraphrases one long sentence or more than one short sentence.
		Objective: The child paraphrases one long sentence into two or more sentences, or more sentences, or paraphrases several sentences by rearranging words and substituting for more than a short phrase.

The paraphrase objectives require the learner to a) change word order, and b) substitute words or use synonyms in restating the meaning of sentences. To change word order, the learner examines a relationship between two or more ideas and then restates them. In making restatements, emphasis is on interpreting the relationship conveyed by function words. Paraphrase through substitution places emphasis on replacing substantive words.

Paraphrasing is introduced at Level C, where the child is expected both to rearrange words and to substitute—for only one word—in simple negative sentences which include directional prepositons. Level D is very similar to Level C, but the child works with passive—as well as active—voice sentences. Because the passive voice tends to be difficult for many learners, the sentence structure used to present this construction is lightly "easier" than that specified for use with the Level D detail skills (see Figure 2), i.e., most of the sentences to be restated are simple sentences.

At Level E the child rearranges or substitutes up to three words within sentences containing two clauses. At Level F, substituting for prepositonal phrases within complex sentences is emphasized. Level G differs from Level F in that the child uses all previously learned paraphrase skills to make both fewer and more sentences from the stimulus sentence(s).

REFERENCES

Chester, R. D.; Askov, E.; Hudson, B.; and Otto, W. *Teacher's Planning Guide: Comprehension*. Minneapolis: National Computer Systems, 1974.

Chomsky, N. Language and the mind. *Psychology Today,* 1969, *1,* 48.

Clark, E. V. How young children describe events in time. In G.B. Flores d-Arcais and W. J. N. LeVelt (Eds.) *Advances in psycholinguistics*. Amsterdam: North-Holland, 1970.

Fernald, J.C. *Connectives of English speech*. New York: Funk and Wagnalls, 1904.

Foust, C.D. The relationship between understanding prepositions and reading comprehension. Unpublished doctoral dissertation, Ohio State University, 1973.

Fries, C.C. *American English grammar*. New York: D. Appleton-Century, 1940.

Gleason, J.B. Language development in early childhood. In J. Warden (Ed.). *Oral language and reading*. Champaign, Ill.: National Council of Teachers of English, 1969.

Gough, P.B. Grammatical transformations of speed of understanding. *Journal of Verbal Learning and Verbal Behavior,* 1965, *4,* 107-111.

Gough, P.B. The verification of sentences: The effects of delay on evidence and sentence length. *Journal of Verbal Learning and Verbal Behavior,* 1966, *5,* 492-496.

Greenberg, J. H. *Language universals*. The Hague: Mouton, 1966.

Just, M.A., and Carpenter, P.A. Comprehension of negation with quantification. *Journal of Verbal Learning and Verbal Behavior,* 1971, *10,* 244-253.

Katz, E.W., and Brent, S.B. Understanding connectives. *Journal of Verbal Learning and Verbal Behavior,* 1968, *7,* 501-509.

Kennedy, G. *The language of tests for young children*. CSE Working Paper No. 7, 1970.

Otto, W. A pragmatic-empirical approach to research in reading. A paper presented at the 20th Annual Convention of the International Reading Association, New York City, May 13-16, 1975.

Otto, W., and Askov, E. *Wisconsin design for reading skill development: rationale and guidelines.* Minneapolis: National Computer Systems. Revised 1974.

Otto, W., and Chester, D. *Objective based reading.* Preliminary Edition. Reading, Massachusetts: Addison-Wesley, 1975.

Otto, W.; Chester, D.; McNeil, J.; and Meyers, S. *Focused reading instruction.* Reading, Massachusetts: Addison-Wesley, 1974.

Robertson, J.E. Pupil understanding of connectives in reading. *Reading Research Quarterly,* Spring, 1968, *3,* 387-417.

Rodgers, D. Which connectives? Signals to enhance comprehension. *Journal of Reading,* March, 1974, *17,* 462-466.

Samuels, S. Hierarchical subskills in the reading acquisition process. In J.T. Guthrie (Ed.), *Aspects of reading acquistion.* Baltimore: Johns Hopkins University Press, 1976.

Smith, F. *Understanding reading: A psycholinguistic analysis of reading and learning to read.* New York: Holt, Rinehart and Winston, 1971.

Stoodt, B. D. The relationship between understanding grammatical conjunctions and reading comprehension. *Elementary English,* 1972, *49,* 502-504.

Wason, P. C. The processing of positive and negative information. *Quarterly Journal of Experimental Psychology,* 1959, *11,* 92-107.

Wason, P. C. Response to affirmative and negative binary statements. *British Journal of Psychology,* 1961, *52,* 133-142.

Wason, P. C. The contexts of plausible denial. *Journal of Verbal Learning and Verbal Behavior,* 1965, *4,* 7-11.

Wason, P. C., and Jones, S. Negatives: Denotation and connotation. *British Journal of Psychology,* 1963, *54,* 299-307.

Comments on
Design for Developing
Comprehension Skills

Irene Athey

It is a pleasure to read and respond to a paper written by
Wayne Otto because I find myself in essential agreement with
so much of what he has to say. However, bearing in mind his
dictum that "controversy keeps us on our toes," I will try to lace
my discourse with a little controversy. I feel particularly
qualified to do this because, having been involved in an
enterprise similar to the Wisconsin Design, namely the
development of the New York State Comprehensive
Achievement Monitoring or CAM system, I can be perhaps
more sympathetic and at the same time more critical toward
the efforts of the Madison team.

Let me begin by saying that I agree wholeheartedly with
Otto that the opposition of holistic methods of teaching
reading and skills-based approaches is a non-issue, an
example of the either-or-fallacy to which psychologists and
educators seem prone. The arguments in which we so
frequently become embroiled, such as phonics versus look-say,
language-experience versus behavioral objectives—in brief,
the "great debates" of reading—are, to my mind, examples of
the *un*desirable effects of controversy, where the antagonists
become entrenched in their extreme positions and are more
concerned with defending their beliefs than in ascertaining the
truth. Neither approach need exclude the other; indeed, one
would hope it would not. Even the most ardent advocate of a
language-experience approach will find it necessary to do some
skill-building in the classroom, so why not make it systematic?
I think the opposite danger is the more likely one, that teachers
become so engrossed in the skills approach that the major goal
is lost sight of. This is the danger to which Samuels refers when

he speaks of the means becoming the end. But we cannot lay the blame for that outcome at the door of the skills approach *per se*. Any method is subject to misuse at the hands of the misguided. The answer lies in a greater appreciation on the part of teachers as to what the skills approach is designed to do, and what it can and cannot accomplish.

Samuels raises another point: "While it is true that [the] sophisticated strategies [of the fluent reader] can be taught to the less sophisticated, these transfers of skills have been accomplished by doing a task analysis of the sophisticated strategies and teaching these subskills to the beginner" seems to imply that the skills approach is only for, or at least more appropriate to, the beginning or intermediate reader. I would like to suggest, on the contrary, that fluency is not an all-or-none state, and that even mature readers could perhaps benefit from sharpening some of the component skills, especially those related to interpretive comprehension.

Let us concede, then, that the skills approach can benefit both beginning and fluent readers, that it is not antagonistic but complementary to other approaches, and is not, therefore, in itself a complete program for teaching reading. Having done so, we can now consider some of the issues and problems involved in objectives-based systems.

The first question has to do with the validity of the particular skills selected. We must remember that "comprehension" is a hypothetical construct like "intelligence." In fact, there is a good deal of evidence to suggest that the two constructs may have considerable overlap, not the least of which is Otto's equation of literal and interpretive comprehension with two aspects of Guilford's model of intelligence, namely Convergent and Divergent Thinking. The problem with hypothetical constructs is that, while everyone knows what it is we are talking about when we speak of "intelligence" or "comprehension," no one can provide a definition which is both exhaustive and universally acceptable. In practice, what one does is to weld existing definitions, factor analytic and other research, and one's own introspections into an overall operational definition one is prepared to stand by. Of course, the operational definition has two limitations: It must not stray too far from conventional wisdom, or it runs the risk of being rejected; and it represents but one of the many possible definitions, especially those which may be forthcoming as a result of future research. The Wisconsin Design followed essentially the same procedure. It looked at existing definitions—those skills teachers emphasize when they say they are teaching comprehension, and the factors generated in research studies, to identify the important components of reading comprehension. I think we should recognize that this leads in some sense to a self-fulfilling prophecy, since the teachers probably have no theoretical rationale on which to base their choice of skills, and the factor-analytic studies simply reproduce what was put into the hopper in the first place, namely scores from tests designed to measure the skills somebody deemed to constitute comprehension. All this is perhaps a torturous way of saying that, while the Wisconsin Design model may have some consensual validation, it should be recognized that it is only one among a number of possible models of comprehension and should be, as I believe it is, open to continuous refinement, or even modification. But beyond this, one must ask the more general question as to what constitutes validation of a construct such as comprehension. The answer seems to lie in the continuous bootstrap operation we call construct validity. This may be what Otto has in mind when he says large-scale, longitudinal studies are the only way we will ever *really* know whether the skill-centered approach is in fact accomplishing the goal of developing reading comprehension.

This brings me to two related points of interest. The first point is somewhat tangential, but it has to do with a concern I have with objectives-based systems in general, and that is what would seem to me their inflexibility. So many decisions are made on the way to preparing a comprehensive system, each one locking one into a particular way of doing things, and since these decisions are interdependent, it becomes a monumental task to change anything because any change in one element involves changes in all the others. Hence the system may become self-perpetuating, shackled by the weight of its own superstructure.

The second point is suggested by the analogy with the construct of intelligence. This is that comprehension, like intelligence, may manifest itself in different ways, or even be differently constituted, at different age levels. For example, in discussing the leveling of objectives with teachers in the course of developing the New York State system, we found that teachers, as a general rule of thumb, do not teach interpretive skills before fourth grade. Without questioning this practice, we may ask on what it is based. Are children below fourth grade incapable of making inferences or interpretations? This does not seem likely. Is it that teachers feel they have enough to do teaching decoding strategies and literal comprehension? Or is it simply tradition? Whether any of these possibilities, or none of them, is the answer, the point is that maybe a single construct—*Comprehension*—is not enough. Maybe we need to look at what constitutes comprehension at various periods in the child's school career, and we need to do it in full recognition of his developmental level in each case, especially, of course, his cognitive level.

I think this is the problem Otto is wrestling with when he talks about hierarchies of skills. If the data do not conform to expectations, he asks, should we conclude that a) the criterion referenced tests are invalid, b) the subjects are atypical, or c) the results might have been different if the prescribed order of skills had been followed from the beginning. I would venture a fourth possibility, namely that the hierarchy, though valid on logical considerations, may violate some psychological or developmental aspect of the child's functioning which must, ultimately, be taken into consideration.

However, this does not mean that the other three alternatives are not highly plausible explanations. In fact, in establishing construct validity, when things go wrong, the first thing to look at is one's tests. Do they indeed measure the constructs they were designed to measure? Even with objectives couched at a "middle level of specificity," it is not easy to construct valid paper-and-pencil tests, especially in multiple-choice format and especially at the lower grades, where passages must, of necessity, be short. But assuming that these skills are, as stated, *essential* skills (essential to comprehension, that is), there remain two assessment problems. The first is to determine the relative contribution of each and every separate skill at each of the different levels. This process is necessary to achieve correct leveling and appropriate emphasis for the various skills. After all, if it is claimed that these are essential skills, then this claim must be demonstrated by showing the relation of each one to growth in comprehension. Face validity or even consensual validity is not enough. Nor is it enough to say that "once we set them, attaining the objectives—not some nebulous number on a general test—ought to be the goal." This is like saying that as long as one's service or backhand in isolation are proficient, one should not worry about whether they improve one's tennis game. Of course, there are fairly well-defined criteria for determining whether one's game has improved; fewer shots go outside the boundary or into the net, and one begins to beat one's opponents. The criteria for determining whether a student's reading comprehension has improved are somewhat less obvious, and I would be the first to agree that a reading test may not be the best way to judge it. Still, this does not get away from the fact that the ultimate value of skills improvement must lie in the extent to which it promotes general comprehension.

The second problem is to determine how the skills interact, in other words how they operate *in unison* to improve general reading comprehension. It comes as no surprise to find that the skills are highly correlated. It would be more of a surprise if they were not. Nor do I think this fact should confront us with the dilemma posed by the cynics of either coming up with discrete, unrelated skills or abandoning the skills approach. But it does suggest that we have an obligation to discover which skills interact and to what effect under what conditions. Perhaps it is not the interaction of skills so much as their flexible deployment which characterizes the fluent reader. I suspect that we know very little about this process, and yet this may be the key to it all. When a fluent reader reads a passage, he does not peruse it first for the main idea, then a second time to note details, then a third time to determine the sequence of events, and so forth. Somehow, in the course of reading, he manages to balance all these factors, just as driving along the street, he keeps control of the accelerator, the clutch, and the brake, constantly reacting to traffic conditions, road surface, and a myriad of other considerations. In fact, it is the intelligent adjustment of his actions to all these factors that makes for a good driver. Similarly, the extent to which a reader can coordinate the skills he may have mastered to perfection in isolation may well determine the depth and breadth of his comprehension of written prose. The importance of skills interaction and its role in reading may have been overlooked in the emphasis on specific isolated skills.

We are really talking about the problem of transfer. How well does the teaching of specific skills transfer to the task of what we might call "real-life reading"? Thorndike long ago pointed out that the more "identical elements" there are between the training situation and the testing situation, the greater will be the transfer of training. Now, as far as the criterion-referenced tests are concerned, there may be a high degree of similarity between training and testing. A student learns to identify a topic sentence in paragraphs which clearly have one, and only one, topic sentence, and he is tested for this skill, on the same kind of paragraph. But when one moves to the world of real-life reading materials, one finds, regrettably, that there are often paragraphs which have more than one topic sentence, or sometimes even no topic sentence. I found this to be true, for example, of several paragraphs in Otto's paper. Similarly, in order to clarify the distinction between literal and inferential thinking, care has been taken to select or construct paragraphs which contain all necessary support for the main idea, in other words to supply all information required for the correct answer, so that reliance on prior experience or on inference is eliminated. Assuming that this can be done (the parallel with culture-free intelligence tests suggests itself here), again the question arises as to how realistic such paragraphs are in relation to the text and trade books children regularly consume. Perhaps we can learn from them how children's books *ought* to be written. Lightening the inferential load of a passage should certainly help children to comprehend its meaning. On the other hand, systematic training in identifying unstated meanings and implications would also seem to be necessary. For this reason, Otto's emphasis on identifying, teaching, and applying the skills *in context* is especially appropriate.

Everything I have talked about seems to relate to the criterion problem, and this may well be because it is the central problem, which gives rise to all the others. At all events, I was intrigued by a statement in the paper to the effect that the authors had been "haunted by the specter of inferential thinking." Many other reading experts have been similarly haunted. Some have chosen to cut the Gordian knot by consigning all such skills to a domain called "thinking," and refusing to consider them under the rubric of reading. Unfortunately this act of bravado accomplishes very little in terms of forwarding our understanding of reading comprehension, because inferential thinking and reading comprehension are inextricably intertwined. By the same token, I hope that the authors of the Wisconsin Design will not relegate inferential thinking to a permanent limbo, because I feel that the inferential skills are at the heart of comprehension, and may be perhaps more pervasive than we think, i.e., operating even when we think only literal comprehension is being called into play.

The inferential skills are indeed many and complex, for they include all the varied activities we subsume under "reasoning,"—making generalizations, inferring cause and effect (with all the ramifications *that* entails, e.g., multiple causation, necessary versus sufficient conditions, causal chaining, etc.), assessing the author's purpose, biases, etc., appreciating the mood of a passage or the delineation of a character, and so forth. Incidentally, I cannot agree that divergent thinking is invariably brought into play in this type of skill. It would be incorrect, for example, to describe a character who stole, cheated, and lied as "honest," or a scene in which the thunder boomed and the wind howled as "tranquil." Of course, it is true that there is sometimes room for a difference of opinion; but, as my old philosophy professor once remarked, "that doesn't make one opinion as good as another." Otherwise, we would all be competent art and drama critics, political experts, and literary connoisseurs. But to return to our "main idea"—we need competent analyses of of the interpretive aspects of comprehension no less than the literal aspects, and objectives, materials, and criterion-referenced tests to go along with them. And, as indicated earlier, we need to determine at what age the inferential skills may optimally be presented, or perhaps adapted to the cognitive and linguistic level of the child. In other words, I am rejecting the statement that criterion-referenced measures are inappropriate in the interpretive domain, which should be assessed by observation or other procedures.

I would like to conclude with a few remarks about the practical aspects of the Wisconsin model. First I would say that a skills approach to reading should be very beneficial to teachers. Teachers cannot teach comprehension in the abstract any more than they can teach students intelligence or happiness; and I agree that we cannot expect diagnostic teaching unless we provide the parameters for the diagnosis. Teachers teach skills anyway, so they should have the benefit of sophisticated analysis of what is involved in reading.

Another advantage of the system is the assistance it provides by keying existing source materials to the objectives, thus preserving the teacher's autonomy to adapt content to local or individual conditions. Teachers certainly need assistance if they are to implement an objectives-based system with all the record-keeping and preparation it entails. On the other hand, a system which provides everything for the teacher neatly labeled and sequenced not only homogenizes the educational process, but strips the teacher of his professional expertise and intiative. The way this problem is handled here seems to be an admirable compromise.

By the same token, I wonder about the role of the teacher in selecting the *objectives* of instruction, and whether there is any provision within the system for a teacher to add to or eliminate objectives from the core bank at discretion. Perhaps the authors might want to debate the desirability of such a provision. However, I have found that teachers are more interested in implementing a system in which they have been directly involved from the beginning. Of course, one must achieve a balance between the amount and kind of teacher involvement and the requirements of research design. When Otto says that the Wisconsin system has been "implemented with success," I wonder by what criteria he makes this statement and what compromises, if any, were made along the way.

Finally, I would like to know more about the testing process and how the data are presented for use by the teacher. In my experience, the construction, administration, and scoring of valid criterion-referenced tests present some of the hairiest problems associated with the objectives approach. I have discussed the procedures followed in New York State in two papers presented at the 1975 conference of the American

Educational Research Association, and would be interested in comparing these with the Wisconsin model.

In spite of the problems I have mentioned, my enthusiasm for the skills approach remains undiminished. I believe it represents a necessary and significant step forward, both in conceptualizing what reading comprehension is and in utilizing that conceptual analysis to improve the teaching of reading. I congratulate Otto and his colleagues on being a part of this new venture.

Cognitive Processes
Fundamental to Reading Instruction

Russell G. Stauffer

Recently Jacques Monod (1971) advanced, as if in summation, what philosophical thought has been voicing for centuries, that while nature is *objective* man as an intelligent human being is *projective*. This provides the base for the scientific method by referring to man's thinking activity as conscious and projective, intentional and purposive. The artifacts that man has made are products of his deliberate, conscious purposefulness as contrasted with the products of nature which are the result of physical forces. Every artifact, whether it be *words* or *things* is a man-made product endowed with a purpose. A hammer or the word hammer is man-made and attests to a conscious and rational intention. The object or the word has about it the structure and organization of knowledge and can, so to speak, cause a person to spin ahead of hammer to predict how it will or might be used and this extends to figurative use. Thus, man predicts or extrapolates as well as interpolates.

If it is the essential task of the human mind to produce, analyze, and regulate concepts and scientific operations, then it must be the task of reading instruction to foster human cognition. Implicit in this is the concept of intention and the process of change premised on the hope of discovery and the discipline of accuracy. One can conclude that "purpose for reading" like "intention in thinking" is crucial to comprehension. This being so, a teacher is obliged to nurture the inquiry process so that readers develop an active intelligence capable of projecting, weighing evidence, making critical decisions, and doing constructive research. This is so because critical reading, like critical thinking, requires cognitive interaction between facts, their values and consequences; between hypotheses and proofs, resulting in the internalization of knowledge and the acumen of self-regulation.

Intention

Observation of children in the sensorimotor stage of infancy provides information about how children first acquire the ability to achieve intentions and reach goals or in brief use "knowledge" as a guide to purposeful action. When a moving object catches the eye of a one-month old baby he may stop sucking the nipple of a bottle and produce ocular convergence (Bruner, 1971). Later, at four months of age, a new principle between sucking and looking develops, when the child merely mouths the nipple but does not suck while watching a lively visual stimulus. Thus early in life the rudiments of dealing with a number of options and part-whole relationships is being pieced together. This suggests that at this early stage a plan or intention exists in the mind of the infant acting and influences the sequence of events that may follow and the ability to benefit from knowledge and may be regulated thereby.

By the end of the sensorimotor period a child is able to attain practical aims, limited though to the time and space restrictions of the immediate perceptual present. Thought rooted in action is directed by the infant toward "success in his manipulations [from the cognitive point of view] and toward personal satisfaction [from the affective point of view]" (Sinclair-de-Zwart, 1969). In time the child develops language symbols to express his intentions, his understandings, his action schemes, and his findings. He acquires an infinite number of phonetic-semantic-percepts or sensori-sound-meaning correlations. Children learn to do this without explicit instruction and without being exposed to a uniform series of experiences (Chomsky, 1971). This tendency for language acquisition and use is a generic mental process and reflects the generalization tendency of the human mind.

Development from the third to the eleventh year shows conservation of properties across invariant changes—amount, weight, volume, horizontality, length, area, number, duration—whereby the underlying cognitive achievements reflect ability to project and hypothesize and to make decisions (Wallach, 1963). As the child matures and organizes objects and events into categories or sorts them in terms of increasing values of some attribute, his performance reflects an increasing ability to project and consider hypothetical possibilities and to test their validity by systematic analysis. In brief, his thinking is capable of formulating problems, possible solutions to the problems, and ways of determining which solutions are correct.

Over this same period of developing maturity, other characteristics develop. Individuals tend to show differences in cognitive style and persistence. These differences are evident in the nature and degree of impulsiveness, **attentiveness, and ability to focus closely on events that** surround them (White, 1963). Undoubtedly, cognitive and affective structures emerge from the interaction between a child and his environment and influence a child's action systems as well as his expectancies.

In addition, individual differences in curiosity reflect strategies for dealing with the uncertainties associated with ambivalent expectancies that vary in their disposition to increase, prolong, and resolve conflicts. D.E. Berlyne (1965: 260) holds that "When directed thinking is used effectively for the relief of conceptual conflict, it seeks information without bias." To this he adds the recommendation that when new material is presented to a child it should be done in such a way that the child's existing expectations are challenged and make him aware of the gaps in his present knowledge structures.

In concept attainment, the predictive capabilities of an individual again play a crucial role. Experiments show that a person's experience and knowledge influence strongly hypotheses ventured. Persons tend to develop a vague plan in a predictable manner and then their intentions keep them at the task until a correct hypothesis is offered (Bruner et al., 1956; Klausmeir et al., 1964).

In summary, then, even though this review is brief, it does provide insight into the nature and value of intention and how it directs and influences cognition. Not only are intentions and strategies that exist in the mind influenced by expectations and uncertainties but also they are influenced by the likely consequences of an action. Thus thought and intention, rooted in reflection and ability to conceptualize, direct mental action whether the stimuli are primarily perceptual or conceptual.

The process of change

The preceding discussion was prepared to show that if the regulated thought of a student is directed in a patterned form in order to comprehend, then reflective reading, being akin to thinking, must also be directed in a patterned form in order for comprehension to occur. To read must mean to comprehend and to speak of "reading comprehension" must be considered redundant terms. Since strategies for sound thinking are learned they can be taught as should strategies for critical and creative reading.

Intrinsic to teaching-learning circumstances is "change". The reader-thinker must know what change he wants to attain, know how to proceed to attain it, and know how to verify and internalize the change. Similarly the able teacher must know how to direct the reading-thinking act so that the *processes* resulting in change are mastered. This requires that the reader like the thinker proceed with intentions clearly declared, with an open mind, with judgment suspended until all the evidence is examined and weighed. Then judgments are made based on the value of facts and a choice of the relevant.

Six aspects of critical reading can be declared. They are: 1) ability to actualize intentions; 2) ability to sift information and determine its relevancy to one's purposes as well as to actively determine an author's intentions; 3) ability to deal with semantic and linguistic constraints in terms of goals being sought; 4) ability to maintain in dynamic equilibrium the personal components of convictions and inclinations; 5) ability to determine truths by choosing among different options; and 6) ability to internalize the knowledge gained and use it in other situations.

Earlier I demonstrated that a basic element in strategies for learning is intention, or a problem, a set, a question. Similarly, the first aspect of reading to learn is "ability to actualize concepts and intentions." In other words, the reading—thinking process must begin in the mind of the reader. He must raise the questions. If he accepts questions someone else raises he must internalize the questions and make them his. This he does by marshalling his experiences and knowledge in such a way that his expectations are challenged and that he is made aware of the gaps in his knowledge. To the reader belong both the responsibility and the tyranny of determining "a right answer."

Because strategies for thinking are learned and can be taught, teaching-learning is best done in "provoked" situations as compared to "spontaneous" situations (Duckworth, 1969). Provoked situations are ones deliberately planned by a teacher to achieve a certain effort. Similarly, strategies for affective reading-thinking are best accomplished in directed reading-thinking activities (DRTAs) provoked for that purpose (Stauffer, 1969).

Because the DRTAs are provoked much depends upon the teacher if the processes to be acquired by the student are to become functional. It is the teacher's attitudes and grasp of DRTA techniques that make the difference. The teacher must be dedicated to the proposition that reading is a cognitive process and that the intellectual disciplines must be taught deliberately.

Recent studies show quite clearly that what the teacher does makes an enormous difference. First is a study done to examine individually formulated purposes for reading in relation to comprehension and purpose attainment (Henderson, 1963). Results justified concluding that pupils differ in the success with which they attain purposes, that pupils who set better purposes are more likely to attain them, and are also more likely to be more successful in attaining purposes supplied by someone else. Second, when children were taught according to Directed Reading-Thinking Activity recommendations and on an open-communication system premise, the quantity, quality, and variety of pupil responses were significantly better than when taught by closed-communication Directing Reading Activity (DRA) procedures as exemplified in basic reader manuals (Petre, 1970; Anderson, 1971). Third, teachers who followed DRTA procedures asked more interpreting and inferring kinds of questions than teachers who did not. As a result, students made responses at higher levels of thinking than a literal level (Davidson, 1970). As might readily be predicted, reading instruction at any level is an independent variable in the reading process. What is done to promote critical reading, regardless of level, is what makes the difference. Said differently, children can be trained to be thinking readers at any level.

A significant study by Taba et al. (1964) was concerned with teaching strategies and thought processes. Her multidimensional analysis of classroom transactions in terms of measurable changes in levels of thinking had several advantages. Results showed that children can learn to make inferences, to generalize, and to make logical assumptions if they receive systematic instruction. The enormous influence of teacher behavior on the thinking of students was most impressive.

The Productive Thinking program of Covington et al. (1966) showed that instructed children were more willing and able to make use of the cognitive skills and strategies common to both creative problem solving and to discerning reflective reading. They developed a general problem solving program of 16 self-contained problem solving episodes. Creative problem solving strategies were taught as well as a number of thinking strategies.

A comprehensive study done at Ohio State University (Wolfe et al., 1967) attempted to determine whether or not children in the elementary grades could be taught to read critically. Bloom's (1956) approach to ways of ordering knowledge influenced the development of a classification system for teachers' verbal behavior, and Guilford's (1965) structure of the intellect proved useful in determining the separate types of thinking of the pupils. Results indicated that teaching critical reading is feasible to children of both sexes and that achievement is influenced by intelligence, general reading ability, and personality and that teaching skill, especially the ability to ask questions and interpret pupil responses, was a key factor (Wolfe et al., 1967). In this latter respect, it is interesting to note that earlier Gallagher (1964) showed how the questions a teacher asked influenced greatly the kind of thinking the student did.

Unquestionably then, the reading-thinking process must begin in the mind of the reader. He must raise the questions. The teacher must keep the inquiry process active by changing the nature and amounts of data to be processed and by the nature of the questions asked. The DRTA teaching-learning process may be outlined briefly as follows:

I. Pupil Actions (P R P)
   A. Predict (set purposes)
   B. Read (process ideas)
   C. Prove (test answers)

II. Teacher Actions (W W P)
   A. What do you think? (activate thought)
   B. Why do you think so? (agitate thought)
   C. Prove it. (require evidence)

If the teacher properly arranges the conditions for student intellectual interaction by instructing in groups of eight or ten members the students can investigate the hidden processes of their own thinking as well as that of other members of the group. By so doing they learn to avoid being docile, unimaginative, and stereotyped in their thinking. Furthermore, authority and dependency are oriented toward the material being read and the group doing the reading rather than the instructor.

Not only is the instructor obliged to nurture the inquiry process by the nature of her questioning but must do so by varying the demands made on the mind to process data and make judgments. This is done by deliberately varying the nature, quantity, and quality of the material to be read using both fiction and non-fiction. Fiction lends itself well to the acquisition of reading-thinking skills because of the nature of plot development and because of the human-interest factor. The former permits proceeding from divergent beginning aspects of a plot and its *who, what, when, where* properties to the convergent concluding aspects of *how* and *why*. The human-interest factor permits young students to identify and project, to marshall their experiences and axioms of life, and deal with plot development and outcome both cognitively and affectively. This type of inquiry process into plot development becomes an active transaction between an individual's expectations as conditioned by his social-cultural environment and by the plot. In turn, children acquire a disposition to be curious, to search for relationships, to seek outcomes. Thus at an early instructional level the focus is cognitive and based on judgment and inference rather than based on an unproductive retelling of isolated story facts.

In nonfiction the search for relationships and patterns of ideas involves facts and their value and the selection and use of the relevant in literature, the humanities, science and mathematics. As the demands of the curriculum spiral in quantity and quality, in complexity and systemization, in fusion and detachment, it becomes increasingly important that students are helped to develop a basis for and a method by which to make judgments. This is the basic strategy of learning and requires the fitting (assimilation) of new information into existing schemes and their alterations (accommodation) so as to make functional (internalize) the extensions and reorganizations. Thus the focus is on the rationale of discovery and inquiry with the emphasis on proof and confirmation.

In reality, DRTA provoked situations become a study in the analysis of variables. The number of variants that a reader may be required to identify, weigh, and make decisions with can be kept quite simple or made quite demanding. (See illustration below.) Thus a reader must be taught to use information to make value judgments objectively. This intellectual power

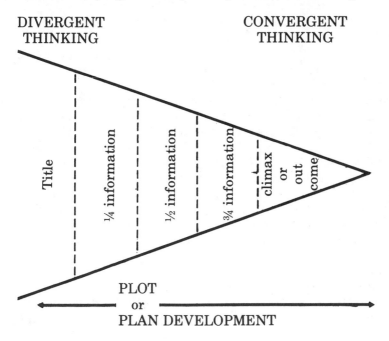

acquisition is accomplished by instruction that varies the quantity, quality, and nature of the material being read. This varying can be done in many ways. In the diagram, judgment periods are declared on a quantity basis or one-fourth the content, one-half, three-fourths, and so on. Doing so varies the number of facts the reader must cope with in decision making. For instance reading one-fourth of a selection may require a reader to identify and weigh as many as ten different facts and use them to determine expectancies. Reading another one-fourth of a selection may add ten more facts to be weighed, to be categorized, and sifted through to determine their value in light of the likely outcome. Each such pause to consider and conjecture taxes the decision making powers of the mind. To acquire functional epistemic orientation requires constant instruction across the years of intellectual maturation and beyond. Pauses for decision making can also be made on a qualitative basis within a page or a paragraph or after a diagram or map or the like. Always the instructional goal is to train the mind.

In brief, it may be said that the regulative principle of directed reading-thinking activities is the *active* search for answers to *genuine* questions. As students become clearer, more articulate, and more sophisticated about raising questions they begin to recognize increasingly that questions and answers, problems and solutions are related reciprocally. As a consequence they see that what is accepted or rejected as solution depends largely on the nature of the problem. Dewey's claim (1938) that when a student's orientation is shifted to inquiry and discovery the scene becomes "... more instruction and humanly dramatic" might be declared as the motto of DRTA instructional-learning strategy. The essential difference between teaching reading as a thinking process in a group situation and outmoded catechetical methods with teacher questions and pupil parroted answers is that in the former the pupil thinks.

The hope of discovery and the discipline of accuracy

The hope of *discovery* is the mainspring of constructive change and is at the heart of question asking. It provides the needed motivation to keep a mind on course in a free and open search for truth. Seneca voiced the regard of most philosophers for intent when he said, "If a man doesn't know toward what port he is sailing no wind is favorable." Socrates, in turn, expressed the hope of discovery succinctly by saying, "A good question is half the answer." Einstein, when asked what was the most important attribute of an innovator, answered quickly, "... a driving spirit of inquiry." Recently Rene Dubos (1968:128) said, "The ability to choose among ideas and possible courses of action may be the most important of all human attributes." For Newton, inquiry was a voyage on the sea of ignorance with the high hope of discovering the islands of truth.

The external forces of man's everyday world generate stimuli faster than he can absorb them. So to resolve cognitive mysteries he must find strategies for reducing their complexities. He learns, because of his innate urge to see cause and effect, to go beyond information swiftly and fallibly. He goes from part to whole, from particular to general, from hypotheses to proofs.

Accuracy is the governing force that transforms ideas into soluble experiences. If the experiences and decisions conform to expected patterns, all is well; but when expectancy is violated the brain is quickly brought to full alertness. All this gives credence to Paul Tillich's conclusion that man becomes really human only at the time of decision, when he exercises free will. No other quest for mind such as the hope of discovery and the discipline of accuracy holds out so great potential rewards to the scholar.

The phrase, "potential rewards to the scholar" raises certain fundamental points. The dynamics of constructive change are not possible without the risk of declaring intentions expressed as tentative hypotheses and representing insightful interpolations and extrapolations. As an epitome it might be said that the dynamics of change is the process of the educated guess. Before new ideas meet the test of accuracy and find their way to the market place, an investment of time, effort, and reflective thought is required. In the final analysis, though, it is *usefulness* (functionality) that represents the potential reward and that leads to intentions that make change and growth possible.

This then is the contribution that sound training in reflective reading and thinking can make to ensure dynamic growth. Students must be trained in the art of asking questions, in open-minded seeking for change through the hope of discovering of new truths that are governed by the disciplines of accuracy. To acquire the needed intellectual refinement in the use of the reading-thinking process described requires constant and consecutive practice under the watchful eye of a master teacher.

Conclusion

Lewis Carroll (1906: 938) in a delightful essay entitled "Feeding the Mind" writes about the proper kind of food for the mind being provided in proper amounts. Then he raises the question, "I wonder if there is such a thing in nature as a *fat mind?* I really think I have met with one or two minds which could not keep up with the slowest trot in conversation, could not jump over a logical fence to save their lives, always got stuck fast in a narrow argument, and, in short, were fit for nothing but to waddle helplessly through the world." The mode of cognitive actions which I have described in this paper as the dynamics of reflective reading-thinking process merit dominating all instruction in reading. The fundamental doctrine of instruction must be directed to the knowing mind and away from a passive taking in of the contents of an author. The mental processes answering to this requires a great exertion to be sure, but the greater the exertion the more valuable is the effect. If it is true that we are what we eat then for minds to remain agile and adept some ideas need to be carefully selected and chewed and digested.

REFERENCES

Anderson, W.W. Study of the effects of self-directed activity upon quantity, quality, and variety of responses in a group directed reading-thinking activity. Unpublished doctoral dissertation, University of Virginia, 1971.

Berlyne, D.E. *Structure and direction in thinking.* New York: John Wiley, 1965.

Bloom, B., et al. *Taxonomy of educational objectives, Handbook I: Cognitive domain.* New York: David McKay, 1956.

Bruner, J.S. *Relevance of education.* New York: W.W. Norton, 1971.

Bruner, J.S.; Goodnow, J.J.; and Austin, G.A. *A study of thinking.* New York: John Wiley, 1956.

Carroll, L. Feeding the mind. *Harper's Monthly.* New York: May 1906, 937-939.

Chomsky, N. Language and the mind. In C. Laird and R.M. Gorrell (Eds.), *Reading about language.* New York: Harcourt Brace Jovanovich, 1971.

Covington, M.V.; Crutchfield; R.S.; and Davies, L.B. *Productive thinking program.* Berkeley, Ca.: Brazelton Printing Co., 1966.

Davidson, J.L. Quantity, quality, and variety of teachers' questions and pupils' responses during an open-communication structured group directed reading-thinking activity and a closed-communication structured group directed reading activity. Unpublished doctoral dissertation, University of Michigan, 1970.

Dewey, J. *Experience and education.* New York: Macmillan Co., 1938.

Dubos, R. *So human an animal.* New York: Charles Scribner's Sons, 1968.

Duckworth, E. Piaget rediscovered. In R. Ripple and V. Rockcastle (Eds.), *Piaget rediscovered, a report on cognitive studies and curriculum development.* Ithaca, N.Y.: Cornell University Press, 1969.

Gallahger, J.L. *Teaching the gifted child.* Boston: Allyn & Bacon, 1964.

Guilford, J.P. Intellectual factors in productive thinking. In J. Ashner and E.Bish (Eds.), *Productive thinking in education.* Washington, D.C.: National Education Association, 1965.

Henderson, E.H. Study of individually formulated purposes for reading in relation to reading achievement, comprehension, and purpose attainment. Unpublished doctoral dissertation, University of Delaware, 1963.

Klausmeier, H. J.; Harris, C. W.; and Wiersma, W. *Strategies of learning and efficiency of concept attainment by individuals and groups.* Cooperative Research Project No. 1442, Madison, Wisc.: University of Wisconsin, 1964.

Monod, J. *Chance and necessity.* Trans. A. Wainhouse. New York: Alfred A. Knopf, 1971.

Petre, R.M. Quantity, quality and variety of pupil responses during an open-communication structured group directed reading-thinking activity and a closed-communication structured group directed reading activity. Unpublished doctoral dissertation, University of Delaware, 1970.

Sinclair-de-Zwart, H. Developmental psycholinguistics. In D. Elkind and J. Flavell (Eds.), *Studies in cognitive development: Essays in honor of Jean Piaget.* New York: Oxford University Press, 1969.

Stauffer, R.G. *Directing reading maturity as a cognitive process.* New York: Harper & Row, 1969.

Taba, H.; Levine, S.; and Elzey, F.F. *Thinking in elementary school children.* Cooperative Research Project No. 1574. San Francisco: San Francisco State College, April 1964.

Wallach, M.A. Research on children's thinking. In H. W. Stevenson (Ed.), *Child psychology,* Sixty-second Yearbook for the NSSE Part I. Chicago: University of Chicago Press, 1963.

White, S. A. Learning. In H. W. Stevenson (Ed.), *Child psychology*, Sixty-second Yearbook for the NSSE Part I. Chicago: University of Chicago Press, 1963.

Wolfe, W.; Huck, C.S.; and King, M.L. *Critical reading ability of elementary school children.* U.S. Department of Health, Education and Welfare, Office of Education, Project No. 5-1040, Contract No. OE 4-10-187. Columbus, Ohio: Ohio State University, 1967.

Comments on
Cognitive Processes Fundamental
to Reading Instruction

Lois Hood

The field of early language development is, at first thought, quite remote from reading comprehension and reading instruction. Three major differences between research in early child language and reading instruction struck me immediately: 1) The orientations of the fields—one being applied and directed toward teaching children; the other being concerned with more basic research, directed toward describing and explaining the behavior of children. 2) The differences in age and cognitive level; certainly a two-year-old child is strikingly different from a six or seven-year-old. 3) The areas under study—one, language, which for all normal children develops without explicit teaching; the other, reading, which for most normal children *requires* explicit teaching.

The key that led me to see points of similarity was, I think, in this last difference. Most children do need to be taught to read, but what kind of teaching was Stauffer emphasizing? As I understand his approach, it is that reading is an active, creative process and should be taught as such. Learning to talk is also an active, creative process. The similarity between the two has in fact been expressed by Stauffer (1969: 288) elsewhere: "Learning to read can be accomplished with the same communication effectiveness motivation as learning to talk."

I want to briefly touch upon three issues raised by Stauffer that have also been addressed in language development research. First, the recognition of the importance of cognitive development. Stauffer has emphasized the importance of action and experience in reading comprehension. He has pointed out the interaction between reading and more general aspects of cognitive development. Similarly, a recent development in language acquisition research has been the realization of the very close connection between language development and cognitive development.

Second is the importance of contextual information. Although not explicitly stated in this paper, the role that the child's experiences play in his ability and motivation toward reading is implicit in the language experience approach to reading. The analogy to language development is possibly a little far-fetched, since the importance of contextual information in language development was realized in terms of a more complete understanding of child language rather than as an aid to the child in learning. However, the realization that children talk about their experiences certainly is similar in focus to the idea that children should read about their experiences.

Finally, central roles are given to intension, alternative strategies, and individual differences in both areas. Stauffer makes mention of individual differences in cognitive style, persistence, and curiosity and the fact that these can all influence and interact with learning to read. The work in language development, describing alternative strategies and individual variation in the form of children's early language and the use of certain non-linguistic strategies, suggests that in reading there might also be individual differences in learning strategies per se. Perhaps just as children appear to have alternative routes to the same end in terms of language, they may have alternative routes to reading. In this regard, it might be useful to investigate the processes that occur with "spontaneous" readers. Perhaps some insight into alternative learning strategies might come from such observations.

REFERENCE

Stauffer, R. *Teaching reading as a thinking process.* New York Harper and Row. 1969.

Five Exemplary Reading Programs

Gita Wilder

In 1971, the United States Office of Education commissioned Educational Testing Service to plan and conduct what was termed a "descriptive and analytic study of compensatory reading programs in U.S. public schools." Actually, the charge was more specific than that. It involved elementary schools only, and within elementary schools, only grades 2, 4, and 6. Since the study was funded by monies allocated for "evaluation," an experimental study was ruled out; thus there was no control at any point over assignment of students to educational treatments. With these as directives, ETS surveyed reading programs in a national sample of 741 public schools during the Spring of 1972. The schools were selected randomly using income (as a measure of socioeconomic status) and percent minority as stratifying variables. The survey was conducted by means of questionnaires sent to each principal and to the teachers of reading in grades 2, 4, and 6.

It had been decided during the planning phase of the study to define compensatory reading as broadly as possible, based on the belief that the only real difference between compensatory and non-compensatory reading instruction lay with the source of the funding support and that, for purposes of this study, *all* types of reading programs should be included. The definition of compensatory reading instruction that was adopted was an arbitrary and purely administrative one; it was defined as any reading instruction provided for students because they were reading below grade level. Thus the definition was free from constraints of funding sources, materials, qualifying characteristics of students, and instructional packages of any sort. The survey covered a wide range of school descriptors, teacher characteristics, and details about methods, materials, and instructional practices.

On the basis of information gathered in the Spring 1972 survey, a subset of the original 741 schools was chosen for more complete study during the 1972-1973 school year. A total of 263 schools, most with compensatory reading programs but some without (to serve as a comparison group), was included in this second phase of the research. In these schools, students were pretested and posttested using two subtests of the grade-appropriate form of the Metropolitan Reading Achievement Test, the grade appropriate Cooperative Primary or STEP test of reading achievement, and a specially designed measure of attitude toward reading. In addition, a daily record was maintained of attendance at reading instruction for each of the 55,000 students in the study, and the questionnaires were administered again to the principals of the participating schools and all teachers of reading in the second, fourth, and sixth grades. On the basis of the test results, a measure of effectiveness was created and applied to all classes, compensatory and non-compensatory, in all of the schools in the second phase of the study. It had been decided, however, on the basis of an analysis performed on the data from the first study year, that reading programs were likely to show greater similarity across grades within schools than by grade levels across schools. The notion of "reading program," then, was a school based one and one with which I suspect many reading people would not be in agreement. There has been some ambiguity in the use this study has made of the term "program" as applied to reading instruction in the schools surveyed. While the questionnaires allowed principals to indicate that their schools offered more than one "reading program" (along with a page of decision rules concerning how to identify such "programs"), in the analysis and reporting of the data, the project staff have also used the term *program* to describe the totality of a school's reading instruction including many of the demographic and sociological features that affect it. In this paper, the term is used for the most part in its broader sense, relating to all of the school and classroom variables that affect but are not traditionally included in definitions of reading programs.

On the basis of the effectiveness data, schools were characterized as having fallen within the predicted range with respect to outcome, or as outliers. That is, a school's posttest scores were examined with respect to its pretest scores. The schools that performed as expected were differentiated from the schools that performed either better or worse than had been expected on the basis of the pretest scores. The outliers were a group that were of special interest to the study staff, and a subset of them were selected for further study during the 1973-1974 school year.

The selection of schools according to an effectiveness criterion was not a simple matter. Effectiveness scores were obtained for each class, for each grade level included in the study, for each school, and for each cluster of schools (schools had been aggregated into eleven clusters by virtue of a factor-type analysis of their essential program characteristics), separately for compensatory students, non-compensatory students, and all students. Needless to say, classes within a grade, a school, or a cluster; grades within a school or a cluster; and schools within a cluster were not uniformly effective. Nor were programs uniformly effective for compensatory and non-compensatory students within a class, a grade, a school, or a cluster. The particular level of effectiveness for the selection of schools to be visited was *cluster effectiveness for compensatory students*. That is, the most and least effective clusters (in terms of a rank-ordering procedure) for compensatory students were selected for representation by schools to be visited. Moreover, within a cluster the most or consistently least effective schools were selected. The procedure was operationalized as follows: clusters were rank-ordered on the basis of the effectiveness of their instruction for compensatory students. Two of the most effective clusters and two of the least effective clusters were selected for visits. Within the clusters, schools were rank-ordered with respect to their effectiveness for compensatory students. From the most effective clusters, a number of the most effective schools were selected for visits. Because schools were not consistently effective across grades, schools that were chosen from effective clusters had to be highly effective (that is, highly ranked in grade-level effectiveness) at more than one grade level. Similarly, from the least effective clusters, the least effective schools (at more than one grade level) were selected for visits.

Twenty-nine schools were visited during the 1973-1974

year, 27 of them were visited twice. During the visits, observers visited all classrooms containing second, fourth, and sixth graders in which reading instruction was taking place, and spoke with principals, teachers, and any other staff involved in the reading programs in the schools. The questionnaires were also administered, for the third successive year, to principals and teachers of reading in the grades in question. The conduct of the observations will be described subsequently; suffice it to say here that the schedule of visits was arranged so as to maximize the number of observers who visited any given site.

At the conclusion of their visits to school, observers were asked to make predictions about the direction of the outlier status of each school they visited, that is, whether the schools were, in their judgment, highly effective or highly ineffective schools. The predictions were discussed at the final debriefings conducted for each school, and divergences and congruences among observers' judgments were noted. The five schools selected for more intensive study in the second year of site visitation were schools that could be considered effective by two criteria. The first was that they were, in terms of the measured effectiveness selection criterion described earlier, among the more effective schools in a most effective cluster. The second was that all observers to a school had predicted it's effective status at the time of the first year visit. The purpose of this final set of visits was to provide a careful and detailed documentation of the features associated with effectiveness in reading instruction.

This, then, was the series of events which led to the selection of the five schools whose reading programs are described in this paper. The conditions of their selection are summarized in Table 1 and should be remembered throughout the observations that follow. First, the five schools were the end result of a process that started with a random national sample of public elementary schools. These were *not* schools selected from among a collection of new and/or exciting innovative schools or sites where experimental curricula were being introduced. They came from the general population of American public schools, and represent a group culled from the range and variety present therein. Second, the criteria by which their effectiveness was measured were quite relative: performance that was better than had been anticipated from their pretest scores on a battery of achievement tests, and agreement by a crew of trained observers that they were among the best schools observed in the group of 29 outliers.

Table 1. A summary of the activities of the compensatory reading project

Year	No. of Schools	Sample	Data Collection
Spring 1972	741	Random sample U.S. public elementary schools	Questionnaires to principals and teachers of reading in grades 2, 4, and 6
School year 1972-73	263	Stratified sample drawn from original 741: strata (1) CR Title I, (2) CR non-Title I, (3) NCR	Achievement and attitude pretest and posttest; attendance records; individual student data; questionnaires as above
School year 1973-74	29	Outliers among 263 schools: higher than predicted achievement and lower than predicted achievement	Site visits; classroom observations; consensus ratings; questionnaires as above
School year 1974-75	5	Schools deemed effective by achievement and observational criteria	Site visits; classroom observations

It had long been the feeling of the study staff that the really meaningful features of reading instruction were not being tapped by either the questionnaires or the test battery, and that in order for any of us to speak with authority about effective reading instruction, we were going to have to get into schools at some point. School and classroom observations were carried out during the third study year for several reasons. The first was to fill in the gaps left by the questionnaires and to provide information about some of the less countable features of instruction. The second was to validate the information obtained from the questionnaires, to determine how the frequency distributions and item responses translated themselves into classroom practices. The third was to document, first-hand, the nature of educational effectiveness by looking at programs whose effectiveness was greater than the average and at the same time, for comparison, looking at programs whose effectiveness was less than the average.

The observations were conceived as a sort of doubleblind experiment in which neither the observers nor the schools being observed knew the effectiveness standings. After the visits, observers were asked to predict from their observations which schools were more and which were less effective. Schools were asked to cooperate with the understanding that the study was attempting to gather more detailed information about a small number of programs; the cooperation rate was reasonably good, although some schools (about 30 percent) did refuse. Observers were selected from a large pool of individuals with an assortment of backgrounds. Among them were several staff members of the project who had been involved with the research from the very beginning, although none had any awareness of the effectiveness rankings. There were also several former teachers and a number of ETS staff members with other major functions: people whose primary areas of interest were measurement, test construction, literature, and educational psychology.

While all of the observers were required to undergo a week of common training in the use of the observation instrument and the general goals of the study, their varying perspectives were helpful in broadening the scope of the observations. A format was developed for rating classroom variables, and a general outline of information to be gathered from interviews was prepared. Visits to schools were flexible enough to be adaptive to school schedules but consistent enough to ensure that comparable data be collected from all sites. As part of the training procedure, a team of reading specialists provided a day's crash course in reading methods and materials in order that the observers, none of whom was trained in reading, would have a common (if limited) background in the field.

Each visit to a school involved two or three days at the school by a team of from two to six observers, the number depending on the size of the school and the number of classes to be visited. Pairs of observers visited each class, taking narrative notes that were later turned into ratings. Once independent ratings had been made, observers conferred about their ratings and produced a third rating form representing the consensus of their individual ratings. Teachers were interviewed informally by one or both members of the pair of observers of the classroom in question. Each evening during the site visit, the site visit team met to share observations and to discuss the following day's schedule; these discussions served to allow for schedule changes in order to provide extra coverage of extraordinary classrooms or events. The classrooms observed were mostly those whose teachers had filled out questionnaires in previous study years, although few of them included the same students as had been tested. The classroom observation instrument included items covering instructional groupings and how these changed during the school year; materials and audiovisual equipment used; such items of teacher behavior as modes of reinforcement and control mechanisms, student handling of wrong answers, use of and type of questions asked; student affect and behavior, level of involvement in the learning process, and degree of autonomy. There were also items covering the time allotted to various kinds of activities and the time spent by both teachers and students in various kinds of groupings. Observers were asked to record all reading materials present in the classroom in addition to those that were actually used.

Each site visit was directed by one member of the observation team charged with making the initial contact with the school; setting up a schedule for the visit; and producing the final document resulting from the visit, a case study report covering all aspects of the school and its reading program. Site visit responsibilities were spread out among the observers so that the number of case studies produced by each person was equalized. When the team returned from the field, a debriefing was held with all team members present as well as members of the project staff who had not been on the trip. All debriefings were tape recorded. The data collected for any single school, therefore, included the following: three observation rating forms for each classroom visited as well as notes taken by each observer in each class visited; tapes of daily on-site debriefings; tapes of final debriefings; and questionnaires that had been administered for the third year. Also available were the previous two years' questionnaires and the test scores from the previous year's testing.

The five schools visited during the 1974-1975 school year were subjected to roughly the same treatment except that the consensus discussions were eliminated in an effort to gain broader coverage including more classrooms and additional interviews. Observers visited classrooms and filled out a somewhat revised form of the classroom observation instrument. Interviews were conducted with teachers and other school personnel connected with the reading program. Debriefings were conducted at the site and at ETS, and case studies were produced as a result of the visits. Because the staff of observers had been pared down to a core group of six people (augmented by some of the former staff where a large school or the illness of a regular observer demanded it), an attempt was made to have all observers see all five schools in order to give the entire group a common perspective. At this stage of the game, everyone knew that the five schools were effective ones; observers were charged with discovering *why*.

So much for the way in which the visits were conducted. Unfortunately, the analytic results of the observations are not yet available for reporting or drawing conclusions. Analyses are planned that will relate the effectiveness rankings for all subtests of all tests to the classroom data gathered by means of the observation instrument. What can be offered at this point are descriptions of and some tentative conclusions about the nature of reading instruction in five schools, from the point of view of one member of the research team who has been with the study from the beginning.

I should tell you something of my own background, since I am about to expose you to some rather biased views of reading instruction and you might like to know the sources of the bias. My academic background is in sociology and anthropology, with some extracurricular work in developmental psychology. I have taught, at various times in my career, second graders in public schools, students of all ages and levels in a foreign language program (Hebrew), and college students in sociology.

Five years of my professional life were spent in the development of tests and other assessment devices. Finally, I've been involved in an assortment of educational evaluation and research projects, including the one I've just described. I possess no credentials in reading or the teaching thereof. I have, however, been a careful observer of my children's educational progress, and I can't help but have had my biases augmented by their experiences learning to read.

Following that digression, let me return to the five schools whose reading programs are to be the subject of discussion. At first blush, the five schools seem to have few features in common. They were, of course, all public elementary schools. All five had kindergarten programs. Four of the five schools served poor children and received some federal funds for reading. Three of the four received state monies for reading as well. The five schools were scattered throughout the United States, one in New England, one in the Deep South, one in a western state, and two in the far west. Two of the schools were located in small, isolated towns, one in a small city, one in a suburb of a major city, and one in a large city. Table 2 presents some of the demographic characteristics of the five schools.

I would like to take some time to describe the reading activity in each of the schools individually, in part to give you a sense of the flavor of each school and in part to define the range covered by the group of five.

School A was a smallish school (335 students in grades K through 5) in a smallish town on the coast of New England. The town was poor, the students were poor, the district was poor. The reading specialist, who had received her training in Boston, remarked that the reading problems among the all-white student population in this school were as severe as any she'd encountered in the ghettos of Boston. The principal described the district as having no money for innovation, the parents as having no tolerance for innovation, and the staff as traditional. Indeed, the school building had a look that observers characterized as "spartan." The principal, a pleasant, easy-going man of fifty or so, was a native of the area who had spent some years in a more cosmopolitan school district and had returned to this area by choice, working for a number of years as a newspaper man until a job opened up in the schools. He and the reading teacher were both new to the school. He

Table 2.   A summary of selected characteristics of five schools with effective reading programs

School	Geog. Reg.	SES	Grades in School	School Enrollment 1973-74	Title I Funds	Racial Composition Student Body
A	NE	-1.7	K-5	335	Yes	100% White
B	S	-1.8	K-6	470	Yes	33% W, 67% B
C	W	—	K-6	700	No	100% White
D	W	-0.8	K-6	610	Yes	30% W, 40% B, 30% Other
E	W	-0.5	K-4	613	Yes	100% White

School	Materials in Use
A	Ginn 360 basals; SRA basals; Scott Foresman basals; Hoffman Readers; EDL flashcards; Bell and Howell Language Master and Autosort; Psychotechnics, Inc. Radio Reading Series; Alpha program
B	Scott Foresman basals; Scott Foresman Open Highways series; Ginn basals; Sullivan Programmed Readers; Merrill Linguistic Readers; LEIR; EDL materials; Aud-X machine with software; Webster Reading Clinic; Macmillan Reading Spectrum
C	ECRI program using Sullivan Programmed Readers; Lyons and Carnahan Young America series; Harcourt Brace basals; Scott Foresman basals; Jr. Scholastic and Weekly Readers; Arrow Books; Distar
D	SRA basal readers; Harper and Row basal readers; Ginn basal readers; Scott Foresman Open Highways series; Bank Street Readers; Appleton-Century-Crofts Reading Learning Center
E	Harper and Row basals; Scott Foresman basals; Supplementary use of Macmillan, Lippincott, Ginn 100, and Scott Foresman basals and Bank Street Readers; Harper and Row Listening-Reading Program; SRA labs; Sullivan Programmed Readers; Fries Linguistic Readers

perceived his role as one of loosening up the school, the teachers, and the approach to education. In the three visits conducted by teams of observers from our project, his progress toward this goal was quite evident.

At the time of the first visit, observers felt this to be the most old-fashioned school they had visited, concluding that the reading classes were being conducted exactly as they would have been twenty or thirty years earlier. Basal readers were used throughout the grades. Students seated at desks arranged in rows and columns were learning to read from basal readers and accompanying workbooks. Classes were divided into three reading groups. The teaching seemed thorough and conscientious, and very, very serious. While new materials had been introduced in the school (the Alpha program for kindergarteners, Ginn 360 in the primary grades, and the Harcourt Brace series in grades 3-5), there was little use of the new materials except in one fourth grade. In this class, a young male teacher had introduced a more informal teaching style and some individually paced activities. A great deal of equipment, much of it electronic, was evident in the Title I reading lab that served 80 students for 30 minutes each day. Nonetheless, students in the lab worked primarily out of basal readers, using the equipment and software and games present for short periods of drill. The atmosphere in the lab was more informal than it was in classrooms, and the informality increased over the course of three visits as the reading teacher seemed to be gaining confidence. At the time of the third visit, many of the activities were teacher-made to meet particular needs (an observer was impressed by the teacher's use of restaurant menus as a device for drill in scanning, for example), and the teacher had instituted a popular lending library of materials for students to take home. More teachers were working with materials other than the basal series that formed the backbone of the reading program. Teachers commented on the change in atmosphere in the school as a whole, and cited in particular the new materials that had been made available to them for the teaching of reading as having contributed to the change. At the time of the third visit, classroom activities included a poetry writing lesson, combined with an art project, and a tape listening exercise; and in one classroom, fourteen different activities were observed to be taking place during the so-called reading period. Still, observers agreed that the essence of reading instruction in this school was the careful and thorough attention given to basics.

School B, in a small city in the Deep South, served a population of 470 students in grades K through 6. The school also had two reading labs and two different types of special education classes. Two-thirds of the school's students were black and characterized as very poor; the principal and more than half of the teachers were white. In this school (a lively, noisy place with an informal atmosphere), a schoolwide emphasis on the language arts was immediately apparent to visitors. The use of Language Experience in Reading (LEIR) had been introduced in the school by the principal midway through the project's testing year, and the whole ambience of the school was colored and shaped by the program. Everywhere student writing was in evidence. In classrooms, the lunchroom, the principal's office, and even the special education classes, student stories, poems, and songs were tacked up, propped up, and hung from clotheslines. With no prompting at all, students would lead visitors to their own contributions to the collection and read their work. The principal's office was decorated with stories about him that had been written after an interview conducted by a second grade class. The work was all treated with obvious pride and respect, laminated in plastic to preserve it before hanging, and frequently fingered and read.

The reading program was conducted mainly out of basal readers, in the standard three-group format, even in the sixth grades. There were also two Title I reading labs providing supplementary reading instruction (mainly drill using an array of hardware and software) for 140 students. Some teachers were more literal in their use of the basal series (Scott Foresman was the series used throughout the school) than others, and the quality of reading instruction was judged to vary among the teachers in the school. Teachers also differed in the ways in which and the extent to which they used the language experience format, ranging from not at all through total immersion in it. Clearly the principal was not forcing anyone to adopt the method, but he seemed to dole out approval of teachers in direct proportion to their use of LEIR. Teachers who were interviewed expressed varying sentiments about the method, from raving enthusiasm through reservations about it for "these children," but all of the teachers were unanimous in their respect and affection for the principal and it seemed clear that sooner or later all of the teachers would have incorporated LEIR to some extent in their instructional programs. Some teachers used LEIR in conjunction with social studies and/or science, some used it as a separate creative activity like art and sometimes combined with art. The special education teachers were using LEIR with great enthusiasm and seeming success.

School B was a happy place to visit and observers felt it was probably a happy place for students. The essence of the reading program at this school was judged to be the overall positive feeling and respect accorded language, spoken and written, and an emphasis on the wholeness of language. One observer concluded that the unique feature of the school was the fact that "Language seems to be the backbone of all instruction and activity."

School C, located in a large city in a western state, was the only school that had a distinctive and easily identifiable "program." You may be familiar with the Exemplary Center for Reading Instruction (ECRI) and the methodology that has come from it. The school in our study was one in which the program had existed for three years at the time of our first visit. The school enrollment was about 700; the students were of approximately lower middle class and middle class origins, and there was no federal funding. The ECRI program involves a series of formulated teacher directives (usually spoken verbatim) for carrying out extensive drill; oral response by students, usually in unison; and a great deal of prescribed positive reinforcement. There is a strong listening component to the program, the rationale behind the oral drills. In this school, the program was being used with the Sullivan materials in the first three grades. In the classes observed using the program (in this instance only second grades), the noise level was very high, the level of student involvement was very high, and the activity seemed unusually brisk and task-oriented. Since the program directives are so specific, there is little chance for individual teacher styles to make themselves apparent.

In other grades in this school, other materials were being used. Distar was in use in the kindergartens; one class of first graders was using i.t.a.; the *Young American* series was in use in grades 4 through 6; and one class used Scott Foresman basals. Classes were grouped homogeneously within grades by reading ability. Observers felt that the ECRI program had affected the school's reading curriculum apart from the classes in which it was actually in use. For instance, the special reading resource teachers (there were two) used ECRI materials and methods. Teachers throughout the school had picked up the positive reinforcement "lingo" and were using it even without the prescriptions of ECRI. There was also a great deal of outloud reading and oral unison drills, a direct spillover from ECRI. Students read aloud to themselves even in the library.

Throughout the school, language arts occupied the bulk of instructional time, up to 3 1/2 hours in some grades. While observers felt that this, in itself, might explain the high effectiveness rankings for the school, it was a source of some concern to the principal and some of the teachers. Their contention was that other areas (social studies, music, art, and science) were receiving short shrift.

It was concluded that the essence of the reading program in this school was the intensive training provided by the ECRI program in basic skills and the spillover of the program to other areas of instruction in the school. The presence of ECRI demonstration teachers and supervisors provided constant external pressure on teachers to be well prepared. The adoption of the program in this school also reflected a stress on reading and on language that carried over into all grade levels.

School D, the fourth school, located in the suburb of a large West Coast city, served students from low-income families. Many of the students came from a high crime area and many of them came from single parent families. The mobility level was extraordinary, topping 100 percent every year. A good deal of federal and state money was available for this school and its effects were very much in evidence. A reading specialist who was responsible for the entire primary grade reading program and a resource center were paid for by state funds. Title I money supplied an Appleton Century Crofts Reading Learning Center for grades 4-6, with a full-time teacher and an aide. There was also a bilingual class at each of the lower grade levels, serving the Spanish speaking population. That amounted to 30 percent of the student body. Students were grouped heterogeneously in an assortment of straight grade and multiage classes. In the primary grades, the reading resource teacher, who was universally praised by teachers and observers, functioned as a kind of master teacher. She visited classrooms and conducted lessons, then provided reinforcement activities for teachers to conduct themselves. Her approach involved a great deal of drill using an eclectic collection of materials. The resource teacher not only maintained the collection of supplementary materials (supplementary to the Harper & Row basal series used throughout the school) but helped the teachers to set up classroom libraries. She had, incidentally, set up a series of what she called "comprehension drills," responding to the relatively poor standing of students in this school on comprehension tests in the statewide testing program in previous years.

The ACC Reading Center, used by the intermediate grades, processed 240 students for 40 minute periods each day. These sessions were given in addition to their regular classroom reading instruction. The ACC procedures included initial testing for placement of students in individual courses of study, and individual work by students on their courses of study in individual carrels. Incentives were provided for completing worksheets correctly. As an innovation added just prior to the visit, students were being asked to read books of their own choosing during the time in carrels when they were waiting to be checked out by the teacher or aide, this because "test results indicated that a greater stress on comprehension was needed." While our observers were horrified by what they considered the "impersonality, mechanization, and isolation" of the carrels, students seemed anxious to get to the center and happy to be there.

In the classrooms observed in this school there were many materials. Bright displays, books and games, and audiovisual equipment were evident in even the most barren (by this school's standards) classrooms. In addition to the Harper & Row series that was everywhere, classrooms might contain any or all of the following: the Ginn 100 series, Roberts English, Basic Goals in Spelling, Bell and Howell worksheets (to accompany some taped material), Bank Street Readers, Scholastic Reader Paperbacks, and the Barnell-Loft Specific Skill Series. All classes had story books in abundance.

There was evidence of communication among teachers

throughout the school. In addition to the strong leadership provided by the primary grades reading resource teacher (leadership that was acknowledged and respected by the teachers), there was evidence that teachers shared ideas and materials. The evidence came from the observed interaction among teachers, their comments in interviews, and from similarities observed in classroom activities. Observers felt the teachers were an unusually professional group.

In this school,, observers attributed what they judged to be the high effectiveness of the reading instruction to two well-organized programs with a wealthy base of materials and a staff that was unusually close, cooperative, and cohesive.

School E by contrast, was one in which evidences of controversy were everywhere. This K through 4 school served over 600 students as the only elementary school in an isolated lumbering town not far from the West Coast. This town, too, was poor, and the school population was described as highly mobile as a result of the vagaries of the lumbering industry. Title I and state funds were available in the school and were used to pay for aides for all classrooms.

The principal of this school was spending his last year at the school when the first visit took place, following a period when he had initiated a great many radical changes in the school. He was a friendly man in his forties who had clearly invested much of his energy in the school. During the years prior to the project's visits, the principal had shifted the structure of the reading program from one of providing special help to selected students on a pullout basis to one in which the responsibility for all reading instruction for students at all levels of ability was placed on the shoulders of the classroom teacher. At that point, a schoolwide effort was made to set up individual goals and prescriptions for students and to change the role of the special reading teacher from one of instructor to one of resource person. She administered tests and developed individual prescriptions, aided in the monitoring of student progress, and provided materials for the reinforcement of skills and competencies. The shift was unpopular in the community and a great deal of public furor ensued. There was also some dissent among the teachers concerning the changes. Somehow the community was mollified, in part, through the principal's involvement of the community in many of the decisions of the school and in his bringing in of new teachers whose instructional goals were allied with his own. By and large the staff was, at the time of our visits, generally supportive of the changes. Even the teachers who were not thoroughly happy with the instructional changes were admiring of the principal and his leadership. The teachers were a lively, articulate bunch; there were still evidences of disagreements among them based as much on style as on differences in educational philosophy; but the total effect was that of a very alive school.

Again, Harper & Row basals were the main vehicle for reading instruction in the school, and the Harper & Row end-of-book tests were the main vehicle for the tracking of student progress. Teachers were under no obligation to use the basals so long as their students could pass the tests at the minimum competency levels, and some teachers indeed did not use the basals at all. Many did, however. In addition to the basals, there was a carefully catalogued and cross-referenced library of resource materials set up by the reading specialist, indicating reading level and skills taught for every piece of material in the place. Among the basal reader series so classified were the Macmillan, Lippincott, Ginn, and Bank Street Readers and the Sullivan programmed materials.

In all classrooms, reading instruction was based on individual "contracts" which were really nothing more than assignment sheets for each student. There were also two instructional aides in every classroom. Teachers varied in the use they made of the contracts and the aides, and the amount of individualization varied with the class as well. In some classes, students worked individually most or all of the time. In other classes, individualized work was interspersed with ad hoc skill groups or groups formed for the purposes of particular projects or activities. One fourth grade teacher expressed his intention to do some group reading every day because he felt that the move away from group discussions had set back comprehension. Observers felt, much as this teacher did, that there was an apparent lack in this school of oral reading by students and of being read to. Individual classrooms appeared to reflect the individual personalities of the teachers and, in this school more than any other, there was considerable variation among classrooms. (In one room, a teacher had done away with conventional classroom furniture and had substituted four couches and a collection of activity centers at tables.) There were more male teachers in this school than in other elementary schools visited, several of them in the lower grades.

Observers were impressed in this school with the degree of task-orientation by students without apparent adult attention. (This observation was made in spite of some teachers' feelings that many of their lower ability students could not sustain interest in individual work for any extended period.)

The principal's next projected change was to establish multiage classes throughout the school. In preparation for this move, he had created three multiage classes as a pilot project during the year of our visits. The teachers of these classes, one a self-contained class of first and second graders and two team-taught third and fourth grade units, were uniformly enthusiastic about the multiage idea although they were all planning changes in their particular set-ups for the following year. Other teachers were still resistant. In planning for the changeover, the principal had set up a series of meetings with parents. Committees that included parents had drawn up some of the preliminary recommendations.

As the program was discussed in interviews with teachers, observers came away with the feeling that the outstanding feature of the program in this school was not the individualized instruction or the contract system, but the shifting of responsibility for instruction to each teacher and the support of that responsibility with a bank of materials, a resource person, and help in the classroom in the form of two aides. Teachers in School E were all unusually thoughtful about their instruction; all of them had contrived plans of one sort or another. There was a great deal of talk about trying things one way or another, and a general willingness to change things within the classroom from year to year.

What conclusions about effective reading programs can be drawn from the descriptions of these five schools? The programs that have been described are all different, and the features that observers concluded were responsible for their effectiveness differed from school to school. What have the programs in common? Much of the dialog that was conducted in the debriefing sessions held during the course of this project was devoted to this question. What follows is some compilation of our collective wisdom about what constitutes good reading programs:

1. All five of the schools described in this paper (and indeed all of the schools felt by observers to have effective reading programs) had defined reading as an important instructional goal. In all of the five schools, reading was accorded top priority among the school's activities. By virtue either of the time spent in reading activities, the money spent for reading materials, or the quality of the resources devoted to reading, the schools indicated clearly that, they considered reading important.

2. In all five schools there was effective educational leadership specific to the issue of reading instruction. In three of the schools, the principals provided the leadership; in one school, the reading leadership came from the reading resource person; in the fifth school, the leadership came from outside the school, but its impetus was felt in all aspects of the reading program.

3. An outstanding feature of the reading programs of all of the five schools observed was careful attention to basic skills, whatever else the programs entailed. In one school, the attention to basics was the essence of the program. In other schools, there were other outstanding components of the program; but in all cases, basic skills were thoroughly and effectively taught.

4. In all of the five schools there was relative breadth of materials. In School A, perhaps the most sparsely supplied of the five, there was an increase over previous years and a growing awareness by teachers that supplementary materials were helpful in reinforcing old skills and broadening the base on which new ones could be taught. Other schools incorporated materials in subject matter areas into their language programs. Our favorite school had students produce their own materials. In all of the schools there was some recognition that there were alternative methods for accomplishing any given goal, and there were materials or resources for obtaining materials to provide alterna-

tives.

5. In all of the five schools described here there was evidence of cross-fertilization of ideas among teachers. In some instances, the impetus for the dialog among teachers was a program (ECRI in one case, the the ACC Reading Center in another). In other cases, the dialog was encouraged by the educational leader, by example or (as in the language experience school) by the conduct of training sessions or discussions about methods and materials. In the school using individual instruction, the dialog was started by the principal's introduction of far-reaching changes; this particular dialog included the community. In any case, it seems that schools in which the reading programs are liveliest and most effective are schools in which ideas about reading are aired and shared among teachers.

"What about teachers?" I hear you cry. Why haven't I said anything about teachers? They were, after all, the primary purveyors of the reading programs in the schools described. I believe that all of us emerged from the experience of the site visits with a sense of awe at the power of teachers to inspire, to bore, to create excitement, to discourage it, and, most important, to create, to enhance, to pass on intact, or to pervert an educational treatment. One of the first orders of analytic business for us will be to examine effectiveness at the classroom level, much of which may be described almost entirely in terms of teacher variables. However, our choice of reading programs to visit was made on the basis of overall school effectiveness, at which level I believe there *is* a program organization that transcends life in individual classrooms. In the five schools I've described to you, we saw a whole range of teacher behavior and quality, from several teachers who were "stars" through one who tacks down the rotten end of my own private teaching excellence scale. In none of the five schools, however, did we feel that the success of the program was due primarily to the quality of instruction in individual classrooms. Instead, we felt in each case that the program somehow had an existence that affected the instruction in individual classrooms, differently perhaps for each class. In one school, for example, we felt that the introduction of the program had injected new life into a receptive but otherwise quite ordinary bunch of teachers. In another school, we felt (somewhat regretfully) that the program tended to eclipse teacher individuality and creativity and substitute for these standardized (albeit effective) teaching practices. I expect that our foray into effectiveness at the classroom level will lead us to a different set of conclusions about reading instruction, conclusions that I suspect will augment rather than contradict our previous findings.

What have we learned from all of this about the nature of effective reading instruction for comprehension? My own observation is that classroom teachers do not conceptualize the area of comprehension apart from any other feature of their reading program. When asked about comprehension, most teachers mentioned something about the comprehension exercises in the materials they were currently using. Most frequently, teachers cited the use of questions, verbal or written, as their method for achieving comprehension or learning whether it has occurred. A few teachers spoke of group discussions, before or after the reading of selected materials, as enhancing comprehension among students. A few teachers spoke of their use of listening exercises as contributing to comprehension (and conversely to the lack of a listening component to their program as being detrimental to the development of comprehension). Others cited vocabulary development and increasing the experiential base of their students as their contributions to comprehension. In short, nowhere among the five schools was there apparent to us a definable, concentrated set of principles or procedures related to instruction for comprehension.

This reflection, achieved through careful reading of the observers' narrative records and the notes taken during interviews with teachers, enhances my belief that a successful reading program is of a piece, and that comprehension is a part of that piece. I have come to believe that an effective reading program includes at the very least successful training in the basic skills needed for decoding and exposure to language in all of its forms (written, spoken, poetry, prose, etc.) and that comprehension is directly related to the amount, intensity, and affect connected with the exposure. This conclusion may, after three years of data collection, serve only to underscore Murray

Kempton's well known definition of a sociologist as one who spends thousands of dollars and develops elaborate methodology to find the nearest house of prostitution.

Comments on
Five Exemplary Reading Programs

Charles A. Perfetti

There is in all research, especially social research, the problem of the observer. In the project reported by Wilder, the role of the observer looms quite large and its effect is somewhat problematical. After all, it was the opinion of the field researcher that determined whether a school was doing well, i.e., whether it would be part of the sample. What of the many others which *objectively* had achieved more than expected but had somehow escaped the observer's selection? What are the characteristics of a school that can arouse unanimous positive feelings from a group of observers? What, if anything, is the effect of their presence on those schools which did make the final sample? I do not have answers to these questions and I do not wish the asking of them to detract from the significance of the project. However, these are things to wonder about.

It would be useful to attempt to suggest how classroom observations can be turned backward to touch theories and ideas concerning comprehension development. Can a successful program be identified that seems to incorporate this or that principle of comprehension? It is easy to see that things are not so simple. School 1 is traditional, school 2 is innovative, school 3 uses a resource person (some don't), school 4 has a total language emersion program, while the others do not. And so on. What do they have in common that would provide some ideas about principles of comprehension or principles of instruction?

On the surface, the only common factor is indeed a very basic one: Reading achievement gains are found where reading achievement is recognized as important. Here there is a logical problem of course. To make strong conclusions from statements like "X is found where Y" depends on observing some non X cases to be sure they aren't found "where Y." The research project described by Wilder does not do this for us. We have no information on nonachieving schools. It's quite possible that recognition of reading achievement as important is not a sufficient condition for improved reading achievement.

None of the methods of teaching can be said to be critical—i.e., phonics method, "total" language experience, and individualized instruction. These are three approaches of reading instruction that seem to be valuable, each containing important (theoretical) principles of how learning works. Yet we cannot affirm their importance because none of them was found in all the favored five schools. Note, however, that we can reach a conclusion of some modest significance, significant at least against the unqualified criticism of various approaches: Phonics won't *hurt* you, and neither will individualized instruction, nor total language experience.

There are two possibilities for this state of confusion. One is that there are hidden regularities. There are variables that determine the probability of effectively teaching a child to read with understanding. It's just that we haven't analyzed the situation in enough detail or perhaps along the right dimensions. For example, perhaps even schools which are not *described* as using phonics, actually did provide substantial instruction in such word decoding skills. Perhaps several schools had rich language experience programs without realizing it, etc. I think this is a very serious possibility and careful analysis is important. New perspectives are also important. Perhaps the critical ingredients are present in all five of the lucky schools, but the description of the variable masked the critical commonalities shared by the schools.

The other possibility concerns the complexity of relationships that get simplified when studying school outcomes. We should keep in mind the powerful qualifier that pervades the physical sciences, but is too often neglected in the social sciences. *Other things equal*, individualization is better than mass prescription. Other things equal, having a reading specialist is better than not. Other things equal, teaching emphasis on spelling-sound correspondence is better than one without such an emphasis, etc. However, other things are seldom equal, and the effect of instructional principles may have been buried under the weight of other variables.

Given either of these possibilities, the outcome is the same. It appears that there is little to be concluded about specific means of instruction in reading. The task of working backward toward conceptualizations of comprehension is of course even more difficult. Here the key is Wilder's conclusion number 3, that the effective schools paid careful *attention to basic skills*. Of course, just what these basic skills are is one problem of theories of comprehension and research into reading processes.

I would suggest that the basic skills emphasized by the effective schools might well have included skilled decoding and attention (and memory) for language. It is likely that the schools who produced good readers produced good comprehenders—children who learned how to listen and write as well as how to read and children for whom decoding became more or less automatic. We need to know what was done in order to more than guess at this, however.

As a research psychologist, I recognize significant gaps in our understanding of reading processes. Theories and models of reading comprehension are either so general as to be more diagrams than theories. Others are so molecular that they fail to give a semblance of an integrated description of reading comprehension. So there is much basic scientific work to do in increasing our understanding of all mental processes, including comprehension.

However, it is possible to suggest some principles applicable to reading comprehension instruction. One is that fast decoding is critical. When there are good ways to teach it, they should be used. It is easy to overestimate a child's decoding skills. Just being able to say the words on a list like the Wide Range is not a very severe test. Decoding has to be fast and automatic.

I do not necessarily advocate prolonged use of phonics-based word instruction. Certainly reading text reinforces the decoding skills. On the other hand, I would not want to rule out the use of extra phonetic training for some children. The problem comes from children who are not so good at basic decoding to enable easy comprehension but not so bad that the teacher can detect it with casual observation.

The second basic process is language comprehension.

What this means is that reading is just a special form of language and that, for human beings, speech is the dominant form of language. The implication is that a reading program, which capitalizes on the fact that reading is a form of language comprehension, is to be recommended over one that goes out of its way to suggest that reading has special characteristics beyond decoding.

The third basic ingredient in reading comprehension is knowledge, knowledge of things and places, knowledge of the world in general. The principle is that "the more you know the better you read." This factor doesn't necessarily have to be separated from language comprehension since language is a primary means for giving information. In fact, it is a subpart of language comprehension. If we want children to be good comprehenders, we have to make them smart about a lot of things. This will increase their comprehension of what they hear *and* of what they read.

While our knowledge of reading processes and principles of instruction is far from complete, there may be adequate information for some purposes. The literacy problem does not exist because reading processes are not well understood. It does not exist because effective methods for teaching have not been discovered. But in both cases, there is at least enough understanding of the basics to be implemented into effective reading instruction. The literacy problem will surely be reduced in proportion to the degree to which individuals who understand reading and understand instruction are in positions both of school leadership and reading instruction. I realize that only part of the literacy problem is solved in this way and that there are major obstacles in the forms of social conditions, family patterns, and so on. But it definitely is a part large enough to work hard at.

Reading Comprehension Processes and Instruction

John T. Guthrie

In the 1920s and 30s major studies of reading were often published by school administrators and practitioners in teaching as well as by researchers (Chall, 1975). Today, although the increasing specialization of research, including the development of new methods of inquiry and statistical analysis, divides the two communities of researchers and practitioners in reading, there are forces at work to close the rift. An increasing proportion of researchers in fields related to reading are interested in societal problems, which is to say, applied research, rather than solely theoretical issues and basic research. Their interest is fueled by many research funding agencies that are demanding a show of relevance in the work they support. On the other side an increasing proportion of administrators, reading specialists, and other practitioners are seeking knowledge from research that will help them in the conduct of schooling.

Communication between researchers and practitioners may be enhanced by posing three questions to each group: 1) Do you have messages for your counterparts in reading? 2) Are these messages consistent? 3) Are the messages important, that is, worthy as a basis for change? In the long run, we should address these questions to both those who are responsible for teaching practices and those who are responsible for basic and applied research. However, the focus of this paper is on the implications of research for practice, and the questions will be directed toward some research on reading comprehension that has been presented in this volume and in the second edition of *Theoretical Models and Processes of Reading* (Singer and Ruddell, 1976).

Are there any messages from research for practice? This question is often couched in terms of whether there is a study that can be identified that has an implication for practice. The popular assumption that an implication may be drawn from an individual study may occasionally be true. Often it is false. Consider the following study. Perfetti and Hogaboam (1975) predicted that, to understand sentences, children must represent several words in memory at the same time, which enables them to be integrated semantically. They predicted that children who could not decode words in a sentence quickly would not comprehend the sentences as readily as children who were fast decoders. After conducting an experiment, they found that, indeed, slow decoders were worse in comprehension than fast decoders, lending some support to their theory. It should be emphasized that a causal relationship between decoding speed and comprehension can be inferred only very tenuously from these data, but for this discussion we will assume that the causal link is fairly secure.

The implications for practice from this study would seem to be that teaching programs and curricula should contain lessons on rapid decoding and rapid word recognition. However, the research was conducted with fifth graders; and neither the researchers nor many teachers would say that rapid decoding should be taught in first grade. Certainly, speed should not be taught before accuracy of word recognition. Certainly, speed of word recognition should not be stressed for those who speak English as a second language and do not understand English when it is presented quickly. And, certainly, speed of word recognition is not useful to a reader who does not understand the meanings of the words he is decoding. In fact, sometimes slow decoding rather than fast decoding is important in reading instruction. These qualifications place into context the implication from the study that lessons in fast decoding are important. This context outlines the limits of the usefulness of the research results.

Illustrated here has been one example that an implication for practice does not automatically flow from the result of an investigation, except in the case of the most applied forms of research. Implications and suggestions for practice are the creations of a synthesizer who combines a vast array of practical needs with available knowledge that is appropriate to these needs. Thus, a study does not have an implication for practice. It has a result. Under some circumstances, this result may be combined with other results and tailored to fit practical needs.

Decoding for comprehension

It is unnecessary to elaborate here upon the fact that reading comprehension usually requires decoding. Since we have an alphabetic writing system, a frequent and efficient method for understanding written materials is to decode the print into spoken language and perform language processing operations to understand the message. While this suggests that students should be taught to decode accurately, recent research suggests that they should also be taught to decode rapidly for optimal comprehension. To illustrate, Perfetti (this volume) proposes that there are three distinct levels of processing during the course of reading. First, printed material is decoded to sound and is held in verbatim form in short term memory for a matter of a few seconds. Second, a semantic analysis is performed on information that was most recently decoded. Third, the newly comprehended information is integrated with information that was previously read or already known by the person.

These three levels of processing function within a limited capacity processor, which means that all processes cannot function at full capacity all the time. One of the characteristics of Level 1 processing is that it includes memory. That is, recently decoded information is maintained in memory until a semantic analysis can be performed upon it. If a child decodes slowly, heavy demands will be placed upon Level 1 processing. A large load on memory will occur since decoded material will have to be maintained for a long time before there is enough information available for semantic analysis. In this situation, a large amount of Level 1 processing occurs and relatively small amounts of attention are available for Levels 2 and 3 processing. Since Levels 2 and 3 relate to comprehension, it follows that the comprehension of a child who decodes slowly will be lower than the comprehension of a child who decodes more rapidly. Although it is mostly hypothetical and requires more research, this general viewpoint about processing during reading is supported by the automaticity theory of LaBerge

amuels (1974) and in the workings of primary memory as
.ned by Gough (1972).

While we may be convinced that the accuracy and even
speed of decoding are important for comprehension, we should
pause to recognize that they are not quite enough to guarantee
it. Not only do we have a host of clinical observations that
children may read aloud quite readily without understanding
what they read, and not only do we recognize that we have all
read at least one complex legal document without
understanding it, we also have experimental support for the
notion that accuracy and speed do not guarantee
comprehension. Anderson et al. (1971) asked adults to read
sentences aloud. Some of them had to fill in blanks at the ends
of sentences; others did not. They presumed that filling in a
blank such as "a circle has neither a _____nor an end"
requires at least some understanding of the sentence. People
were tested by being required to say the last word of the
sentence (which some of them had not seen) when they were
given the subject noun (circle) in the sentence. Subjects who
filled in blanks recalled the sentences better than those who did
not. This result illustrates that when people are required to
attend to the meaning of a sentence, understanding and recall
are facilitated. The influence of attention on processing and
memory occurred even though everyone was fast and accurate
in decoding.

Purpose in comprehension

Since it is apparent that understanding written material
requires directed attention, it is important to note that
attention pertains to purpose in reading. For many years,
Stauffer (this volume) and more recently Gibson (1972) have
emphasized purpose as the driving force of the inquiring mind,
as the basic motivation for reading. We seek to comprehend
written materials, especially when we need the knowledge they
contain and the information they can supply. At the heart of
the language experience approach to teaching is the detection
and nourishment of this motivation, although the scientific
study of the topic has just begun.

One analysis of purpose has been forwarded by Frase
(this volume). He proposes that purpose has two dimensions:
focus and form. The focus of purpose is the content of the

reading matter towards which the reader is oriented. Frase shows that the more specific and positive the focus, the more is learned about the area under focus. For example, if a child is reading about primitive tribes, he will learn most about the marriage rites if he is told specifically to look for information about marriage rites. The form of purpose, which is also important, refers to the sequence of information in which the purpose is framed. For example, if we suggest that the child read about the marriage rites in nomadic tribes, the sequence in which he represents the purpose will determine the order in which he searches and processes information in the material he is reading. This shows that purpose plays a selective role, increasing the learning of information within the focus and decreasing learning of information outside the focus. Clearly, a price must be paid for the benefits of purpose in reading, but that is probably justified since there are few of us who wish to learn everything about everything.

Syntax and semantics in meaningful processing

During the course of reading, after purpose has caused attention to focus on a certain aspect of the meaning, what happens next? We should probably expect common language operations to occur. Among others, Carroll (this volume) argues that reading comprehension is a special case of language comprehension. Ruddell (1976) supports this position by illustrating that children understand written materials more clearly if they are similar to the child's prevalent oral language patterns than if they are different from these patterns. Ruddell adds that words in print are understood more readily if they have rich, semantic counterparts in the child's oral language than if they are ill-defined, barren items.

What aspects of language are useful for understanding and facilitating reading comprehension? Although the very existence of syntax is debated in some quarters, it is nevertheless a useful aspect of language description. In a review of early literature on language, around 1965, before generative semantics had surfaced, Ruddell (1969) pointed out that linguistic constituents have psychological reality. That is to say, linguistic descriptions of sentences divide them at clause boundaries, phrases having more unity than clauses. Psycholinguistic research has shown that phrases are perceived and processed as a unit more readily than clauses. In the sentence "The wild timberwolves howled all night," adults group first the noun phrase and then the verb phrase, and combine the two in attempting to understand its meaning. A first step in reading comprehension is to perceive the grammatical structure as a basis for the meaningful interpretation of the sentence.

It is additionally stressed by Athey (this volume) that comprehension depends upon knowledge of the world as well as language functioning. She gives an example of knowledge of causal relations that may be signalled by the word "and." In the sentence "The wing healed and the bird flew away," there is an implied causal relationship; whereas, in the sentence "The wing healed and the legs grew strong," there are two concurrent events that are not causally related. The child's information and knowledge of birds, combined with the cognitive processes needed for grasping the difference between sequence and causality, determine how well he can understand these two uses of "and." Limits of knowledge and cognition are more likely to be the source of misunderstanding these sentences than limits of language competence.

Transformation of meanings in comprehension

After a sentence has been initially understood with a distinct reliance on grammatical factors, the information is likely to be transformed such that the meanings but not the grammatical structures are stored in memory. It has been illustrated that when adults are presented sentences on a topic, the sentences are integrated semantically into a complex idea. Recall is then based on this complex idea, rather than on specific sentences that were originally presented and perceived (Franks and Bransford, 1974). For example, when adults are presented several sentences containing different information on the same topic, all of the information is combined. Later, the specific sentences that were presented or their specific structures such as the inclusion of subordinate clauses cannot be recognized; but the information as a whole will be remembered. Furthermore, the more complex the information that is presented, the higher degree of integration that occurs. Simple materials may be learned rotely, whereas complex materials require more elaborate transformations.

Rearrangements of information of this sort are dependent on knowledge of the material that is being read. Semantic organization and transforms cannot occur for a topic about which we have little prior information (Peterson and McIntyre, 1973).

Confirming these findings with children, Pearson (1974-75) showed that third and fourth graders recalled causal relations in unified, subordinated chunks rather than in discrete units regardless of the form in which they had been presented. For instance, consider the sentence "Tom slept all day because he was lazy." Children recalled that information in the form of one sentence whether it was presented to them as one sentence or as two sentences, such as "Tom slept all day. Tom was lazy." In other words, children unified the separate sentences to aid their recall. Children also remembered information with the causal cues present whether or not the cues had been contained in the original sentences. Recall of the information "Tom slept all day, because he was lazy" usually contained the word "because" even though the original sentence did not have this cue and, instead, was presented as "Tom slept all day and he was lazy." Apparently, children transform and supplement information to give it some cohesive meaning.

Reading to learn

The previous sketch of some of the language and cognitive processes involved in reading represent a few of the messages that seem to be coming from the research community and may be useful in practice. At this point, we may question whether the messages are consistent and lead to similar practices, or whether they are conflicting and contradictory in their implications for practice. At first it may seem there is a conflict. It has been emphasized that reading is a process requiring language and cognition. From this it is sensible to suggest that the materials presented to children should be at or below their level of language and cognitive development. But in the same breath it has been emphasized that processes of language and cognition must be taught by teachers or at least practiced in classrooms if children are to improve in reading, which suggests that materials should be linguistically challenging. However, we do not have to choose between accommodating reading materials to the language of children on the one hand and attempting to facilitate language development on the other. We should include both as goals in school curricula. The distinction between reading to learn and learning to read may serve to highlight the differences between these goals.

Occasions often arise during teaching when we want children to read primarily for knowledge or pleasure. At these times we usually want to provide materials that are easily comprehended. In line with this purpose, Athey (this volume) argues that since reading comprehension depends upon the apprehension of grammatical structures and knowledge of the real world, books should be suited to children in terms of these factors and should not exceed their level of development. For example, written stories should not assume, necessarily, that children use the word "and" in the same way as adults. In the sentence, "The branch broke that the boy was sitting on and he fell," there is a causal relationship. But in the sentence, "The branch broke that the bird was sitting on and it rotted," there is more of an emphasis on sequence than causality. Children who cannot process the grammatical and cognitive complexities needed to distinguish between these sentences should not be given materials at this level if they are expected to read for new knowledge or pleasure.

This is not to say that simplifying the grammatical and cognitive load of written materials is the whole answer to comprehensibility. Pearson's work (1974-75) illustrates that, up to a point, syntactic complexity is beneficial to comprehension. He shows that improving comprehension does not necessarily require reducing the complexity of materials. Rather, it requires providing cues to make the semantic relations in written materials explicit. The basic ideas and relationships that we want children to learn from written materials should be presented in not only a simple but also a salient manner. The important information should emerge as the figure from the ground. The emphasis on goal orientation provided by Frase (this volume) also pertains to this issue. Children will learn those things from written text most readily that are included most specifically in their most important purpose for reading. We should not leave to accident or inference what we wish children to learn from materials. We should set purposes, questions, and signposts that will provide sharply defined guides to children when they are attempting to comprehend written materials independently.

Materials designed to impart new knowledge should be embellished. They should include a host of appropriately placed questions; numerous headings, spaces, and other signposts to meaning; organizational characteristics that are matched to the purposes of the teacher; and language structures that are similar to those of the readership.

Learning to read

Often the goal of instruction is to improve processes of reading comprehension, which is placed in contrast to the goal of increasing knowledge of a specific content area. Research by Ruddell (1969) and Anderson (1974) suggests that, in teaching children reading comprehension, we should first teach all of the word meanings in as concrete and denotative a manner as possible. Anderson found that adults learn sentences more accurately when the subject nouns are modified with concrete adjectives than when the nouns are not modified or are modified with redundant information. In other words, the concreteness, image-evoking value of words determines how easily they are learned and recalled. These studies should be replicated with children before implications for teaching may be drawn confidently. But assuming for the moment that the results would be the same, it would seem to be extremely important in teaching new vocabulary meanings to give a very specific context that can be imagined in pictured form, to provide examples, and to provide many modifiers. Representing abstract concepts and words with metaphors, analogies and graphs may be more important to good instruction than we have previously recognized.

In teaching children to understand sentences, the pupils should also be taught grammatical structure, not in the sense of verbalizing grammatical rules, but rather in the sense of being able to answer verbatim questions over a sentence. For instance, in the sentence, "The weary cuckoo flew to the judge's chamber," the child should be able to answer, "What flew? Where did it go? What was the bird like?" Being able to answer literal questions shows that the children can locate grammatical constituents accurately.

Pearson (1974-75), Perfetti (this volume), and Franks and Bransford (1974) present research which implies that children should be taught how to transform material they have understood at a literal level. They should be taught how to impose their own signposts of meaning on sentences by adding connectives or qualifications or changing the syntax. For this purpose, teachers should require children to rewrite sentences or passages inserting cues of various kinds that would give the information meaning without changing its substance. Children could be given a paragraph containing three topics that are highly interwoven. They could be asked to list the number of topics, to list all of the sentences (or all of the information) on each of the topics separately, to rewrite the material from each topic into a coherent treatment, and so on. Such activities would give children practice in integrating and organizing information which are vital processes of memory.

The language demands of the materials used for the purpose of teaching comprehension processes should be slightly higher than the language capabilities of the learners, since language instruction is essential to reading improvement. The signposts of meaning should be absent and, rather, the children should be expected to impose them on the materials, in specifically planned classroom activities. Purposes should not be provided in the materials, but should be developed by the students with assistance from teachers in order to learn the art of goal-setting and resetting during reading. If purposes or goals were presented in all of the materials given to children they might never learn to set their own purposes effectively. Needless to say, this distinction between two types of materials—one for reading to learn and another for learning to read—should not be drawn to a ridiculous extreme. There will be many instances in which children will both learn new information and new reading processes from the same set of materials. However, we cannot expect that this would occur at an optimal level for all of the children all of the time.

Importance of implications

The final question that should be posed to research implications is whether they are important for education. While we do not know of criteria for significance that have been devised by group consensus, we can suggest three critical dimensions. Implications from research for practice would qualify as significant if they: 1) suggest bold new practices, 2) enable us to select the most promising among an array of prevailing practices, or 3) serve as an explanation of why certain educational activities are effective. Two investigations and their relationships to practice may be used as examples. In 1962, Singer presented a version of the substrata factor theory of reading. At that time, he suggested that reading curricula should contain each factor in his theory as an objective for instruction. Educational goals would include vocabulary, matching sounds in words, suffixes, understanding words in context, blending word sounds, spelling, and understanding prefixes. He noted that teachers should teach these factors and enable students to switch between factors during reading. It is curious that, at the same convention, Barton and Wilder (1962) reported the current practices of teachers. Based on a study of about 1,500 teachers in about 150 schools, they found that the following activities were mentioned by the following percentages of fourth- to sixth-grade teachers as "very important or absolutely essential" in their reading programs:

Basal reading series	88%
Classroom library of varied books	90%
High-interest materials for retarded readers	88%
Graded workbooks	80%

Teachers in grades four through six also reported that the following activities were used half or more days in their reading programs:

Learn new words as wholes (flashcards, etc.)	61%
Learn to use context to guess new words	54%
Sound out words from letters and letter combinations	64%
Divide words into syllables	73%
Noticing similar sounds in words	54%

Compared to this picture of practice, Singer's research did not provide any radical new departures. The components emphasized in his theory are all included as major practices common to teachers. The implications for teaching did not fulfill the selective function, since all of the activities were already in practice in reasonably similar frequencies. However, they provided a supportive and explanatory function indicating at least partially why reading instruction was successful at all.

A recent model of cognitive operations that may occur in adult reading has been proposed by Frase (1975). It was induced from a large variety of studies published since the late 1960s. The model includes the components of: 1) goal orientation; 2) encoding, which is attending and storing information in memory; and 3) rehearsal and integration, which is essentially going over what you have read and combining it with information that you already knew. Two memory components, short-term and long-term memory, are appropriately included. Frase himself notes that this is remarkably similar to the SQ3R method of teaching. Standing for Survey-Question-Read-Recite-Review, this approach was popular among teachers in the early 1960s. Thus, the method of instruction had been used long before its components were studied scientifically. However, Frase's model shows that the components of reading that are encouraged in this method are extremely useful for adults in understanding written materials. Therefore, the general method receives some support. In this case, research served a selective function by emphasizing the cognitive components of one approach to instruction. The research model also provides some rationale for why the teaching method should work, which illustrates its explanatory function. It was neither the author's intent nor his accomplishment to provide new teaching methods from the model. Whether new instructional practices may be generated from it is a challenge for the future.

What of the implications for practice that were presented earlier in this chapter? Do they serve an innovative, selective, or explanatory function for instructional practice? The answer lies in the knowledge and purpose of the reader.

REFERENCES

Anderson, R. C. Concretization and sentence learning. *Journal of Educational Psychology*, 1974, *66*, 179-183.

Anderson, R. C.; Goldberg, S.; and Hidde, J. Meaningful processing of sentences, *Journal of Educational Psychology*, 1971, *62*, 395-399.

Athey, I. Syntax, semantics and reading. In J. Guthrie (Ed.), *Cognition, curriculum, and comprehension*. Newark: International Reading Association, 1977.

Barton, A., and Wilder, D. The Columbia-Carnegie Study of Reading Research and Its Communication—An Interim Report. *Proceedings of the International Reading Association*, Newark, Delaware, 1962, 170-176.

Carroll, J. Developmental parameters of reading comprehension. In J. Guthrie (Ed.), *Cognition, curriculum, and comprehension*. Newark: International Reading Association, 1977.

Chall, J. Restoring dignity and self-worth to the teacher. *Phi Delta Kappan*, 1975, *57*, 170-174.

Franks, J., and Bransford, J. Memory for syntactic form as a function of semantic context. *Journal of Experimental Psychology*, 1974, *103*, 1037-1039.

Frase, L. Prose processing. In G. Bower (Ed.), *Psychology of Learning and Motivation* (Vol. 9). New York: Academic Press, 1975.

Frase, L. Purpose in reading. In J. Guthrie (Ed.), *Cognition, curriculum, and comprehension*. Newark: International Reading Association, 1977.

Gibson, E. J. Reading for some purpose. In J. Kavanagh and I. Mattingly, (Eds.), *Language by ear and by eye*. Cambridge: The MIT Press, 1972.

Gough, P. One second of reading. In J. Kavanagh and I. Mattingly (Eds.), *Language by ear and by eye*. Cambridge: The MIT Press, 1972.

LaBerge, D., and Samuels, S. J. Toward a theory of automatic information processing in reading. *Cognitive Psychology*, 1974, *6*, 293-323.

Pearson, D. The effects of grammatical complexity on children's comprehension, recall and conception of certain semantic relations. *Reading Research Quarterly*, 1974-1975, *10*, 155-192.

Perfetti, C. Language comprehension and fast decoding: some psycholinguistic prerequisites for skilled reading comprehension. In J. Guthrie (Ed.), *Cognition, curriculum, and comprehension*. Newark: International Reading Association, 1977.

Perfetti, C., and Hogaboam, T. Relationship between single word decoding and reading comprehension skill. *Journal of Educational Psychology*, 1975, *67*, 461-470.

Peterson, R. G., and McIntyre, C. W. The influence of semantic "relatedness" on linguistic integration and retention. *American Journal of Psychology*, 1973, *86*, 697-706.

Ruddell, R. Language acquisition and reading process. In H. Singer and R. Ruddell (Eds.), *Theoretical models and processes of reading*. Newark: International Reading Association, 1976.

Ruddell, R. Psycholinguistic implications for a systems of communication model. In K. S. Goodman and J. T. Fleming (Eds.), *Psycholinguistics and the teaching of reading*. Newark: International Reading Association, 1969.

Singer, H. Substrata-factor theory of reading: Theoretical design for teaching reading. *Proceedings of the International Reading Association*, Newark, Delaware, 1962, 7, 226-232.

Singer, H., and Ruddell, R. (Eds.) *Theoretical models and processes of reading*. Newark: International Reading Association, 1976.

Stauffer, R. G. Cognitive processes fundamental to reading instruction. In J. Guthrie (Ed.), *Cognition, curriculum, and comprehension*. Newark: International Reading Association, 1977.

Author Index

Anderson, R.C. 48, 55, 58, 59, 286, 291
Anderson, W.W. 246
Askov, E. 200, 203
Athey, I. *x*, 288, 290

Baaker, D.J. 33
Baele, E.R. 90
Bartolome, P.I. 65
Barton, A. 293
Bates, E. 105
Beck, I.L. *x*, 122, 123, 125
Bellugi, U. 102
Berger, N. 36
Berko, J. 101
Berlyne, D.E. 244
Bever, T.G. 32, 87, 106, 107
Biddle, W.B. 48, 58, 59
Bloch, O. 101
Bloom, B. 247
Bloom, L. 103, 104, 105, 106, 107, 108, 109
Bloomer, R.H. 66
Blount, H.P. 92
Bormuth, J.R. 7, 10, 23, 76, 89, 93
Botel, M. 92
Bowerman, M. 103
Boyd, W.M. 48
Braine, M. 102
Bransford, J. 90, 288, 292
Brassard, M.B. 5
Brent, S.B. 74, 224
Brown, C.C. 165
Brown R. 101, 102, 103, 104, 109
Brown, W.R. 165
Bruner, J.S. 243, 244
Buchanan, C.D. 114
Burke, C.L. 167
Bushell, D. 164

Calfee, R.C. 5
Carpenter, P.A. 227
Carroll, J.B. 2, 7, 9, 10, 16, 21, 32, 59,
    128, 287
Carroll, L. 252
Cedergren, H. 109
Chall, J.C. 116, 283
Chao, Y.R. 101
Chester, R.D. 199, 205
Chomsky, C. 75, 83, 89
Chomsky, N. 221, 243
Clark, E.V. 106, 107, 108, 225
Clymer, T. 171
Coleman, E.B. 6, 93
Cooke, D.A. 65
Coomber, J.E. 27
Corey, J.R. 164, 165

Corsaro, W.A. 105
Coulson, D. 56
Covington, M.V. 247
Crabbs, L.M. 6
Craik, F. 21
Crane, S. 166
Cunningham, B.V. 154

Danks, J.H. 84
Davidson, J.L. 246
Davis, F.B. 160
Denner, B. 75
Dewey, J. 42, 250
Diederich, P.B. II 122
DiVesta, F.J. 48, 56
Donaldson, M. 79, 81, 85
Downing, J. 75
Dubos, R. 251
Duckworth, E. 246
Dulaney, S. 166
Durost, W.N. 120, 154
Durrell, D.D. 5

Eaton, M. 165
Edwards, P. 93
Eichelberger, R.T. 123
Eischens, R.R. 48
Endicott, A.L. 92
Entwisle, D.R. 86
Epstein, W.A. 84
Ervin, S. 102
Etzel, B.C. 165

Farley, F.H. 66
Ferguson, C.A. 108
Fernald, J.C. 224
Fodor, J.A. 32, 80
Foust, C.D. 222, 225
Franks, J. 90, 288, 292
Frase, L.T. *x*, 43, 44, 45, 48, 50, 54, 56,
    57, 60, 62, 286, 287, 290, 294
Fraser, C. 102
Friedman, M.P. 56
Fries, C.C. 221
Furth, H.G. 89

Gagne, E.D. 58
Gallagher, J.J. 247
Garrett, M.F. 32, 80
Garvey, C. 105
Gates, D. 171
Gibbons, H.D. 84
Gibson, E.J. 286
Glaser, R. 114
Gleason, J.B. 225